TEACHING THE LEARNING-DISABLED ADOLESCENT

CONTRIBUTORS

VIRGINIA L. BROWN

JOHN F. CAWLEY

DONALD D. DESHLER

PATRICIA H. GILLESPIE

LIBBY GOODMAN

DONALD D. HAMMILL

PAUL IRVINE

THERESA LAURIE

JANET W. LERNER

LESTER MANN

RITA SILVERMAN

MERRILL C. SITKO

J. LEE WIEDERHOLT

JAMES E. YSSELDYKE

NAOMI ZIGMOND

TEACHING THE LEARNING-DISABLED ADOLESCENT

EDITED BY

LESTER MANN
EDITOR, *JOURNAL OF SPECIAL EDUCATION*

LIBBY GOODMAN
DIRECTOR, PHILADELPHIA PUBLIC SCHOOLS

J. LEE WIEDERHOLT
UNIVERSITY OF TEXAS, AUSTIN

HOUGHTON MIFFLIN COMPANY   BOSTON
Dallas   Geneva, Illinois   Hopewell, New Jersey   Palo Alto   London

Library of Congress Catalog Card Number: 77–074377

ISBN: 0–395–25434–5

3893222

CONTENTS

v

PREFACE

For professionals and parents concerned with the education of the learning disabled, the learning-disabled adolescent poses a complex challenge. The field of learning disabilities has, for the most part, focused its attention on elementary education and has directed its major remedial efforts toward the young learning-disabled child. There has been a general neglect of the problems facing the secondary-level learning-disabled student. It will not be possible to correct the effects of this neglect by mere extrapolation of earlier work done at the elementary or primary level. Optimal education for the older learning-disabled student is not simply a repetition or upward extension of the work done at earlier levels; the learning-disabled teenager and the learning-disabled elementary school student are separated by more than age. Expanded personal, social, and academic experience makes the older student a much more difficult subject for intervention than is the younger student with learning deficiencies.

Years of mislearning, frustration, and failure are a formidable barrier to successful remediation. But no one doubts that we must try to help older students cross this barrier. Answers to the problems of secondary learning-disabled students will be found in new areas of inquiry, areas that begin to be defined in *Teaching the Learning-Disabled Adolescent*. This book will introduce readers to the emerging field of secondary learning disabilities.

The book is the work of many individuals. Our contributing authors have distinguished themselves in a variety of endeavors, no less the present book. We are grateful to them for their willingness to attack problems in areas that are still without definition. Thanks to them, this book has achieved a breadth and scope appropriate to an introductory text.

We are indebted, too, to our reviewers, whose suggestions guided us at all stages of manuscript preparation. To Tanis Bryan of the University of Illinois at Chicago Circle, Robert F. Busch of the University of Missouri, Dorothy Drysdale Campbell of the University of Georgia, David Dawson of Central Connecticut State College, and Patrick T. Mullen of California State College at San Bernardino we offer our thanks.

Finally, we wish to acknowledge the Montgomery County Intermediate Unit #23, under whose auspices the preparation of this book proceeded.

TEACHING THE LEARNING-DISABLED ADOLESCENT

INTRODUCTION

LESTER MANN

The education of secondary-level pupils has recently become one of the most pressing concerns in the field of learning disabilities. Two facts help to explain why this is so. First, many people, from government officials to the couple next door, are expressing alarm that many secondary school graduates are poorly educated in the academic fundamentals required for effective everyday living. By the criteria used to identify and establish learning disabilities, a considerable number of these graduates are learning-disabled; yet they were not identified as such during their school careers. Second, it has become increasingly —often painfully—apparent that many pupils who *were* diagnosed in elementary school as being learning-disabled have not responded adequately to the training and remedial efforts provided them during their earlier grades. They will require continued help as they move into adolescence and young adulthood.

Why are learning disabilities at the secondary level a new concern? Why didn't the field of learning disabilities begin long ago to deal with adolescents? The answer lies in the fact that the field of learning disabilities, so recent in its development and popularity, has been largely committed to developing basic skills in young children, that is, those in nursery school through sixth grade. This commitment was based upon the reigning philosophy of intervention programs—the earlier the better! We believed that if we could identify children with learning problems at an early age, we could provide them with sufficient remediation to correct their problems. If this were done, there would be little need to be concerned with secondary-level learning problems; they would be few and minor. The learning-disabled elementary school child, once remediated and made productive, would be a non-learning-disabled pupil by the time he or she entered secondary programs.

Alas, magic always reveals itself as illusion on closer examination. While workers in the field of learning disabilities did indeed produce some remarkable remedial efforts, they are now forced to confront the reality of learning problems that did not go away despite their best efforts.

We most surely cannot fault the learning-disabilities field for its commitment to early intervention. For early intervention appeared and still appears to be the major focus for our efforts. Nor can we fault the field now for not having solved all the problems it has faced. One of the more recent, if belated, awarenesses of the American public is that not all problems can be solved. Yet the commitment made by specialists in learning disabilities, by professors, publishers, technicians, teachers, instructional aides, physicians, psychologists and social workers, occupational therapists, physical therapists, and optometrists to problems of younger students has had most serious consequences. Now that learning-disabilities professionals are ready to deal with secondary-level learning disabilities, they are confronted with a bare cupboard. Only a minuscule literature discusses the problems of secondary-level learning-disabled pupils; only the most limited technologies of test and instructional materials provide for these pupils' needs.

The almost exclusive attention that learning-disabilities professionals have paid over the years to young pupils has meant neglect for older ones. People in the field who are concerned with the learning-disabled preadolescent and adolescent must now start from scratch in attempting to help older students with their learning problems.

Students of secondary learning disabilities need an overview of their large but relatively unexplored field. They need a basis on which to erect methodologies of instruction and evaluation. It was with this in mind that the present book was conceived. A panel of experts in the field was asked to examine and discuss problems, needs, techniques, and even tentative solutions.

A book like this, developed from the efforts of a number of authors, has a peculiar advantage. It offers readers the chance to hear different authors speaking at length and for themselves on aspects of secondary-level learning disabilities that have interested them. Readers will hear polemics on one side, sober research on the other, ivory tower speculation, meat-and-potatoes concretism—in short, widely different approaches that together are contributing to the growth of a discipline.

Chapter 1, by J. Lee Wiederholt of the University of Texas, provides a historical orientation to the field of learning disabilities and a perspective on the problems of secondary-level learning-disabled pupils. Professor Wiederholt discusses the perplexities of assessment of and programming for these pupils. He also confronts the problems of developing helping services for older learning-disabled pupils and offers some recommendations toward their solution.

Donald Hammill, prominent in the field of learning disabilities, has made many contributions to the professional literature, particularly in the area of remedial education. In Chapter 2 Dr. Hammill addresses himself to difficult questions of definition and diagnosis. There is little doubt that these two issues are among the most problematical that the field of secondary-level learning disabilities faces. Who are the learning-disabled, how do we identify them and distinguish them from other types of handicapped individuals? What is the incidence of secondary-level learning-disabled pupils? Hammill's chapter provides the learning-disabilities specialist with important information and some rationales essential to the development of understanding of these pressing questions.

Donald Deshler, of the University of Kansas Medical Center, is a new and bright light in the field of learning disabilities. He directs Chapter 3 to the psychoeducational aspects of learning-disabled pupils. The reader will find Dr. Deshler's chapter a welcome relief from the usual litany of learning problems found in many journal pages. Deshler is interested in the pupil as a person: how he or she functions in the classroom, home, and society. His focus is particularly important, I believe, to efforts to help secondary-level learning-disabled pupils, who are educationally more a creature of their environments than are younger learning-disabled pupils. Deshler's examination of secondary learning-disabled pupils and his recommendations for new areas of exploration can provide useful guides for research and service in a relatively neglected corner of learning-disabilities work.

Virginia Brown is a professional who moves with ease between the school system and the campus (she is on the faculty of the University of Minnesota at Duluth). From her experience in both types of settings, she is aware of both the theoretical and practical issues confronting specialists working with secondary-level learning-disability pupils. Dr. Brown's expertise in curriculum development and clinical management is shared with us in Chapter 4. We know that what she recommends will *work*. Her chapter differentiates educational programming at the secondary level from that at the elementary level, and she provides a wide choice of curricular options for the learning-disability specialist attempting to develop programs and resources in middle, junior, and senior high schools.

Janet Lerner of Northeastern Illinois University is the author of a major text in the field of learning disabilities and is known for her systems approach to learning disabilities. Her learning-disability model in Chapter 5 provides a threefold taxonomy of teaching approaches toward the learning-disabled preadolescent and adolescent. Presented are three major categories of analysis: (1) approaches that concentrate on individual pupil differences—the student himself or herself; (2) those that emphasize the content of instruction ("analyze the subject matter of the content to be learned, rather than the pupil"); and (3) those that analyze the environmental conditions of learning—for example, psychotherapeutic intervention and behavior modification. Readers of Professor Lerner's chapter will gain insight into the many dimensions of remediation.

Professor James Ysseldyke of the University of Minnesota is a scholar of learning disabilities with a background in both special education and school psychology. His contributions to the field are noted for their usefulness in resolving difficulties in measurement and decision making. Professor Ysseldyke's work in aptitude-treatment interactions is a model of clear exposition. In Chapter 6 he addresses the problems of defining and diagnosing learning disabilities and abilities, first in broad perspective and then in special application to the secondary-level learning-disabled. Can one formulate programs for the secondary school learning-disabled pupil on the basis of process deficits? Those who plan on so doing should at least be aware of the pitfalls and dangers of such an approach. Ysseldyke's recommendations provide a most useful guide to the wary.

Professors Sitko and Gillespie (Chapter 7) and Gillespie and Sitko (Chapter 8) deal first with speech and language deficits and then with the acquisition of reading skills by learning-disabled pupils. These are certainly major areas of concern to learning-disability specialists working at the secondary level. Gillespie and Sitko, who are both at Indiana University, are well equipped to deal with these problems, as they have labored in both the classroom and the university research laboratory. Readers will probably be as disappointed as their authors are with the relative dearth of language research with older pupils that Chapter 7 reports, but the chapter may at least inspire some systematic attacks on the disability areas it investigates.

Chapter 8, on the reading problems of learning-disabled pupils in secondary schools, is direct and informative. Again the reader will find that, while many authors have addressed themselves to reading problems and their remediation, few have approached these issues from the standpoint of the secondary-level learning-disabled pupil. Nevertheless, Gillespie and Sitko's review of the state of the art of reading instruction with learning-disabled pupils, the diagnostic instruments, the instructional technology and the results thereof, and the problems of measuring change and improvement provides us with an important overview of the most pressing instructional area in learning disabilities. Our authors also provide appropriate and useful guides for future interventions.

Mathematics is a relatively neglected field at all levels of inquiry in learning disabilities. Few learning-disabilities specialists have made a systematic approach to the problems of teaching children and youth who have a learning problem in mathematics. Dr. John F. Cawley of the University of Connecticut is an exception. He provides readers of Chapter 9 with a much needed perspective and then presents a model of unusual depth to aid in the analysis and correction of mathematical learning disabilities at the secondary level. Learning-disabilities specialists who have found themselves perplexed with mathematical instruction for secondary learning-disabled pupils will be far better equipped to tackle this problem as a result of having heard Professor Cawley's wise and innovative thinking on the subject.

Educational programming for secondary-level learning-disabled pupils means program and career planning of a breadth that goes beyond the more specific issues of education and diagnosis. Dr. Libby Goodman, of the Montgomery County Intermediate Unit in Pennsylvania during preparation of this book, is one of the few major writers in the field of learning disabilities who has had direct public-school program responsibilities in the field of secondary learning disabilities. Her Chapter 10 deals with actual projects for the learning-disabled secondary-level pupil. It makes us aware of the realities, difficulties, and opportunities that confront us when we deal with learning disabilities beyond the elementary school level.

Paul Irvine, whose experience as a Board of Cooperative Educational Services (BOCES) director makes him an authoritative writer on many subjects, and Dr. Goodman contribute Chapter 11, on the vocational and postvocational training of secondary pupils with learning disabilities. This is a difficult area to deal with, since it requires us to distinguish the learning-disabled pupil at this level from any other pupils who may have learning problems—and indeed from normal students—if appropriate adjustments of curricula are to be made. Yet the student of secondary-level learning disabilities must be aware of the issues and problems at this level of operation. Chapter 11 will meet that purpose.

Finally, in Chapter 12, Professor Naomi Zigmond and two of her fellow workers at the University of Pittsburgh—Rita Silverman and Theresa Laurie—deal with the matter of preparing competent teachers to work with secondary-level learning-disabled pupils. They come to grips with such questions as whether secondary learning-disabled pupils have specific learning characteristics or problems that warrant their being treated differently from youth with other handicaps or with no handicaps at all. Professor Zigmond is among the first in the United States to investigate specifically teacher preparation within the field of secondary learning disabilities. We can expect that many advances in teacher preparation for this field will result from her pioneering efforts.

And now, with our introductions over, let us on with the book!

CHAPTER 1

ADOLESCENTS WITH LEARNING DISABILITIES: THE PROBLEM IN PERSPECTIVE

J. LEE WIEDERHOLT

The rapid growth of the field of learning disabilities during the past decade was a remarkable phenomenon in special education. But although it brought about a great deal of progress with preschool and elementary children, it paid little attention to adolescents with learning disabilities. Today, as children once identified as having learning disabilities pass from childhood into adolescence, many concerned parents, legislators, and professionals are beginning to focus on the older student. They now realize that, even with early identification and treatment, many learning-disabled pupils simply cannot be "cured."

This chapter examines critical aspects of the field of learning disabilities. The first section is an overview of accomplishments in the field. The second section deals with issues that educators must confront in establishing secondary school programs. These discussions are meant to prepare the reader for additional study, both in this book and elsewhere, of the literature pertaining to the education of learning-disabled adolescents.

■ PERSPECTIVES ON THE PAST ■

From the early nineteenth century, pioneer physicians, psychologists, and educators have been concerned about individuals with learning disabilities. Early interest in the learning-disabled is described by many writers (Lerner, 1971; Kirk, 1972; Hallahan & Cruickshank, 1973; Wiederholt, 1974; Wallace & McLoughlin, 1975; and Myers & Hammill, 1976). Their work shows that, while the basic premises and issues in the field have remained remarkably consistent, the semantics and trappings have changed periodically. For example, the terminology used to label the learning-disabled has been modified throughout the decades. Early contributors tended to use medically oriented terms such as *brain damage, brain crippled, cerebral disorders, neurological impairments, dyslexia,* or *dysphasia* in describing this handicap. Within the last two decades, however, the term *learning disabilities* has predominated.

Although terminology has changed, most professionals still approach disabilities with the same basic premise. That is, they believe that persons with this condition have learning problems that are rooted in dysfunctions within the central nervous system.

10

In my 1974 work I noted that the contributions of individuals and the events that marked the development of the field of learning disabilities could be organized within two dimensions. The first dimension deals with the type of disorders manifested by the learning-disabled. These disorders can be grouped under three broad categories: (1) disorders of spoken language, (2) disorders of written language, and (3) disorders of perceptual and motor processes. The second dimension deals with the developmental phases through which the field has progressed. During the first developmental phase—the foundations period —physicians were speculating about the causes (the etiology) of learning disabilities. During the second developmental phase—the transition period—psychologists and educators translated the theoretical postulations derived by the contributors of the foundations phase into diagnostic and remedial procedures. The third developmental phase— the integration period—is characterized primarily by educators' development of public school programs for the learning-disabled.*

THE FOUNDATIONS PHASE

During the foundations phase (about 1800–1930), physicians investigated the etiology of specific learning disorders, classifying and categorizing the different types. They provided treatment for adults with severe disorders in spoken or written language and/or perceptual-motor processes. For the most part, the information they used in their work was derived from the study of adults with acquired brain damage —people such as war-wounded veterans and stroke patients. The physicians made a concerted effort to describe the deviant behavioral characteristics of these patients and to localize the deviant behavior in specific parts of the brain.

Information was obtained by correlating the observed behavior

---

* Growth through the sequential contributions of these three professional groups (physicians, psychologists, and educators) is hardly unique to special education. For example, in the field of retardation, physicians such as Itard, Sequin, Montessori, and Decroly were initial contributors to the field. Psychologists such as Descoudres, Goddard, Kirk, Wallen, and Witmer later provided more emphasis to the growth of the field. Using the theories and programs developed by the medical and psychological professions as a base, educators are currently improving and modifying services for the retarded in the schools.

patterns of the brain-injured with data acquired through autopsy at the patient's death. These findings were then generalized to a larger population. For example, if a war-wounded patient lost his ability to speak after a head injury, and an autopsy showed that a particular part of his brain had been damaged, it was assumed that other, similar cases of dysfunction in spoken language were caused by damage to that area of the brain. Using this reasoning, Alfred Strauss, Samuel Orton, and other physicians hypothesized that children who demonstrated delays in the development of written language, spoken language, or perceptual-motor processes suffered from a brain dysfunction similar to the dysfunctions found in brain-injured adults. They stressed, therefore, that special treatment must be provided for these children with "cerebral dysfunctions."

During this period Franz Joseph Gall, John Baptiste Bouillard, Pierre Paul Broca, John Hughlings Jackson, Henry Charlton Bastian, Carl Wernicke, Paul Pierre Marie, and Henry Head made major contributions to the study of disorders of spoken language. Physicians James Hinshelwood and Samuel Torry Orton investigated disorders of written language, while Kurt Goldstein, Alfred Strauss, and Heinz Werner, among numerous others, studied disorders of perceptual and motor behavior.

The work of Luria (1966), Schuell, Jenkins, and Jimenez-Pabon (1964), and others shows that the pioneers of the field were in frequent disagreement about the specific etiology, classification, and treatment of the learning disorders they studied. Despite its lack of agreement, the early work in learning disabilities served to alert parents and professionals to a group of handicapped individuals who needed special services.

The brain-injured teenage and adult soldiers studied during the foundations period were not like most learning-disabled adolescents identified in the secondary school today. The records of the soldiers indicate that the specific abilities impaired as the result of brain damage had originally been intact. Their disabilities were *acquired* disabilities. Most of today's learning-disabled adolescents, by contrast, have *developmental* disabilities. They have never learned some specific skills, or, at least, their achievements in these areas are well below their perceived capabilities. In spite of marked differences between individuals with acquired and developmental disabilities, many pro-

12

fessionals still believe that both disabilities are anchored in dysfunction of the central nervous system.

THE TRANSITION PHASE

During the transition phase (about 1930–1960), psychologists and educators attempted to translate many of their predecessors' theories into diagnostic and remedial practice. Charles Osgood and Joseph Wepman relied on the work of Bastian, Wernicke, and others to develop models that, they believed, explained the process of communication through speech. Wepman then developed the Language Modalities Tests for Aphasia (Wepman & Jones, 1961), while Kirk, McCarthy, and Kirk (1961) utilized a modification of the Osgood model in the development of the Illinois Test of Psycholinguistic Abilities (ITPA). These models and tests were then used to identify specific disorders in spoken language, and numerous programs were developed to remediate any noted deficits. Other contributors in the area of spoken language during this period include Helmer Myklebust, Mildred A. McGinnis, and Jon Eisenson.

The development of tests and programs for students with disorders of written language (reading, writing, and spelling) were undertaken by Grace Fernald, Marion Monroe, Samuel Kirk, Anna Gillingham and Bessie Stillman, and Romalda Bishop Spalding. Other professionals, like Laura Lehtinen, William Cruickshank, Marianne Frostig, Newell Kephart, Gerald Getman, and Raymond Barsch, were concerned with perceptual-motor assessment and program development.

The tests and remedial programs developed were based primarily on the theories of the foundations period and the individual clinical experiences of the transition-phase authors. Since they believed that their work was constructed on sound medical, psychological, and educational principles, these professionals believed that it would benefit children with suspected minimal cerebral dysfunction. In each area of their work, they were concerned with a subset of specific skills that they believed was necessary for overcoming learning deficits. They studied phonemic sound discrimination and spoken language, sound-symbol association and written language, eye-hand coordination, and perception. The tools they developed were extremely helpful in the expansion and rapid growth of the field during the sixties and seventies;

these tools have been reviewed by Lerner (1971), by Myers and Hammill (1976), and by me (1974).

As in the foundations phase, little consideration was directed toward the learning-disabled adolescent. With the exception of Eisenson's test, Examining for Aphasia (1954), which was developed specifically for adolescents and adults, most other tests and remedial programs were geared toward young students. While some of the techniques prescribed by these tests and programs might conceivably be modified for use with adolescents, the validity of such an approach remained (and continues to remain) largely untested.

THE INTEGRATION PHASE

The birth of the field of learning disabilities can be dated April 6, 1963. On this day Samuel A. Kirk stated in a speech at a conference sponsored by the Fund for Perceptually Handicapped Children, Inc:

Recently, I have used the term "learning disabilities" to describe a group of children who have disorders in development of language, speech, reading and associated communication skills needed for social interaction. In this group, I do not include children who have sensory handicaps such as blindness or deafness, because we have methods of managing and training the deaf and blind. I also exclude from this group children who have generalized mental retardation. (Kirk, p. 3)

This speech had two major effects. First, it served as a catalyst to existing interest in the field; second, it isolated the general characteristics of the population to be subsumed under the label "learning disabilities."

Kirk's speech also precipitated a vote by the convention members that resulted in their reorganization as the Association for Children with Learning Disabilities (ACLD). ACLD grew rapidly during the last decade, becoming primarily a forum for parents of learning-disabled children. The organization plays a major role in influencing legislation and the allocation of monies for service to children with learning disabilities.

The next few years saw landmark publications and organizational growth. Three task force reports were funded by the National Society for Crippled Children and Adults, and by the National Institute of Neurological Diseases and Blindness, Public Health Service, U.S. Department of Health, Education and Welfare. Task Force I dealt with terminology and identification in the field of learning disabilities. In its report (Clements, 1966) the Task Force identified the ten characteristics of learning-disabled children most frequently cited in the literature.*

(1) hyperactivity, (2) perceptual-motor impairments, (3) emotional lability, (4) general coordination deficits, (5) disorders of attention, (6) impulsivity, (7) disorders of memory and thinking, (8) specific learning disabilities (reading, arithmetic, writing, spelling), (9) disorders of speech and hearing, and (10) equivocal neurological signs and electroencephalographic irregularities.   (p. 13)

The First Annual Report of the National Advisory Committee on Handicapped Children was published in 1968. It estimated that, although there were approximately one to two million children who could be defined as learning-disabled, only a few were receiving special education. The report also gave a formal definition of learning disabilities:

Children with special learning disabilities exhibit a disorder in one or more of the basic psychological processes involved in understanding or in using spoken or written language. These may be manifested in disorders of listening, thinking, talking, reading, writing, spelling or arithmetic. They include conditions which have been referred to as perceptual handicaps, brain injury, minimal brain dysfunctions, dyslexia, developmental aphasia, etc. They do not include learning problems due primarily to visual, hearing, or motor handicaps, to mental retardation, emotional disturbance, or to environmental disadvantage.   (p. 14)

During the same year, 1968, the Division for Children with Learning Disabilities (DCLD) was organized within the Council for Exceptional Children (CEC). DCLD's stated purpose is to promote the education and general well-being of the learning-disabled. It currently comprises over 10,500 professionals throughout the nation. One of the youngest divisions in CEC, it has quickly become the largest.

In 1969 the second and third of the three task force reports were published. The report of Task Force II contained an analysis of

---

* These characteristics are not necessarily in order of frequency of occurrence. The characteristics are those that were of most interest to writers during a specific period in the development of the field of learning disabilities.

educational identification, assessment, and evaluation procedures; educational programs; administrative and classroom procedures; professional preparation; and legislation for the education of the learning-disabled (Haring & Miller, 1969). Task Force III (Chalfant & Scheffelin, 1969) contained a review of the research on central-processing dysfunctions in children relative to the analysis and synthesis of sensory information and on dysfunctions in symbolic operations.

These various reports, as well as individual and organizational pressure, served as a foundation for legislative action. On February 28, 1969, Senator Ralph Yarborough of Texas introduced the Children with Learning Disabilities Act of 1969 in the U.S. Senate (Senate Bill 1190). Representative Roland Pucinski of Illinois introduced a similar bill in the House of Representatives (House of Representatives Bill 8660). The Children with Learning Disabilities Act amended Title VI (known as the Education of the Handicapped Act of 1967) of the Elementary and Secondary Act by specifically providing authority to the U.S. Office of Education to establish programs for the learning-disabled.

Two years later the first major national effort was made by the Bureau of Education for the Handicapped (BEH), U.S. Office of Education, to provide services to learning-disabled children throughout the nation. The legislative mandate and appropriations enabled BEH to award grants to state educational agencies for the purpose of developing Child Service Demonstration Centers (CSDCs). Eight state education agencies were awarded grants on the basis of their proposals for the fiscal years 1971–1973. At the time of this writing (1977), forty-four states have centers that are funded by BEH. After undergoing vigorous evaluation and refinement, these centers are being used as models to stimulate statewide service to learning-disabled children. The BEH also provided monies for research and teacher preparation programs.

In addition to the CSDCs, a Leadership Training Institute in Learning Disabilities (LTI) was also funded by the BEH in 1971. The purposes of an LTI are threefold: to survey and analyze the learning-disabilities field in relation to present knowledge and services; to survey and analyze teacher preparation activities; and to develop national plans for implementing strategies in research, training, and service (Bryant, 1972). Additional government-funded reports on the characteristics of children enrolled in the CSDCs, summaries of research, listings of tests, program evaluation techniques, and administrative considerations in the operation of learning-disabilities programs were also made available through the LTI.

During the late sixties and seventies, most states passed legislation and established school programs specifically for learning-disabled children. Numerous universities and colleges developed programs to prepare teachers working with this handicapped population, several textbooks on children with learning disorders were written, and untold numbers of tests and instructional materials were generated. In all, phenomenal advances were made in providing a wide variety of services to children with learning disabilities.

Unfortunately, throughout this period (about 1963–1973) learning-disabled adolescents were again virtually ignored. While a few articles, chapters, and monographs on older students were made available to the interested professional or parent (Anderson, 1970; Schloss, 1971), they were the exception rather than the rule. However, since the beginning of the learning-disabilities movement, some pioneer individuals had been working with teenagers and trying desperately to get programs established to meet their unique needs. The efforts of these workers began to have an effect on the field during the early seventies.

■ PERSPECTIVES ON THE PRESENT ■

By the mid-1970s, members of the learning-disabilities discipline had begun to place a high priority on school services for adolescent pupils. At the federal level the BEH, again utilizing Title VI-G funds, specified that proposals for Child Service Demonstration Centers that focused on adolescents would receive high priority in consideration for funding. In addition, the BEH funded a state-of-the-art document on the teenage learning-disabled population. That report was completed by me in 1975.

In many state educational agencies, program development for adolescents also became a high priority, and special projects began to be funded in many school districts. The Texas Educational Agency, Division of Special Education, made secondary programming one of their top three priorities. In 1975, five special projects were funded in Texas. The purposes of these projects were to investigate the field, to plan appropriate programs for students in special education, and to evaluate the efficiency of various service-delivery systems.

The Texas Education Agency also received a federal contract for a Service Demonstration Center for fifteen-year-old learning-disabled adolescents in 1972. During 1976 at least six innovative programs were in operation throughout the state. Personnel in Pennsylvania, Iowa, Oklahoma, and South Carolina, just to mention a few states, were also involved in experimental program development for learning-disabled adolescents.

The literature of the field began to contain numerous discussions of learning-disabled adolescents. Siegel (1974) published one of the first books on the subject, *The Exceptional Child Grows Up*. In their books on the learning-disabled, Brutten, Richardson, and Mangel (1973) and Weber (1974) included chapters about the specific problems of adolescents. Articles in professional journals appeared with increasing frequency by the mid-1970s.

National, state, and local conferences began to devote more and more sessions to the unique problems of learning-disabled adolescents. A major example of this shift in emphasis from the young child to the teenager was the New Orleans Invitational Caucus held in 1975 by the Division for Children with Learning Disabilities of the Council for Exceptional Children. Those attending the caucus specified that adolescents should be a primary topic of discussion. As a result, a subcommittee was formed within the caucus to deliberate on secondary school programming throughout the meeting.

Members of the subcommittee stressed the need for the division to consider the following critical recommendations: (1) that operational criteria for the identification of adolescents with learning disabilities be developed, (2) that the types of school programs needed at the secondary level be defined, (3) that a continuum of services from preschool to adulthood be established, (4) that adolescents' academic, social, emotional, and career needs be the focal point of school programs, (5) that competencies of secondary learning-disabilities teachers be defined and appropriate training programs instituted, (6) that a model for evaluating instructional strategies be developed, (7) that increased communication between parents and professionals be established, and (8) that funding and legislative agencies seek input from parents and professionals regarding the needs of learning-disabled adolescents.

It is apparent from just these few examples that adolescents with

18

learning disabilities have finally become a major concern of educators. Yet this move into a priority position has raised certain serious issues. The remainder of this chapter will address these issues. They include (1) defining, identifying, and determining the incidence of learning disabilities among adolescents, (2) implementing the range-of-services concept, (3) developing tests and instructional materials, (4) developing curricula, and (5) determining teacher competencies needed to serve learning-disabled adolescents adequately.

DEFINITION, IDENTIFICATION, AND INCIDENCE

The definition of learning disabilities that was proposed by the National Advisory Committee on Handicapped Children in 1968 has been adequate in securing funds and establishing laws governing support of handicapped children. This definition, however, is conceptualized and acted upon very differently throughout the nation.

In Chapter 2 of this book, Hammill characterizes the divergence of opinions on this topic. He describes, at one end of a wide continuum, professionals who believe that learning-disabled individuals must demonstrate obvious behavioral symptoms of brain dysfunction. At the other end of the continuum, he places professionals who consider as disabled any pupil experiencing significant school failure who does not fit any other category of exceptionality, such as the mentally retarded, blind, or deaf. Of course, the definition of learning disabilities one uses determines to a great extent the numbers and types of students who will be eligible for learning-disabilities services. If one adheres to the criteria of severe manifestations of suspected brain dysfunction, the identified number of pupils is likely to be small. On the other hand, if one accepts underachievement as the single criterion, the number of students identified as being eligible for services is likely to be very large—especially in districts noted for poor scholastic achievement.

Currently, several investigators (the Departments of Education in Iowa and in Kentucky, among others) are attempting to define criteria for identification that would yield a realistic number of pupils who will be eligible for learning-disabilities services and, at the same time, delineate students with the more severe disorders. While many current studies appear promising, it will remain for national and state organizations to select from the various studies the criteria and accompanying incidence figures that they are willing to include under the learning-disabilities label. I suspect that guidelines will soon be accepted by the majority of members in the field.

Unfortunately, those who would establish secondary learning-disabilities programs at this time are faced with acting upon a definition that is without clearly defined boundaries. Until a good working definition has been established, identification criteria should be viewed as experimental. Extreme caution should be taken in labeling a teenager as learning-disabled. You are encouraged to read Hammill's chapter in this book (Chapter 2) to obtain more detailed information on the issue of definition, identification, and incidence.

RANGE-OF-SERVICES CONCEPT

Advanced ideas about services in special education embody the range-of-services concept. In essence, the range-of-services idea is based on the belief that no single school service program can efficiently and effectively meet the needs of all handicapped pupils. In addition to resource room programs, there is need for medical and welfare programs, residential schools, full-time special schools and classes, and consultation services to regular education teachers if the unique needs of each handicapped student are to be met.

Range-of-service models have been presented by Reynolds (1962), Deno (1970), Brown (1973), Minskoff (1969), and myself (1975). Of these authors, Minskoff and I have developed our models specifically for adolescents with learning disabilities. Minskoff proposed three curriculum "tracts." Tract A was designed for adolescents with severe learning disabilities in addition to social and emotional problems. Tract B was designed for adolescents with less severe disorders. Essentially, Tract B provided educational opportunities for non-college-bound adolescents; it focused heavily on vocational education. Tract C, designed for mildly disabled adolescents, concentrated on modification of regular education programs. My study suggested that six types of programs are necessary to meet the unique needs of learning-disabled adolescents. These are (1) noneducational services (medical, welfare), (2) residential schools, (3) full-time special classes, (4) part-time special classes, (5) resource programs, and (6) consultation to teachers of handicapped students in regular education programs.

Those involved in establishing secondary school programs are faced at the outset with two imposing financial and personnel questions:

How can a school district support each of these programs? Where will the teaching staff be found? Consequently, most program developers probably need to focus their initial efforts on developing only one or two of the various service arrangements available.

Currently, the most popular procedure for serving disabled pupils in public elementary schools is the resource program combined with consultation to the regular classroom teacher. While this service model appears to be useful at the elementary level, some problems may occur in transferring it to the secondary schools. First, the secondary school curriculum is different from the elementary school curriculum. In the elementary schools, the goals of both special and regular educators are often the same—that is, to teach language, reading, writing, spelling, and arithmetic. But in the secondary schools, the goals typically differ. The curriculum offered in the junior and senior high schools includes English and language arts, social studies, science, higher mathematics, foreign languages, fine arts, health education, and clerical, business, and vocational education. Regular secondary education teachers often assume that their students are already proficient in basic academic skills taught in the elementary schools. Unfortunately, most, if not all, learning-disabled adolescents are seriously deficient in some basic skills and thus find orderly advancement through the secondary school curriculum very difficult.

Other factors also make the mainstreaming of the learning-disabled adolescent into regular education difficult to implement at the secondary level. For example, regular education teachers see approximately 20 to 40 students in each class and may see as many as 120 students a day. Even with resource support, these teachers are not likely to be able to provide as much individual attention to learning-disabled students as is necessary. The academic failure that often accompanies this problem is likely to damage a student's self-concept and to quash interest in continued formal education. Also, unlike their colleagues in the elementary schools, few secondary teachers are sufficiently trained in developmental, remedial, or corrective teaching. As a result, their ability to provide special teaching of basic academic skills is seriously impaired. As these problem areas indicate, secondary educators will need to consider the utility of mainstreaming before instituting it for all their learning-disabled students.

It is my considered, but admittedly unvalidated, opinion that the part-time special class may best meet the needs of most adolescents with learning disabilities. This type of class allows the adolescent to be mainstreamed into nonacademic classes (homeroom, vocational and career education, gym, and art) whenever possible. It also allows some integration into content-oriented subjects where appropriate. But, at the same time, this service delivery system allows the special educator the opportunity of providing the intensive and extensive individualized remedial education that is appropriate to students' disabilities.

Those educators who are given the responsibility of establishing secondary school programs are encouraged to consider the part-time special class as the first type of program to be established. Nonetheless, special educational support to the adolescent can never be considered adequate until a full range of services is available within the school system. Plans should be made, therefore, for a full implementation of services as soon as possible.

TESTS AND INSTRUCTIONAL MATERIALS

In the area of standardized assessment, the selection of appropriate tests of intelligence, academic aptitude and performance, vocational or occupational interests, and social-emotional development offers some difficulty. For the most part, only the individually administered tests of intelligence appear to be adequate for their stated purposes; standardized tests in other areas generally suffer from critical weaknesses. Few diagnosticians would plan to use any standardized devices for planning a specific individual program of instruction. And yet good standardized devices are necessary in determining the degree of disabilities a student is experiencing in relation to normed performance standards. Such information is very helpful (and often required by funding agencies) in validating that a student has problems necessitating special education services. In addition, standardized tests are extremely useful for research purposes and/or objective evaluation of a learner's progress.

Unfortunately, many of the standardized tests currently available for use with adolescents suffer from one or more of the following shortcomings:

1. Some of the tests are poorly constructed with regard to item selection. This results in low reliability and poor validity. Many simply lack statistical data on these dimensions.

22

2. Often these devices are poorly normed or not shown to be useful with the handicapped population; that is, the reliability of the devices is undetermined for problem learners.

3. In many cases, the grade or age equivalents are not normed low enough to provide a specific score for an adolescent with learning problems.

4. Many tests rely heavily on reading and consequently are unsuitable for many learning-disabled students to take. For example, the score that poor readers obtain on a science or history test probably reflects as much the students' inability to read as their ability to handle scientific concepts or historical facts.

While some measurement devices appear more appropriate than others, most will need to be used carefully and critically and, where necessary, to be modified. Professionals who administer standardized tests should be aware of the weaknesses in these devices; they should avoid being overly confident of the scores yielded.

Instructional materials appropriate for adolescents with learning disabilities also appear wanting. In the literature of the field, a great deal of stress is placed upon the need for remedial materials, particularly reading materials, for older students. It is also emphasized that these materials must be of high interest but at a low instructional level. Some instructional materials are available (see Chapter 8), and new ones are currently being developed. None, though, appears to be well designed, researched, and/or studied for its efficacy in teaching learning-disabled adolescents.

In short, the future energies of researchers and educators should be directed toward developing and evaluating new assessment and instructional techniques and critically evaluating the instructional materials currently available.

CURRICULA

Almost all learning-disabled adolescents lack functional proficiency in language, reading, handwriting, spelling, or arithmetic. As a result, the secondary program in special education should emphasize either the development of these important skills or the ways to compensate for their absence. In addition, secondary students need to be assisted in selecting realistic careers and to be given opportunities to learn the skills to do well in them. These two components should form the core of the curriculum for most learning-disabled adolescents.

The Carnegie Unit should be considered, when appropriate, in selecting curricula for students. For sixty years it has been the most widely used method for evaluating student progress from high school entrance to graduation (Roush, 1970). In 1909 the College Examining Board, the National Conference Committee, and the Carnegie Foundation defined the Carnegie Unit as follows:

A unit represents a year's study in any subject in a secondary school, constituting approximately a quarter of a full year's work. This statement is designed to afford a standard measurement for the work done in the secondary schools. It takes the four-year high school courses as a basis, and assumes that the length of a school year is from thirty-six to forty weeks and that the study is pursued for four or five periods a week; but, under ordinary circumstances, a satisfactory year's work in any subject cannot be accomplished in less than one hundred and twenty sixty-minute hours or their equivalent.   (Savage, 1948, p. 4)

A student who does not meet the standard course requirements of the Carnegie Units probably will not be eligible for a standard high school diploma. Those responsible for establishing curricula for learning-disabled adolescents will need to consider the Carnegie requirements carefully and to be critically aware of the constraints of the units. In some cases, an adolescent may simply not be able to complete the units for a diploma; in other cases, the best interests of the student's present needs and future career opportunities may lie in working for the diploma.

TEACHER COMPETENCIES

Perhaps one of the most glaring areas of weakness in special education today is the lack of college programs that prepare teachers expressly for working with adolescents. This is particularly true for the field of learning disabilities. The field is so new to public education that only recently have programs been developed for training teachers to work with learning-disabled adolescents. Consequently, professionals establishing learning-disabilities programs in the secondary schools need to be aware that adequately trained teachers are not immediately available.

Today any discussion of teacher preparation usually raises two very basic issues. First, what are the specific competencies that teachers should have before working with the learning-disabled? Second, how can these competencies be trained in pre-service and in-service programs? Relative to the first point, it is clear that teachers will need to be skilled in assessing and teaching basic academic skills and contents, managing disruptive behaviors, and dealing with a variety of social-emotional problems. In addition, they will need to be well aware of career education programs and know how to adapt available programs to the special needs of their students. Perhaps it is this latter set of competencies that most makes learning-disabilities teachers in secondary schools different from their elementary colleagues. Because of the lack of educators specifically trained to work with learning-disabled adolescents, most new programs for this population are likely to be staffed by inexperienced or inadequately prepared teachers. Though these teachers may be certified in either elementary or special education, their training is not adequate for their full responsibilities. We need, then, first of all, to delineate the necessary qualifications for secondary learning-disabilities teachers. We need, too, to develop corresponding mechanisms for training teachers in these competencies. And until these two areas are adequately developed, teachers will have to be flexible, experimental, and ever ready to learn new skills. Chapter 12 in this book will be especially helpful to those educators who must deal with this problem.

■ CONCLUSION ■

When we read the current literature on the learning-disabled population, we realize that there is much we do not know. It is equally apparent, however, that we are making much progress. The state of the art in learning disabilities is not unlike the state of every other field of human endeavor: some information is known, other information is tentative and experimental, and much remains to be discovered.

Those who are concerned with the learning-disabled adolescent must face several issues. First, research needs to be undertaken regarding the definition, identification, and incidence of learning-disabled students. Second, a range of services ought to be developed in the nation's public schools. Third, available tests and instructional materials need to be modified and/or evaluated and new techniques need to be developed following sound procedures. Fourth, the components of a basic curriculum of academic and career education for the adolescent need to be defined and implemented. Fifth, teacher preparation programs must be instituted at both pre- and in-service levels. The remaining chapters in this book will investigate these five issues—and others—in detail.

■ REFERENCES ■

Anderson, L. E. (Ed.). *Helping the adolescent with the hidden handicap.* Belmont, Calif.: Fearon, 1970.

Brown, V. *A range of comprehensive services concept in special education.* Madison, Wis.: Madison Public Schools, 1973.

Brutten, M., Richardson, S. O., & Mangel, C. *Something's wrong with my child.* New York: Harcourt Brace Jovanovich, 1973.

Bryant, N. D. *Final report: Leadership training institute in learning disabilities* (U.S.O.E. Grant No. OEG-0-71-4425 604, U.S. Office of Education). Tucson: University of Arizona, Department of Special Education, 1972.

Chalfant, J. C., & Scheffelin, M. A. *Central processing dysfunctions in children: A review of research* (phase three of a three-phase project) (NINDS Monograph No. 9). Bethesda, Md.: National Institute of Neurological Diseases and Stroke, 1969.

Clements, S. D. *Minimal brain dysfunction in children: Terminology and identification* (phase one of a three-phase project) (NINDS Monograph No. 3, U.S. Public Health Service Publication No. 1415). Washington, D.C.: U.S. Government Printing Office, 1966.

Deno, E. Special education as developmental capital. *Exceptional Children,* 1970, 37, 229–237.

Eisenson, T. *Examining for aphasia.* New York: Psychological Corp., 1954.

Hallahan, D. P., & Cruickshank, W. *Psycho-educational foundations of learning disabilities.* Englewood Cliffs, N.J.: Prentice-Hall, 1973.

Haring, N. G., & Miller, C. A. (Eds.). *Minimal brain dysfunctions in children: Educational, medical and health related services* (phase two of a three-phase project) (N&SDCP Monograph, Public Health Publication No. 2015). Washington, D.C.: U.S. Department of Health, Education and Welfare, 1969.

Head, H. *Aphasia and kindred disorders of speech* (Vols. 1 & 2). London: Cambridge University Press, 1926.

Kirk, S. A. Behavioral diagnosis and remediation of learning disabilities. *Proceedings of the Annual Meeting of the Conference on Exploration into the Problems of the Perceptually Handicapped Child* (Vol. 1). Chicago: Perceptually Handicapped Children, Inc., 1963.

Kirk, S. A. *Educating exceptional children*. Boston: Houghton Mifflin, 1972.

Kirk, S. A., McCarthy, J. J., & Kirk, W. D. *Examiner's manual: Illinois test of psycholinguistic abilities*. Urbana: University of Illinois Press, 1961.

Lerner, J. W. *Children with learning disabilities: Theories, diagnosis, and teaching strategies*. Boston: Houghton Mifflin, 1971.

Luria, A. R. *Higher cortical functions in man*. New York: Basic Books, 1966.

Minskoff, J. G. Modifying and restructuring academics for secondary school special education. *Adams School Bulletin*, 1969, *3*, 1.

Myers, P. I., & Hammill, D. D. *Methods for learning disorders*. New York: Wiley, 1976.

Reynolds, M. C. A framework for considering some issues in special education. *Exceptional Children*, 1962, *1*, 367–370.

Roush, R. E. The Carnegie unit—how did we get it? *The Educational Forum*, 1970, *35*, 71–74.

Savage, H. J. The Carnegie Foundation and the rise of the unit. *Forty-third annual report of the Carnegie Foundation for the advancement of teaching*. Boston: Merrymount, 1948.

Schloss, E. *The educator's enigma: The adolescent with learning disabilities*. San Rafael, Calif.: Academic Therapy Publications, 1971.

Schuell, H., Jenkins, J. J., & Jimenez-Pabon, E. *Aphasia in adults*. New York: Haeber Medical Division, Harper, 1964.

Siegel, E. *The exceptional child grows up*. New York: Dutton, 1974.

Wallace, G., & McLoughlin, J. A. *Learning disabilities: Concepts and characteristics*. Columbus, Ohio: Charles E. Merrill, 1975.

Weber, R. E. *Handbook on learning disabilities*. Englewood Cliffs, N.J.: Prentice-Hall, 1974.

Wepman, J. M., & Jones, L. V. *The language modalities test for aphasia*. Chicago: University of Chicago Education Industry Service, 1961.

Wiederholt, J. L. Historical perspectives on the education of the learning disabled. In L. Mann & D. A. Sabatino (Eds.), *The second review of special education*. Philadelphia: JSE Press, 1974.

Wiederholt, J. L. *A report on secondary school programs for the learning disabled. Final report* (Project No. II12-7145B, Grant No. OEG-0-714425). Washington, D.C.: Bureau of Education for the Handicapped, 1975.

CHAPTER 2

ADOLESCENTS WITH SPECIFIC LEARNING DISABILITIES: DEFINITION, IDENTIFICATION, AND INCIDENCE

DONALD D. HAMMILL

As we saw in Chapter 1, the field of learning disabilities first became an integrated and organized area of interest in 1963 at a conference sponsored by the Fund for Perceptually Handicapped Children. The Association for Children with Learning Disabilities was formed there, and an advisory board was created. The members of the board held a broad spectrum of opinions about specific disorders of spoken and written language and about deficits in perceptual-motor functioning. Five years later, educators from the Council for Exceptional Children who were interested in learning-disabled students met and formed another group, the Division for Children with Learning Disabilities. These two national organizations have generated much public interest in the learning-disabled. Partially as a result of their efforts, school programs have been established, and funds to support Child Service Demonstration Centers, teacher training programs, and research have been obtained. For the most part, these organizations have emphasized programming for the preschool and elementary school student. Efforts on behalf of the adolescent youngster with learning disabilities have been less emphasized.

From the start some parents and professionals have balked at this neglect of the older student. At every convention they would justifiably complain that the program contained little or nothing of interest to them. Although they had contributed their fair share to the organizational efforts to make government officials, public school administrators, and teachers aware of the unique instructional requirements of individuals with specific learning disabilities, often they were forced to watch with resignation as programs were initiated only at the elementary levels. Time was on their side, however; children in elementary schools eventually became adolescents. With each passing year the ranks of those interested in adolescents with specific learning disabilities have become larger and increasingly more vocal.

Only now, twelve years after the founding of the learning-disabilities movement, are the problems of young adults with specific learning disabilities beginning to receive a fair proportion of attention. This belatedness is ironic because the entire field is conceptualized on the study of adolescents and adults with learning and behavior problems. The basic principles and definitions, most of the assessment devices, and many of the remedial and treatment procedures associated with the movement today are readily traceable to the work done between 1800 and 1930 by researcher-clinicians who studied mostly adolescents and adults (Goldstein, 1936; Head, 1926; Jackson, 1915; Hinshelwood, 1917).

The belated interest in programs for secondary students with specific learning disabilities is raising a number of questions. First, how are "learning disabilities" to be defined? Second, how are affected individuals to be identified? And, third, how many students are there with serious learning disabilities?

■ LEARNING DISABILITIES: A DEFINITION ■

The majority of professionals in the field have no difficulty defining "specific learning disability." They simply accept one of the many existing definitions, referring to it every time they are asked "What kinds of students will you serve in this new program? What is the target population for your research project? What kinds of students are you preparing teachers to teach?" The particular definition selected matters little, since all the definitions are similar in their basic points.

The definitions offered by Kirk and Bateman (1962), Myklebust (1963), Bateman (1965), the National Society for Crippled Children and Adults (1966), the Association for Children with Learning Disabilities (1967), or the National Advisory Committee on Handicapped Children (1968) fundamentally incorporate the same ideas. First, there must be a significant disparity between the abilities that the student does well and those that he or she does poorly (for example, between reading and speaking ability or between measured intelligence and academic performance). Second, this observed disparity must somehow be caused by a disturbance involving some basic psychological process. Finally, the problem cannot be caused directly by such conditions as mental retardation, blindness, or deprivation. This last component in the definition is usually referred to as the exclusion clause. These three elements appear in one form or another in almost all the definitions commonly used today.

The most popular definition of all—the one offered by the National Advisory Committee on Handicapped Children—is quoted in Chapter 1 of this book. This particular definition is the one most frequently used by teacher trainers, school administrators, and researchers when they are asked to specify the population in which they are interested.

Because it was developed by a committee sponsored by the U.S. Office of Education (USOE) and is written into the guidelines governing the operation of programs for the learning-disabled in several states, it has an official aura about it.

While definitions may serve various administrative purposes, this one and others have a basic shortcoming (or a saving grace, depending on your point of view). They are actually projective devices, for every professional person interprets the definition in terms of his or her own background, orientation, interests, and school needs. Because they conceptualize the field of learning disabilities differently, educators also interpret the definition differently. The importance of this observation to educational practice is discussed in the next section.

Actually, choosing a satisfactory definition to describe the adolescent with specific learning disabilities causes few problems. There are many suitable definitions; any of those referred to in this section will suffice. Putting the definition into operation, however, is another matter. The manner in which the definition is *interpreted* determines two critical aspects of educational programming: who is to be included, and how many are to be served. Considered in this light, the choice and interpretation of a definition become more significant.

■ IDENTIFICATION OF LEARNING-DISABLED STUDENTS ■

In his survey of the development of the field of learning disabilities, Wiederholt (1974) suggested that the ideas, orientations, and procedures that influenced the growth of the field could be divided into three relatively distinct stages—the foundations phase, the transition phase, and the integration phase. (See Chapter 1 of this book.) During the foundations period, the work was dominated by physicians studying adults with acquired brain injuries. In the transition period, when attention shifted to the study of pupils with developmental disorders, the investigations were undertaken mostly by psychologists and educators. During the integration period (today's stage), the theories and practices of the previous stages are being widely applied to students. Educators are now becoming increasingly prominent in the field of learning disabilities, although psychologists and physicians are still making significant contributions. Given the divergence of training of those who have structured the field, it is not surprising that today's professionals are tending to operationalize the concept of learning disabilities quite differently from their predecessors, even though they may adhere to the same definitions.

Throughout the development of the field, the younger professionals have built on the work of those who went before. Consequently, many of the concepts about learning-disabled individuals that were postulated in the 1800s continue to affect current educational policies and programming. Although these early contributions have naturally undergone varying degrees of alteration and face lifting, they are still clearly visible. Their influence is most critically felt in the area of identification.

There seem to be two clearly defined approaches to identifying learning-disabled students. The first is a "strict-constructionalist" interpretation that conceives of learning disability as including little more than the "hard core," or classically defined clinical types, especially dyslexics, dysphasics, and those with Strauss syndrome. The second, more liberal interpretation permits the inclusion of underachieving, unmotivated, and poorly taught students of the "soft core" variety. In practice, most educators probably attempt to implement programs that incorporate aspects of both approaches.

THE STRICT-INTERPRETATION APPROACH

The basic ideas of the advocates of the strict-interpretation approach are remarkably similar to those espoused by the founders of the field of learning disabilities. The adolescent's problems are interpreted within a psychoneurological frame of reference, the etiology is either demonstrated or suspected brain dysfunction, and the terms used to describe the observed problems have unmistakable pathological undertones. Thus the cause of an individual's difficulties might be said to be rooted in brain injury, heredity, cerebral dysfunction, or some similar area; and the specific problems that the young person may evidence are diagnosed as developmental dysphasia, dyslexia, strephosymbolia, dysgraphia, dyscalculia, catastrophic syndrome, Strauss syndrome, and the like. This approach, the most enduring of all, has been present at every stage in the development of the field. Its advocates interpret the definition strictly in terms of criteria set down by professionals who worked in the foundations stage.

There is little need to speculate about how the founding fathers would operationalize the USOE definition. Conjecture is unnecessary because the fathers have described precisely the characteristics of the affected persons they studied and have followed up these descriptions with clear explanations of their significance. An example in the area of disorders of spoken language is provided by Gall:

In consequence of an attack of apoplexy a soldier found it impossible to express in spoken language his feelings and ideas. His face bore no signs of a deranged intellect. His mind (esprit) found the answer to questions addressed to him and he carried out all he was told to do; shown an armchair and asked if he knew what it was, he answered by seating himself in it. He could not articulate on the spot a word pronounced for him to repeat; but a few moments later the word escaped from his lips as if involuntarily. In his embarrassment he pointed to the lower part of his forehead; he showed impatience and indicated by gestures that his impotence of speech came from there. It was not his tongue which was embarrassed; for he moved it with great agility and could pronounce quite well a large number of isolated words. His memory was not at fault, for he signified his anger at being unable to express himself concerning many things which he wished to communicate. It was the faculty of speech alone which was abolished. (Head, 1926, p. 11)

Like Gall and others, Hinshelwood (1917) studied persons who had sustained cerebral insult and, as a result, had lost a basic ability. His area of primary interest was reading. This interest in *acquired* disabilities in written language, however, expanded to include two *developmental* forms as well. These Hinshelwood called "congenital word-blindness" and "hereditary congenital word-blindness." He described an example of the former type as

a boy, aged fourteen years, bright, intelligent, and quick at games and in no way inferior to others of his own age, unless in his inability to learn to read. The greatest difficulty was experienced in teaching the boy his letters, and it was thought that he never would learn them. He had by constant application acquired a knowledge of the letters, but though at school and under tutors for seven years, and in spite of the most persistent efforts, he could only with difficulty spell out words of one syllable. Words written or printed seemed to convey no impression to his mind, and it was only after laboriously spelling them that he was able by the sound of the letters to discover their import. He read figures fluently, and could do simple sums correctly. The boy himself said that he was fond of arithmetic, and

34

found no difficulty with it. The boy's schoolmaster, who had taught him for some years, said that he would be the smartest boy in school, if the instruction were entirely oral.   (pp. 41–42)

It is apparent that the characteristics associated with the conditions observed by Gall (about 1802) and by Hinshelwood (about 1895) are consistent with the key provisions in the 1968 USOE definition of specific learning disability. First, both Gall and Hinshelwood noted the presence of discrepancies between their subjects' reading, math, and/ or speech abilities, thus demonstrating the principle of disparity. Second, either by inference or by documentation, they both maintained that the individual's problem was the direct consequence of actual brain dysfunctioning—that is, a process deficit involving the neural capacity of the brain to permit the orderly performance of certain neural events. Third, they both felt obligated to show that their cases were not caused by other conditions, notably mental retardation or deafness. This effort represents an early adherence to the intention behind the exclusion clause.

It should be pointed out that most of the founding fathers worked in fairly controlled clinical environments, such as a physician's private practice, a veterans hospital, or a university laboratory school. Moreover, they were mostly interested in studying "pure" or relatively pure cases. These two factors of control and purity made the problems concerning identification fewer and less perplexing than those that face a public school diagnostician today. Then, as now, it was a relatively simple matter, using clinical judgment or test scores, to establish the presence or absence of significant gaps or imbalances in a youngster's learning patterns. Acting upon the exclusion clause was no problem for these early researchers, because they usually selected only those subjects whose observed problems were likely to be independent of, or at least not seriously affected by, other contaminating conditions.

The strict interpretation of the process clause would not cause them any appreciable difficulty, either. Since they worked primarily with severely impaired adolescents and adults with acquired rather than developmental problems, it was usually possible to build a solid case in support of the presence of a neurologically defined process deficit. In most of their cases, they could provide more or less convincing evidence that the individual's lost abilities had been intact prior to a particular trauma (an automobile accident, say, or a shrapnel head

35

wound). Since the probability of nerve damage in such incidents is high, and since the loss of the ability corresponded with the approximate time of the trauma, it was thought that the neural damage had likely caused a disruption in the processes necessary for proficient speaking, thinking, and reading. The early workers' criteria for diagnosing developmental problems were also straightforward and rigorous. For example, if a youngster was bright, had been exposed to talented teachers, was motivated and achieving in other subjects, and was impaired seriously only in a single skill, it was considered probable that he suffered from congenital word-blindness, strephosymbolia, developmental dyslexia, or some form of dysphasia.

This approach to identification was never really popular among professionals oriented to public schools, but it is still an influence on many other people. Personnel in private schools and clinics and private practitioners have a penchant for the approach. Needless to say, educators and psychologists who are employed in medical facilities also gravitate toward acceptance of this orientation; and it is certainly not uncommon to find a class or two for "aphasic" or "brain-injured" students in a public school. Many parents are practically addicted to the principles and terminology associated with this approach. I believe that it is fair to assert that the strongest advocates of this position tend to accept, for the most part, theoretical positions, assessment procedures, treatment techniques, and identification criteria suggested by Strauss, Lehtinen, Cruickshank, McGinnis, Shedd, Orton, Myklebust, Wepman, and Eisenson, among others.

THE LIBERAL-INTERPRETATION APPROACH

The public school system is the stronghold for advocates of a liberal interpretation of the learning-disability definition. To understand why, one needs to know something about the realities of present-day public school administrative practices involving nonachieving students.

There are four *major* kinds of nonachieving students in the schools: the retarded, the learning-disabled, the disturbed, and a large mass of the nonhandicapped who for a variety of reasons are simply not meeting the academic or behavioral expectations of the school. Adolescents in the first three of these groups have handicaps that represent fundable categories. Adolescents in the last and much larger group, not being handicapped, do not qualify for special education services in most states, even though they are a constant source of problems for teachers and may well be more difficult to handle than are youngsters with handicaps.

Of course, public school administrators, diagnosticians, and teachers all recognize that in practice this system does not operate with clearly defined examples of each category. "Pure" or even relatively pure cases of retardation, disturbance, or learning disability are relatively few and usually readily identifiable. However, identification becomes much more difficult in the case of students who are experiencing moderate or mild difficulty. Is a particular student mildly disturbed, mildly retarded, mildly learning-disabled; or is she a nonhandicapped youngster who is merely experiencing school-related difficulties?

The majority of students who have difficulties in school do not evidence either serious problems or purity of symptoms. Consider the hypothetical case of a thirteen-year-old girl from an impoverished home with a history of prematurity and an equivocal EEG who reads three years behind CA level. Her measured intelligence is indicative of dull normal functioning, though her performance of a few cognitive tasks is normal for her age. Very uninterested in school, she does not want to attend. As a result, she is often involved in disruptive episodes with fellow students and teachers.

Is this student handicapped? If so, is she retarded, disturbed, learning-disabled, or all three? Who could say with appreciable confidence? The reality of the situation is that, as the degree of school failure becomes milder, the confusion among categories becomes greater. But because present-day administrative policies require that students be classified as having some type of handicap before they can receive special educational services, school personnel are forced to pretend that they can sort problem students into discrete categories with some degree of accuracy.

Hard-pressed school administrators and diagnosticians have greeted as a godsend government's recognition of the learning-disabled as a category of the handicapped who should receive educational funds. By applying a liberal interpretation to the learning-disabilities definition, they can provide special services to all students who are experiencing any kind of significant problem in school. Included are students with severe learning disabilities, as well as countless other individuals who would otherwise be called educable retarded,* mildly disturbed, disadvantaged, underachieving, unmotivated, and so on. Administratively, all these newly acquired "learning disability" cases would be considered "mildly handicapped."

The advocates of a liberal interpretation of the USOE definition dismiss its ambiguous and superfluous statements. Students with special learning disabilities, they say, exhibit problems in listening, thinking, reading, writing, spelling, and/or arithmetic. This is the operational definition of learning disabilities that is used in many, perhaps most, schools today. The criterion for identification is basically low achievement in school work.

There is some evidence that this approach to identification is being used extensively in the schools. Kirk and Elkins (1974), investigating the nature of the pupils referred to the Title VI-G projects across the nation, reported that the majority of the cases enrolled were not at all learning-disabled according to their criteria. Their conclusion confirms my own suspicions, which are based on observation of many learning-disability programs in public schools. In my experience, students enrolled in learning-disability classes evidence an almost total absence of hyperactivity, distractibility, linguistic, or specific conceptualization problems. A reading of the cumulative folders of these students all too often leads me to conclude that the majority of those enrolled are either dull-normal pupils achieving at expected levels or children with comparatively high IQs who are simply underachieving. Besides a low IQ, other causes for poor achievement may be poor teaching, insufficient support for school at home, and the pupil's lack of interest.

---

* The situation regarding educable mentally retarded (EMR) students deserves special mention. For years, the EMR classification was the "wastebasket" for regular education, and problem children of all varieties were enrolled in EMR classes. This was evidenced in the Garrison and Hammill (1971) study of 450 eleven-year-old children attending educable classes. The authors reported that 44 percent of these pupils actually had IQs greater than 75, and 61 percent were performing at at least the lower range of normal in the spoken-language variables investigated. Clearly, more than just EMR children were being enrolled in these classes. Today there is a strong movement in many areas toward eliminating the EMR classes or at least toward restricting enrollment to children who are in fact mentally retarded. A result of this procedure is that large numbers of pupils previously diagnosed as EMRs are being returned to the regular class, from which many of them are reassigned eventually as learning-disabled cases.

The same definition used by those adhering to a hard-core position is applied to those youngsters who are represented as soft-core learning-disabled. In other words, these pupils are regarded as having milder forms of the conditions associated with the strict application of the definition, such as dyslexia or dysphasia—a dubious conclusion, to say the least. However, those who would apply a liberal interpretation can easily satisfy the principle of disparity. They argue: Do not all under-achievers, including those from impoverished or affluent homes, show a discrepancy between their estimated intellectual potential and their actual school performance? Could not all cases that presently qualify for remedial reading and arithmetic also satisfy the disparity clause in the definition?

Proponents of a liberal interpretation satisfy the exclusion clause by pointing out that the intent of the phrase is to exclude cases in which retardation, disadvantaged background, and the like are primary causes of the specific learning disability. Surely it was not the intention of the definition that retarded individuals who had learning disabilities in addition to their retardation would be arbitrarily excluded. The process-deficit clause is dispatched by broadening the meaning of the term. These advocates reject the idea that the processes mentioned in the definition are to be equated exclusively with psychoneurological processes. Instead, they assert that many abilities, such as arithmetic and oral reading, are collections of sequenced skills and that these can be referred to as the "processes" of reading, of speaking, of writing, and so on. In this sense, can't individuals who fail to achieve in these areas be said to have some kind of process deficit? It could also be argued, of course, that reading, spelling, and speaking are as much psychoneurological processes as those described in the other approaches to identification.

Advocates of this liberal interpretation are quick to point out what they consider to be its advantages:

1. Since diagnoses in terms of assigning students with mild to moderate problems to discrete categories of handicaps are at best suspect, one might just as well treat all such students as a single category.

2. Since most students with mild to moderate problems are good candidates for mainstreaming efforts, it is convenient to consider them administratively as members of a single group.

3. Regardless of whether they are diagnosed as retarded, learning-disabled, or disturbed, students with mild to moderate problems resemble each other remarkably in their symptoms and instructional needs. For example, a student diagnosed as mildly learning-disabled may be more like a student diagnosed as mildly disturbed than he is like a student diagnosed as a severe learning-disability case (using the strict interpretation).

4. Finally, for reasons of their own, many parents of handicapped students prefer the label *learning-disabled* to the labels *retarded* or *disturbed*.

In all honesty, however, I believe that most school personnel who advocate a liberal interpretation of the definition would prefer a basic change in the rules governing funding, identification, and placement. This change would take them, to a considerable extent, out of the "diagnosing-as-handicapped" business and would permit students (especially those with mild to moderate problems) to receive services without having to be labeled as handicapped. Under such a system, school personnel would simply assign these students to the program that they need (for example, vocational education or college preparation) and provide whatever supportive services are necessary to accommodate problems interfering with the course of study (limited intelligence, poor reading and speaking ability, and so on). Appropriate supportive services might include the availability of a resource room or a consulting teacher. In all probability the school could manage successfully most of the handicapped and nonhandicapped students who evidence mild and moderate learning and behavior problems. Under such an arrangement, special education would provide special services to all students who needed them rather than confining its attention exclusively to handicapped populations.

In this approach students who are truly learning-disabled would be diagnosed and labeled properly so that their progress in school could be carefully monitored. Honest diagnosis would ensure that the unique and often serious difficulties associated with some learning-disabled youngsters are being remediated or compensated for and that the students are receiving the services that are in their best interest, whether these are provided in self-contained or mainstream programs.

The practice of defining all children who have school-related problems as learning-disabled may prove to be no more than a passing administrative convenience—a conceptually indefensible but practical necessity at the present time for getting services to nonhandicapped students who need them. The expansion of noncategorical approaches in education, an increased concern about the individual needs of problem learners on the part of regular education teachers, and successful mainstreaming and zero-reject programs may one day make it possible for many public school professionals to forego the liberal interpretation of the learning-disabilities definition.

These two approaches, the strict and the liberal interpretation, represent the extreme positions in putting a definition of learning disability into operation. For several reasons most educators, in implementing their programs, incorporate elements from both interpretations. On the one hand, many educators feel that, although the strict definition may be excellent when applied to adults who have become brain damaged and subsequently lost a specific ability, it is inappropriate when applied to children with developmental problems. On the other hand, they reject many of the pragmatic solutions that some of the advocates of the liberal approach feel compelled to make. They fear that the relatively small group of learning-disabled students will be lost in the thrust to accommodate the hordes of students who would be identified as learning-disabled by this interpretation. They argue that state legislators will not endure an interpretation that could permit 50 to 60 percent of the scholastic population of many schools to be administratively diagnosed as "handicapped." They prophesy that when a legislative reaction comes, as it eventually will, the interests of the real learning-disabled students will suffer.

What is needed today is a set of objective criteria for use by public school personnel and others to identify the population of students with specific learning disability. Fortunately, many professionals are considering various approaches. The tack taken by Wiederholt (1975) seems most promising. His five criteria relate to the student's (1) school or language achievement, (2) intelligence, (3) sensory intactness, (4) emotional status, and (5) environmental background. In short, a learning-disabled teenager enrolled in the eighth grade or higher would perform in academic areas below the fourth-grade level, would have an IQ above 85 or 90, would have normal hearing and vision after correction, would be more or less emotionally stable, would have a reasonably good school attendance record, and would be English-speaking. Conceivably, there are learning-disabled adolescents who have truancy records and who speak languages other than English, but such cases should be considered individually. The stated criteria certainly cannot be applied to non-English speakers, for the necessary tests are patently inappropriate in such instances.

These criteria would identify a group of students who were seriously underachieving in academic or language performance, though not all "underachievers" would be included. Presumably, the true handicapped learners would be caught in the net along with undetermined numbers of seriously involved problem cases. If this group were to number not more than 3 to 5 percent of the population, the criteria could be used for an operational definition of "learning disability" in the schools. Should the criteria identify more than 5 percent, additional criteria could be formulated in an attempt to reduce the percentage so that only the clear-cut cases of learning disability would be identified.

Wiederholt spells out in detail just how the criteria could be used and what the limitations are. He points out that these criteria are actually screening procedures and that they are to be used as guidelines, rather than as rigid, arbitrary standards. Wiederholt also cautions his readers that the criteria are still in an experimental stage of development; he recommends that they be field-tested and evaluated before being accepted. The criteria should be applied experimentally in a few representative schools (whose enrollments reflect a cross-section of mental abilities, races, and social classes) to determine just what kinds of, and how many, learning-disabled adolescents are identified. A variation of these criteria is found in Hammill (1976). McNutt (1977) is a source for readers interested in experimental validation of both sets of criteria on an adolescent population.

■ THE INCIDENCE OF LEARNING DISABILITIES ■
AMONG ADOLESCENTS

While some attempts have been made to determine the incidence of learning disabilities among school-aged students in general, I know of no studies undertaken specifically at the secondary level. The number of adolescents who have learning disabilities is, therefore, unknown at present.

Even if one were to accept the incidence figures associated with the overall school population as reasonably valid estimates for the secondary-aged subgroup, the question of incidence would still be far from resolved because of the general lack of agreement among the figures that have been proposed. After specifying the difficulties involved in estimating the incidence of learning disability, Kirk (1972) suggested that "the best guess is that from one to three percent at the least, and possibly seven percent at the most, of the school population require special remedial education." The validity of this estimate has received some support from Wissink (1972), who surveyed one hundred "leaders" in the learning-disabilities area (of which thirty-nine responded) regarding their estimates of the incidence of learning disabilities in a school population. Half the respondents estimated the incidence to be 5 percent or less, though almost one-third thought it was 15 percent or higher. Several comprehensive surveys of school populations have tried to establish an exact incidence but have had little success in establishing a set figure. After reviewing twenty-one of these studies, Bryant and McLoughlin (1972) concluded that the incidence of learning difficulties ranged from 3 to 28 percent, with half of the studies reporting an incidence above 13 percent.

Ultimately this lack of agreement among studies can be traced back to the absence of an agreed-on, definitive, and operational definition of "learning disabilities." Since educators who use a strict interpretation conceive of the category of the learning-disabled as including little more than classically defined students who are more likely to be found in private schools or clinical settings than in public school operations, they believe that no more than 3 percent of the school population is learning-disabled. To supporters of the liberal interpretation, an incidence figure of 15 to 30 percent seems minimal. In urban school districts with large concentrations of minorities and economically impoverished people, the figures reported by liberal interpretationists are sometimes higher.

Until there emerges an operational definition that can be used to develop specific criteria to identify precisely the pupil under question, we shall have to be content with widely disparate "guesstimates" regarding the incidence of learning disability in the school population. Unfortunately, school administrators cannot wait until the definitional questions are fully resolved. They are now being required to specify the percentage of students in their schools for whom they intend to provide services under the "learning disabilities" label. They are required to have a set figure in mind before implementing any programs so that adequate teachers, funding, and materials can be located. Therefore, it is recommended that administrators follow Kirk's suggestion and plan to serve approximately 3 percent of the school enrollment, and in no case more than 7 percent.

■ **REFERENCES** ■

Association for Children with Learning Disabilities. The Annual Conference, New York City, meeting of executives of the organization and selected professionals, 1967.

Bateman, B. An educator's view of a diagnostic approach to learning disorders. In J. Hellmuth (Ed.), *Learning disorders.* Seattle: Special Child Publications, 1965.

Bryant, N. D., & McLoughlin, J. A. Subject variables: Definition, incidence, characteristics, and correlates. In N. D. Bryant & C. E. Kass (Eds.), *Final report; Leadership training institute in learning disabilities* (Vol. 1). Tucson: University of Arizona Department of Special Education, 1972.

Garrison, M., & Hammill, D. D. Who are the retarded? *Exceptional Children,* 1971, *38,* 13–20.

Goldstein, K. The modification of behavior consequent to cerebral lesions. *Psychiatric Quarterly,* 1936, *10,* 586–610.

Hammill, D. D. Defining "learning disabilities" for pragmatic purposes. *Academic Therapy,* 1976, *12,* 26–37.

Head, H. *Aphasia and kindred disorders of speech* (Vols. 1 and 2). London: Cambridge University Press, 1926.

Hinshelwood, J. *Congenital word blindness.* London: Lewis, 1917.

Jackson, J. H. On the physiology of language. *Brain,* 1915, *38,* 59–64.

Kirk, S. A. *Educating exceptional children* (2nd ed.). Boston: Houghton Mifflin, 1972.

Kirk, S. A., & Bateman, B. Diagnosis and remediation of learning disabilities. *Exceptional Children,* 1962, *29,* 73–78.

Kirk, S. A., & Elkins, J. *Characteristics of children enrolled in the Child Service Demonstration Centers.* Tucson: University of Arizona, Department of Special Education, 1974.

McNutt, G. L. *The identification of learning disabled adolescents.* Doctoral dissertation, Department of Special Education, University of Texas, Austin, 1977.

Myklebust, H. R. Psychoneurological learning disorders in children. In S. A. Kirk & W. Becker (Eds.), *Conference on children with minimal brain impairment.* Urbana: University of Illinois Press, 1963.

National Advisory Committee on Handicapped Children. *First annual report, Special education for handicapped children.* Washington, D.C.: Department of Health, Education and Welfare, 1968.

National Society for Crippled Children and Adults and the National Institute of Neurological Diseases and Blindness of the National Institutes of Health. *Minimal brain dysfunction in children* (NINDB Monograph No. 3). Washington, D.C.: U.S. Department of Health, Education and Welfare, 1966.

Wiederholt, J. L. Historical perspectives on the education of the learning disabled. In L. Mann & D. A. Sabatino (Eds.), *The second review of special education.* Philadelphia: JSE Press, 1974.

Wiederholt, J. L. *A report on secondary school programs for the learning disabled. Final Report* (Project No. H12-7145B, Grant No. OEG-0-714425). Washington, D.C.: Bureau of Education for the Handicapped, 1975.

Wissink, J. F. *A procedure for the identification of children with learning disabilities.* Unpublished doctoral dissertation, University of Arizona, 1972.

CHAPTER 3

PSYCHOEDUCATIONAL ASPECTS OF LEARNING-DISABLED ADOLESCENTS

DONALD D. DESHLER

A major problem confronting professionals in the learning-disabilities field is the identification of characteristics that differentiate learning-disabled pupils both from other problem learners and from pupils who do not evidence learning disorders. There has been much studying of the characteristics of learning-disabled students in the elementary grades (Clements, 1966; Myklebust & Boshes, 1969; Deutch & Schumer, 1970; DeRuiter, 1973), but little data exist on older learning-disability pupils (Anderson, 1970; Deshler, 1974). Before we can set up appropriate remedial programs for older disabled students, we must first learn what distinguishes this target population from the larger group. Some educators warn about the ill effects of categorizing pupils on the basis of their primary disability. Being aware of the limitations of this practice does not, however, preclude our using it in determining the characteristic deficiencies that result from specific disabilities. Recognizing these characteristic deficiencies is relevant to understanding the means by which students learn and perform.

■ THE STUDY OF CHARACTERISTICS ■

Current information on the characteristics of secondary learning-disabled students is primarily based on clinical or classroom observations of adolescent learners (Hagin, 1971; Strother, 1971; Siegel, 1974; Wilcox, 1970; Drake & Cavanaugh, 1970). The research and observational literature, though, often does not clearly define target populations. Consequently, comparing different research and observational findings is difficult.

Bryant and McLoughlin (1972) emphasized that the variables characterizing learning-disabled pupils are a function of the definition of criterion levels for inclusion and exclusion. Specifying these criterion levels in research and observational reports would seem to be a logical first step in the search for the identifying characteristics of a given population.

Delineating variables that characterize learning-disabled students is a complex undertaking. The identification of variance is *not* accomplished by the common practice of citing elaborate lists of characteristics popularly associated with learning disabilities. Such an approach often results in the inappropriate and eventually meaningless application of terms such as *hyperactivity, perceptual deficit, distractibility,* and *disorders of thinking.*

In studying the characteristics of learning disability, one should weigh the relative importance and prevalence of various characteristics at different age levels, in different types of disabilities, in different settings, and in different combinations. The intricacies of the situation demand the following considerations:

1. The presence of any given characteristic is neither conclusive nor required in determining if a youngster has a learning disability. Conversely, all characteristics commonly associated with learning disabilities need not be present in order to cause a reduction in a student's educational and social adjustments.

2. A critical element in identifying and operationally defining handicaps is cut-off points. Although cut-off points on general characteristics, such as visual or auditory acuity, can be used to define blindness and deafness as handicaps, many misclassifications have resulted from using cut-off points on intelligence tests to define mental retardation. In the case of learning disabilities, even if a cut-off point from a single measure could be established, it would not be sufficient to explain the disability, since the characteristic could also be present in part of the population that is not learning-disabled. Thus, delineating differences between learning-disabled and non-learning disabled populations is more complex than the either-or solution implied by using cut-off points to locate learning-disabled students in the lower portion of a learning continuum.

3. In redefining learning disability, Kass (1974) suggested that one of the conditions of a learning disability is that it persists past maturity. Similarly, Rogan and Lukens (1969) stated that a learning disability is characterized by a persistence or chronicity. They also noted that the disability may manifest itself in changing ways as the pupil matures and the school demands change. The question of how manifestations of a disability vary as a function of chronological age is a critical one, because it has not been fully determined if characteristics commonly associated with learning disabilities at younger ages exist in adolescent populations. For example, Clements (1966) has listed, in order of prevalence, ten differentiating characteristics* of minimal brain dysfunctions. This listing is based primarily on research conducted with children rather than with adolescents. Thus, any generalization of characteristics from a younger age group to an older one should be made with caution.

4. Characteristics associated with learning disabilities are often closely related. Myers and Hammill (1969) emphasized the influence of one characteristic on another and the interrelation and progressive debilitating influence of given characteristics on behavioral and academic outcomes. In a study of forty component disabilities thought to be correlated with learning disabilities, Wissink (1972) found that none of the factors was judged as being totally independent. Banks and Finlayson (1973) also discovered a high degree of interrelatedness between characteristics associated with success and failure in secondary schools. Thus, the high probability of overlap of characteristics should be considered, and characteristic groupings should not be treated as mutually exclusive.

5. While it is possible to conceptualize every learned behavior as a potential area of learning disability, only a few areas are regarded as basic to the field. Typically, the areas of emphasis have involved the use of spoken or written language in an academic setting and the implications of deficient academic skills for educational opportunities. This emphasis may be appropriate when the target population consists of elementary-age students, since dysfunctioning in learning calls attention to itself primarily in poor performance in academic skill areas. As students with learning disabilities enter adolescence, however, inadequate academic performance may be accompanied by nonacademic characteristics caused by social demands and pressures external to the classroom. Consequently, any discussion of the characteristics of learning-disabled adolescents must include those factors that would diminish their employment adjustment and social adjustment as well as their academic success.

✳ **6.** Learning-disabled secondary school students are adolescents, sub-

---

* The ten most commonly cited characteristics resulting from Clements' review are (1) hyperactivity, (2) perceptual-motor impairments, (3) emotional lability, (4) general coordination deficits, (5) disorders of attention, (6) impulsivity, (7) disorders of memory and thinking, (8) specific learning disabilities (9) disorders of speech and hearing, and (10) equivocal neurological signs and encephalographic irregularities.

ject to the demands and influences unique to that particular period of development. While educators should be cautious in making generalizations about adolescence, they do need to be aware of some of the unique pressures encountered by students in this age group. For example, a young person's sexual maturation and the desire to become autonomous and independent from adult domination may precipitate certain kinds of behaviors. However, a normal falling short of a perceived ideal standard on any given developmental trait should not be misinterpreted as a characteristic unique to learning-disabled students at this age level. When a pupil's performance on a given attribute is below the standard expectation, the challenge of the assessment process is to determine if the performance is within the range of normal variation, or if it is a significant deviation from the perceived standard. If the deviation is a significant one, the probability that the student is learning-disabled is increased but not ensured. An educator aware of the pressures and changes in adolescent development will have further insight into a youngster already saddled with a learning disability. Since there are innumerable unanswered questions on the effects of adolescence on behavior, perhaps the best posture for educators is to develop an awareness of how developmental pressures may precipitate a problem in learning or adjustment. The characteristics of a handicapping condition should be examined in the larger milieu of external and internal factors such as adolescent development.

The discussion on psychoeducational characteristics that follows delineates subject and environmental characteristics that account for and describe learning disabilities in adolescents. The characteristics are arbitrarily categorized as academic-cognitive factors, personality-social factors, and perceptual-motor factors. Such a classification is obviously subjective; the placing of a component in a particular category does not imply that the component is independent of other components or that the categories are mutually exclusive.

■ ACADEMIC-COGNITIVE FACTORS ■

The characteristics that define the learning processes of disabled learners have not been adequately researched (Bryant & Kass, 1972), but disability at the high school level does appear to show a lack of hierarchical acquisition of functions associated with normal academic

51

achievement. By the time students reach high school age, previous developmental functions should have been systematically integrated so that students are capable of performing complex tasks with high efficiency. When basic skills have not been integrated by high school age, performance on curriculum requirements will most likely be affected, because academic materials at this level are more complex and demand a synthesized, efficient application of skills. The aim of the elementary academic program for all children is the acquisition of academic skills in reading, spelling, language, and arithmetic. Learning-disabled secondary students often need additional training in these basic skills, but the regular curriculum focuses more on various content areas that demand the *application* of basic academic skills rather than their *acquisition*.

To promote the acquisition of these skills, educators should be aware of three basic academic and cognitive factors: performance profiles and cognitive abilities, language and communication, and skills for independent functioning.

PERFORMANCE PROFILES AND COGNITIVE ABILITIES

Learning-disabled students are commonly thought to have a profile of academic abilities that reflects both strengths and weaknesses. Authors who have described the learning-disabled pupil have noted that these students also show a jagged profile in achievement level and inconsistency in performance (Gordon, 1969; Siegel, 1974). Using a Bayesian analysis* of test scores on learning-disabled and normal adolescent samples, I found significant overlap in the performance of the groups (1974). This supports the notion of a profile of variant abilities and indicates that learning-disabled adolescents do not have a suppressed profile in all areas of academic functioning.

Some authors have noted that measures of cognitive abilities of reading-disabled and learning-disabled populations show a decrease as a function of age. Myklebust (1973), for example, has indicated that

---

* Bayesian statistics provide a means of updating probability statements about the presence of given characteristics by combining prior probabilities (which represent the state of knowledge prior to observations and data gathering) with test score data to produce revised posterior probabilities (which reflect the confidence with which learning disabilities have been identified).

the highest scores on the Primary Mental Abilities Test and the Draw-a-Man Test were attained by nine- and eleven-year-old reading-disability groups, and the lowest by the fifteen-year-old group. Myklebust does not feel that this trend indicates a decrease in potential but rather an inability to achieve at a normal rate.

Others who have noted lower measures of cognitive abilities among older students attribute this performance to delays in maturation. Brutten, Richardson, and Mangel (1973) stress that logical-reasoning and abstract-thinking skills do not develop as early in learning-disability pupils as they do in nondisabled students. A Stanford Research Institute report entitled *Compensatory Education and Early Adolescence* (1974) speaks of maturational deficiencies in describing the poor performance of some high school students. This report notes that intensive educational efforts with certain older pupils may be equally effective as early intervention with other segments of the population, because in the adolescent period some students experience accelerated rates of cognitive development.

The long-term effect of exposure to remedial strategies that emphasize working with a student's weaknesses while ignoring his or her strengths may be another explanation for lower performance measures at the secondary level. The neglect of areas of integrity for a prolonged period may result in a depression of these areas. Thus, instead of bringing weaknesses into closer proximity with strengths, remediation may result in reducing strengths toward the level of weaknesses.

Apparent changes in cognitive abilities as a function of age may also be the result of the assessment procedures used to measure these changes. Most measures of cognitive functioning rely on product-oriented data—that is, data that depend highly on knowledge of culturally based facts. Such measures unfairly discriminate against students who are unable to benefit fully from the middle-class base of knowledge or who have "tuned out" the instruction that provides them with the necessary "products" of information. Assessment procedures that emphasize the *process* by which one learns may be a more meaningful index in measuring cognitive abilities, since process data are not as likely to be contaminated by previous cultural learning. The work on learning potential by Budoff (1968) gives promising direction to the problem of assessment of adolescent populations and may be considered a favorable alternative to traditional product assessment.

LANGUAGE AND COMMUNICATION

In order to achieve in the secondary curriculum, a student must demonstrate basic integrities in reading, spelling, writing, and language. Learning-disabled students, however, continue to encounter difficulties in some or all of these areas in the secondary grades.

Many learning-disabled adolescents fail to master basic reading skills. Hagin (1971) states that the pervasive difficulty of the learning-disabled adolescent is an inadequacy in dealing with symbols. This may manifest itself in difficulties with chemical symbols or the phyla in biology. A comprehensive study citing the difficulties experienced by clinic cases (age ten to fourteen) of reading disability was reported by Doehring (1968). Her factor analysis of seventy-nine variables related to reading indicated that the members of the reading-disabled group differed in their proficiency in various reading skills such as word discrimination, work recognition, and decoding. She also found, however, that these students generally tended to perform poorly on all measures of reading and spelling.

High school students have also been found to be deficient in blending ability. Drake and Cavanaugh (1970), for example, found that secondary students who score fifteen or more points higher on the Performance than on the Verbal scale of the Wechsler frequently exhibit auditory problems such as blending, discrimination, and serial-order memory. My study (1974), using the Blending test from the Stanford Diagnostic Reading Test, Level II (Karlsen, Madden, & Gardner, 1966), found that learning-disabled high school students perform much more poorly in blending tasks than do non-learning-disabled students. Among the learning-disabled, the ability to synthesize word parts into wholes remains unmastered at the secondary level. Blending facility figures importantly in mastery of the secondary curriculum because of the importance of speed as a performance variable. Also, the ability quickly to synthesize parts into wholes aids comprehension of content material.

While most research on disabled populations has emphasized reading difficulties involving skills of decoding and accuracy, the secondary curriculum also demands competency in comprehension, vocabulary development, and speed. Research is needed to define the exact nature of deficits evidenced by adolescent learning-disabled populations in these skill areas.

Spelling difficulties often accompany reading disabilities or problems in decoding words. Boder (1971) devised a diagnostic screening procedure in which reading and spelling are jointly analyzed as interdependent functions. Her procedure identified three atypical reading-spelling patterns that are characteristic of dyslexic students. She found at least one of the patterns in all the problem readers she studied, but none in normal readers and spellers.

Bryant and McLoughlin (1972) suggest that spelling problems frequently remain after a child who has had a reading problem has overcome that difficulty. Some authors indicate that spelling is a more sensitive indicator of a language handicap, because fewer means of compensation are available and because poor spelling may persist past maturity. My work with high school students (Deshler, 1974) lends support to these notions. I analyzed the ability of high school students to detect spelling errors in words. The results, when analyzed with a signal detection model,* indicate that the ability of the learning-disabled group to find spelling errors is not much better than chance performance. More important, virtually no overlap was noted in the performance of the learning-disabled and the normal groups. This suggests that the task of detecting spelling errors was extremely effective in discriminating learning-disabled students from normal students. On reading comprehension measures, by contrast, the samples in my study evidenced considerable performance overlap.

Written expression is of paramount importance at the secondary level. Curriculum requirements at the secondary level rely heavily on written responses. Note taking, test taking, and assignment completion are largely a function of one's skills in written expression. Unfortunately, problems of written language have often been neglected in the study of development deviations. A significant contribution has been made by Myklebust in the development of the Picture Story Language Test (1965), which was designed to study written expression in normal and exceptional children. This test analyzes three dimensions of written expression: productivity (total words, total sentences, words per sentence), correctness (of syntax), and ideation (degree of abstractness or concreteness in written expression).

In a 1973 study using nine-, eleven-, thirteen-, and fifteen-year-olds,

---

* Signal detection theory provides a means of analyzing a student's sensitivity to the presence of an error as well as the criteria used by the subject to say that an error is present or absent.

Myklebust compared the written language of a reading-disabled population with that of a normal population. At all ages the reading-disabled group was found to be markedly deficient in output of written language as measured by total words written and total sentences. In most cases the reading-disabled group produced about one-third the output of the control group. This suggests a lack of fluency and a laboriousness in written expression. The reading-disabled group was also deficient on the syntax measures, such as correct use of tense, punctuation, and word order.

Myklebust also noted an interesting trend in syntax facility as a function of age. At nine years of age, the reading-disabled syntax quotient was seventeen points below average; but at eleven, thirteen, and fifteen years, it was only about seven points lower than average. Thus deficiencies in syntax seem to be somewhat improved by age eleven; and, like the normals, the reading-disability group reached a plateau at eleven years and evidenced few gains in syntax after this age.

The reading-disabled group was also found to be retarded in the use of abstractions. This use is closely related to language fluency and to the magnitude of the word pool available to the student. The ability to use and understand abstractness in communication is of critical importance in successfully meeting secondary curriculum demands. The fifteen-year-olds were markedly inferior to the normal controls on this index. Myklebust underscored the problems that youngsters disabled in written expression encounter as they grow older. Deficiencies in written expression can greatly diminish a student's chances for successfully fulfilling curricular demands in the secondary schools.

Oral language, writing, speaking, and listening have been identified as the primary language forms. Unfortunately, we know little about the oral-language characteristics of language disorders, about delayed language development, and about the best methods of teaching oral-language skills. The ability to speak effectively is a required skill for success in classroom activities and social situations. A student may partially compensate for reading or writing deficiencies by employing effective speaking skills in group settings. These skills include building a speaking vocabulary, learning linguistic patterns, and formulating sentences. Lubach (1975) found that learning-disabled junior high school students have deficits in the use of past-tense verbs when compared to normal peers. Lubach suggests that incorrect past-tense usage is still effective for conveying the basic thought, since the incorrect form is often similar to the correct form. My study (1974) found the vocabulary skills of learning-disabled high school students to be inferior to their normal peers in a synonym identification task, using vocabulary terms from secondary-level text materials.

The successful completion of curriculum requirements in secondary school is facilitated if students have the listening skills needed to handle the information that comes through lectures, directions, and normal conversation. Listening skills, as categorized by Wilt (1964), include understanding words and concepts; building a listening vocabulary; understanding sentences and other linguistic elements of language; auditory memory; and listening comprehension, which includes following directions, understanding a sequence of events through listening, recalling details, and getting the main idea. Hagin (1971) has described the learning-disabled adolescent as one who may have difficulty listening in school and who may become confused and be unable to take effective notes during discussions or class lectures. Siegel (1974) sees the ramifications of poor listening skills in an even broader context. He contends that social interactions and peer acceptance, job performance, and academic success are highly dependent upon keen listening skills; therefore, development of these skills should be a high priority in teaching learning-disabled adolescents.

SKILLS FOR INDEPENDENT FUNCTIONING

One goal of adolescence is independence of action, both in and out of the classroom. Successful social adjustment and successful classroom performance depend, in part, on the degree to which a student can function autonomously. Typically, secondary students do not have the close interaction with, and supervision by, teachers that they enjoyed in the elementary grades. The imposed structure and organization that provided direction to students in elementary school is reduced to a subtle, more flexible structure in high school.

In elementary school many of the study assignments and test reviews are conducted under the watchful eye of the teacher. Secondary-level students are expected to assume more responsibility for such activities and to impose their own structure. For many youngsters with a learning disability, the absence of structure and organization and an inability to function independently can prove devastating.

Academic success in secondary school is largely a function of one's study and test-taking skills. Learning-disabled youngsters in secondary situations are often deficient on both accounts. Study skills that may be absent include planning a study schedule, reviewing frequently, understanding that there is a difference between being familiar with material and knowing material, and knowing which persons to ask for help and how to ask. Test-taking skills that may be absent are these: determining the type of questions a teacher may ask, answering easy questions first, allotting time properly during the test session, answering all questions, and checking answers. Hudson (1974) has stressed that highly structured schedules and routines in academic settings can favorably affect school adjustment of learning-disabled high school students. Especially helpful are teachers who show students how to organize an approach to problems (and who assist them in systematic planning and following through).

A student's ability to function independently in an academic or social setting is facilitated if activities are accompanied by a constant process of self-monitoring. The role of monitoring, or the detection of errors, is a crucial one in both learning and performance. Wissink (1972) found that learning-disability specialists estimate that a monitoring deficit occurs in a learning-disabled population. To learn a skilled, highly integrated response and to perform accurately and rapidly, one must respond both to feedback data generated from one's own response and to external information. Siegel (1974) has suggested that a faulty feedback mechanism in older learning-disabled students may impede their ability to interact appropriately in social situations. My study (1974) found that learning-disabled high school students evidenced a monitoring deficit on academic tasks that require the detection of self-generated and externally generated errors.

On a creative-writing task, for example, learning-disabled students detected only one-third of the errors that they committed. The normal group detected twice as many errors on the same task. The repercussions of such performance in academic and future employment situations are obvious. Learning-disabled adolescents should be made aware of the quality of their performance in written work. They should learn monitoring strategies and how to be selective in their written words and sentences so as to limit the number of errors.

Finally, independent functioning assumes the application of intact thinking skills. Thinking skills are difficult to define, but through research we are learning a great deal about problem solving. Havertape

(1976) noted that learning-disabled adolescents exhibit perseveration, disinhibition, and qualitatively different approaches to problem solving. Whimbey (1976) noted that college students with low IQs failed to use abstractions in making systematic comparisons of data, applied "one-shot" thinking, and willingly allowed gaps of knowledge to exist. Other thinking skills in which learning-disabled adolescents may be deficient are organizing information, dealing with abstractions, questioning, and evaluating information.

This review of academic-cognitive factors suggests a high priority should be given to gathering data on characteristics that relate to learning and educational performance. Of equal concern is the need to consider those variables that relate to adequate social adjustment as well as to educational success. These will be discussed in the next section.

■ PERSONALITY-SOCIAL FACTORS ■

Determining the effects of a learning handicap on an individual is difficult, if not impossible. Nevertheless, [there is evidence that students with learning disabilities experience significant problems in social adjustment, social perception, self-concept, and motivation.] Authors who have written about learning disorders in adolescents have stressed the concomitant emotional and personality difficulties that beset these individuals (Gordon, 1970; Griffin, 1971; Rosenthal, 1973; Silver, 1974). These accompanying difficulties warrant the full attention of those involved in the educational process of learning-disabled pupils. Such problems are potentially more of a hindrance to success and adjustment in life than is the mastery of certain academic concepts. Whether these problems result from, give rise to, or are independent of the given learning disability is difficult to resolve. What is certain, however, is that socioeconomic and family variables influence school achievement and related emotional and personality adjustments. This means that failure in secondary schools should be considered in light of the highly complex and dynamic pattern of relationships among the variables internal and external to the learner.

On entering junior or senior high school, a learning-disabled student with a history of failures may react within a wide continuum of behaviors ranging from inner-directedness to outer-directedness. These behaviors may be seen as no more than discrete affective behaviors. But if a behavior is predominant and consistent—that is, if it occurs systematically—it constitutes an affective *style*. For example, a student who simply gives up whenever demands she perceives as inappropriate are placed on her is acting according to an affective style. If, however, a student's behavior is erratic from one day to the next, it should not be considered an affective style. Take the student who is overly dependent on a teacher for help in a resource setting but denies having difficulty or needing help when in the regular classroom. His initial reactions to the demands of the classroom situation may be to withdraw by sitting in the back of the class and not participating. As the situation increases in stress, though, he may sleep in class, leave class while it is in session, or choose more and more often not to come to class at all. Finally, under severe stress, his behavior may become purposeless and entirely disorganized.

The desired affective style has been labeled "interdependence." Dyer (1972) suggested that the ideal style is not choosing between independence and dependence but knowing when to be dependent on someone else and when to be independent. The erratic behavior of many learning-disabled students seems to indicate that they will have to be taught this style.

My coworker G. R. Alley and I believe that affective behavior is an action or a reaction aimed at overcoming a real or perceived obstacle. When facing situations that an adult would consider stressful, adolescents frequently carry their behavior to the extreme. Extreme behaviors are identified with adolescents because it is during this developmental period that the limits of behavior are tested. Behaviors such as overeating, oversleeping, extreme outbursts of temper, extreme withdrawal, oversensitivity, time panic, or overactivity are generated or extinguished according to the level of stress that an adolescent associates with an obstacle.

To cope with these obstacles, pupils need both the understanding of adults and the tempering reactions of the peer group. Under optimal circumstances students can use their own resources *and* the input from "significant others." The significant others can assist in perceiving the reality of the stress associated with the obstacle or in communicating options to overcome the obstacle.

The inability to achieve, the lack of success, the nonreinforcing experiences—all may lead to undesirable behaviors in learning-disabled adolescents. Siegel (1974) attributes impulsivity, low frustration threshold, irritability, low self-esteem, and suggestibility to learning-disabled adolescents and further suggests that these behaviors can, under certain conditions, result in antisocial criminal acts. Juvenile delinquency has historically been regarded as primarily a social or legal concept, but delinquents evidence many characteristics similar to those of learning-disabled youngsters. Mauser (1974) has noted similarities in the following areas: negative self-concept, low frustration tolerance, higher ratio of males to females, directional orientation problems, minimal brain dysfunction, similar intelligence level, and difficulties in school beginning in the primary grades. While a causal relationship between learning disabilities and juvenile delinquency has not been demonstrated, it appears that juvenile delinquency is an outlet for some learning-disabled adolescents (Jacobson, 1974; Stenger, 1975; Roman, 1957).

A comprehensive study by Banks and Finlayson (1973) illuminated the effect of certain nonacademic variables on success and failure in the secondary schools. This study represented a thorough attempt to come to an understanding of the relationships among social structure, parental and home practices, educational variables, and the personality of secondary-aged students. (Since the authors' intent was to look at the interrelatedness of the factors studied, their findings should not be cited in isolation and their data should be interpreted with caution.) In summarizing their findings on twenty-nine variables studied, Banks and Finlayson stated:

The items . . . found to be related to success tended . . . to fall into two main clusters. In the first of these, the emotional climate of the family, parental approval and satisfaction with perceived progress, and parental aspirations were found to be interrelated with certain measures of pupil personality and motivation. These included dependence on adults, intellectual curiosity, homework orientation and introversion.

The second . . . clustering of items suggests the possibility not only that love-oriented techniques of discipline are a factor in school achievement in so far as they influence pupil motivation, but also that the differences in school achievement between the social classes are related to the differences between them in patterns of child-rearing. . . . In general, the pattern of responses with respect to disciplinary techniques was strikingly different in the successful and in the unsuccessful groups. Parents of unsuccessful boys

61

followed a pattern of discipline in which smacking was combined with material deprivation, shouting, nagging and telling off. . . . It was very rare for [parents of successful boys] to use this particular combination of techniques. Parents of successful boys also tended to have a warmer, more approving and less critical relationship. . . .

. . . Parent/child relationships and techniques of discipline were more important in differentiating between successful and unsuccessful working-class parents than factors of a socio-economic nature.   (pp. 148–150)

These findings underscore the critical role played by family-related variables in facilitating the success of high school students. Others have also noted the importance of these factors during the adolescent years. In a study comparing the family relationships of overachieving and underachieving high school students, Morrow and Wilson (1967) found that the parents of bright high achievers share more activities, ideas, and confidences and are more approving and encouraging of achievements than are the parents of bright underachieving boys. Cervantes (1965) compared the home conditions of high school dropouts with high school graduates. He concluded that the dropout is generally the product of a family deficient in stable primary relations. Conditions favoring high school success were intrafamily understanding and acceptance, family encouragement of students' educational and occupational plans, communication within the home, spending leisure time together, and happiness within the home.

In discussing parent-adolescent relationships, most studies suggest a linear relationship between parental authority and student achievement; that is, the more authoritarian the parents, the lower the achievement. Bronfenbrenner (1961) contends, however, that a curvilinear relationship may be a more accurate description of child-rearing techniques and achievement—too much or too little discipline may have negative effects on achievement.

Hollon (1970), in his work on masked depression, recommends that special educators direct their attention to social and emotional factors as they relate to school performance. He reported that depression may be the underlying cause of some adolescents' poor school achievement. Teachers' attempts to motivate through exhortation or criticism may only increase the depression. Instead, teachers should direct their intervention efforts toward the adverse social or home conditions causing the depression.

If skills in interaction and communication can facilitate adjustment even within unfavorable social or family situations, then adolescents should be taught these skills as strategies for coping with adverse conditions. Dyer (1972), for example, has defined elements essential to effective communication and contends that knowing what factors interfere with communication can significantly enhance the communication process.

Repeated academic failures, whether related to adverse social/family conditions or not, are certain to mark the learning-disabled student's personality. Siegel (1974), for example, feels that the greatest single handicap of the older learning-disabled pupil is an aversive personality that repels rather than attracts people. The negative ramifications of such a personality for school success, social adjustment, and employment opportunities are evident.

✳ Poor social perception, one of the most apparent problems of many older learning-disabled students, may surface in several ways—all of which may neutralize the progress made in academic areas. Forms in which poor social perception may manifest itself include inability to generalize from one situation to another, oversensitivity to the reactions of others, inflexibility in acting, difficulty in accurately interpreting the moods and communications (verbal and nonverbal) of others, and difficulty in determining the impact of one's actions on others. Since the ability to monitor one's actions and the reactions of others is a prerequisite to social sophistication, all these difficulties in social perception may actually be another manifestation of a monitoring deficit.

Repeated academic failure almost always leads to a damaged self-concept and the development of defenses. Drake and Cavanaugh (1970) stress the devastating effects that failure in school settings has on self-concept. They observed feelings of depression and even guilt in learning-disabled adolescents. Furthermore, they noted that continual academic failure causes students to doubt their intelligence; consequently, fears of mental subnormality develop.

A student's feelings of mental inferiority may be compounded as curriculum requirements become more difficult and failures more frequent. Each failure results in a heightened fear of more failure. Russell (1974) states that learning-disabled adolescents may suffer an identity crisis after repeated failures because the feelings of inadequacy that are generated cause them to question their place in the world.

63

Defense mechanisms provide a means by which humans can cope with pressures. Adolescents with learning disabilities who survive twelve years in the educational system have usually refined their defense and coping mechanisms and their ability to deploy them. Defenses may vary in form from sweet, manipulating personalities to rationalizations suggesting that teachers are the primary reason for lack of success. A possible danger of relying too heavily on defenses is a detachment from reality to the point of being unable to be honest with oneself. Dyer (1972) maintains that a prerequisite to "authentic behavior" is a willingness to admit weaknesses to others so as to facilitate an honest engagement in action that may eliminate, change, or compensate for the weakness. He also suggests that some people hide behind façades in certain areas for such a long period of time that it becomes difficult even to talk about the precipitating weakness, let alone take actions to overcome or circumvent it. This may account for the oversensitivity or avoidance demonstrated by some learning-disabled adolescents toward school problems.

One of the most obvious aspects of personality associated with success or failure, either at school or in later life, is the presence or absence of the motivation to succeed. Though it has been analyzed in a variety of ways and under different labels, achievement motivation is frequently overlooked in educational and vocational planning. Teachers often incorrectly assume that all students, the learning-disabled included, have the same desire to achieve success in school and work. Bradfield (1970) suggests that learning-disabled adolescents who have faced constant failure and frustration have a high fear of failure and, in turn, evidence low motivation to achieve. Drake and Cavanaugh (1970) point out that continual failure eventually discourages students from even trying to perform academically related tasks. The empirical evidence of Banks and Finlayson (1973) basically supports these contentions. Using both projective and questionnaire measures, they found successful boys to have significantly higher "need for achievement" scores than unsuccessful boys do. Parents' aspirations for their sons were also found to be highly related to the students' achievement motivation. In addition, internal motivation in the form of intellectual curiosity markedly favored successful boys, and achievement motivation was associated with social class variables and techniques of discipline applied in the home. Obviously, the study of achievement motivation as a factor of success in high school is a highly complex undertaking. We need comprehensive theories of motivation applicable to education; and because motivation is multidimensional in nature, the accompanying theories and formulations for research must be equally as complex.

Strategies for studying the characteristics of learning-disabled adolescents must include careful consideration of personality and social-related variables. The role of these variables in explaining the profile of the older learning-disabled student is crucial, and their importance should not be minimized in the interest of studying only variables more directly related to academic work.

■ PERCEPTUAL AND MOTOR FACTORS ■

This section discusses some of the perceptual and motor variables that are found with greater frequency among learning-disabled populations than among students without learning handicaps. These variables may (but do not necessarily) contribute to, or result from, the learning disability itself. Some of them may diminish or change as the student grows older, but they do not vanish entirely. Research specifically relating to perceptual and motor disability in secondary learning-disabled populations is negligible, so our attention must go to clinical and classroom observation of perceptual and motor factors in order to understand their ramifications for academic performance and social adjustment. Perceptual-motor correlates to learning disability that may continue to manifest themselves in older students include hyperactivity, distractibility, poor attention, incoordination, and perceptual irregularities.

Hyperactivity, one of the most frequently identified and spoken-of correlates of learning disabilities, has been defined and studied in a variety of ways. Bryant and McLoughlin (1972) note that hyperactivity generally decreases with age. In describing hyperactivity in neurologically handicapped teenagers, Wilcox (1970) notes a contrast in bodily activities between younger and older students. The behavior of a five- or six-year-old, she says, might be described as "frantic to-and-fro purposeless motor activity," whereas the behavior of an adolescent who is hyperactive is usually characterized by subtler actions such as finger or object tapping, grimacing, or tics. Others have also noted a reduction in hyperactive behavior as subjects grow older (Schulman, Kaspar, & Throne, 1965; Werry, Weiss, Douglas, & Martin, 1966). In a follow-up study on hyperactive children, Menkes, Rowe, and Menkes (1967) found hyperactive behavior to disappear by adolescence in all but a few cases. Werry (1968), however, stresses that though the prognosis for hyperactivity is favorable, the prognosis for overall social adjustment may not be. He also notes that preliminary results from a longitudinal study suggest that, except for hyperactivity, residual problems such as learning difficulties do persist into adolescence. Behavior manifestations that are sometimes caused by, or associated with, hyperactivity should be considered in older learning-disabled students. These may include problems in attention, distractibility, or concentration.

As students grow older, they are less prone to distractibility and poor attention to tasks. The improvement may be the result of maturation, or it may be brought about indirectly by peers who are less accepting of interruption behaviors that they themselves have outgrown. Wilcox (1970) has observed, however, that the improvement in attention span noted in older students is often not sufficient for the long class periods and lectures common in many secondary schools. She contends that attention disorders may be manifested in two types of behavior: distraction of others when attention lapses from the task at hand, or a paralysis of effort that includes failure to concentrate on the given task.

Hagin (1971) has brought out a possible ramification of distractibility problems—namely, a difficulty in tuning out extraneous stimulation. Concentration may be affected by movement of other people, environmental noises, or distracting noise components in the central nervous system (Senf, 1972). This can pose particular problems for a secondary student who is expected to complete class assignments at home. If the home environment is one of constant activity with no room available for quiet, uninterrupted work, the learning-disabled adolescent may experience great difficulties in concentrating. Even a normal home environment may not be sufficient for the learning-disabled youngster who is readily distracted by internally generated stimuli, such as tangential thoughts and daydreams. School schedules that are modularized into segments of time smaller than the traditional fifty-minute blocks may help students with concentration and attention problems.

Fine and gross motor coordination also improve in the teenage years with maturation (Wilcox, 1970; Siegel, 1974), but significant problems may still persist. I noted (1974) that the writing samples of learning-disabled high school students were generally more illegible and evidenced poor spacing and cramping. Note taking in classes may be impaired because of laboriousness in writing. Typing has frequently been proposed as an alternative communication vehicle for handicapped students to use as they prepare written assignments. The perceptual and coordination demands of typing, however, may preclude it as a workable solution for many learning-disabled youngsters.

Gross motor difficulties may be detected through clumsiness in physical education activities or social activities such as dancing. Myklebust (1973) administered the Health Railwalking Test (designed to measure locomotor coordination) to normal and reading-disabled children. The poor readers in the thirteen- and fifteen-year-old groups performed approximately 20 percent below the normal controls. He found that disturbances in locomotor coordination remained deficient to about the same degree from ages nine to fifteen. Poor performance resulting from incoordination problems may confirm a student's feeling of not fitting in with the physical world and further hamper his self-esteem.

Perceptual irregularities, like other correlates discussed above, appear to improve with age. Nonetheless, students may avoid, or effectively compensate for, certain activities that would reveal perceptual deficits in the teenage years. For example, students may not choose mechanical drawing as an elective because of problems resulting from poor depth perception, or they may learn to handle left-right discrimination problems by relying on a right-hand mole for a cue. Problems with time perception may be particularly devastating to older learning-disabled students as they try to meet many schedule demands of school and everyday life.

In all the perceptual and motor matters discussed in this section, the learning-disabled show general improvement with age. An important point to remember, however, is that the nonhandicapped also demonstrate refinements and improvements with maturation. A central issue is whether the improvement shown by learning-disabled adolescents are sufficient to change both their self-perceptions and the way that others perceive them.

■ FUTURE DIRECTIONS ■

The present dearth of data on characteristics makes it difficult to construct a *complete* learning, social, and emotional profile of the learning-disabled adolescent; however, a partial profile is beginning to emerge.

First, the profile of learning-disabled adolescents reflects a pattern of both strengths and weaknesses. Since these students function normally in some areas, their educational treatment and prognosis will be markedly different from that prescribed for pupils who are suppressed in all areas of functioning.

Second, many skills basic to the academic process are still lacking or have been incorrectly acquired. Success in the academic curriculum will be limited until the student masters skills sufficient for functioning independently in an academic setting.

Third, by adolescence there is a high probability that learning-disabled students will experience the indirect effects of a learning handicap as manifested by poor self-perception, lowered self-concept, or reduced motivation. Disability in a basic learning process may be the root problem, but it must be considered not only by itself but also in relation to other problems that it may precipitate.

Finally, maturation and/or compensation tends to refine and integrate many psychological, perceptual, and motor functions. Consequently, problems of incoordination, hyperactivity, distractibility, and poor attention may manifest themselves in more subtle or controlled ways in older students. Still to be resolved, however, is whether these functions are refined significantly through maturation and/or compensation, so as to become normal behaviors rather than remaining as deviant characteristics.

Much research and theoretical work must be done on the characteristics of learning-disabled populations. Some of the areas that need attention are these:

1. If research efforts are to be productive in delineating and clarifying learning-disability characteristics at the secondary level, research samples must be carefully defined. Criteria for inclusion and exclusion must be described in detail. Such procedures will facilitate the comparison and replication of research findings, as well as provide an operational definition of the population.

2. Research on characteristics should analyze the performance of learning-disabled, other handicapped, and normal students on specific

psychoeducational variables. These variables should also be studied at different ages during the adolescent period to determine the effect of age on given characteristics. The high degree of interrelatedness among characteristics must be accounted for in the study of academic and nonacademic factors. Variables in each grouping should be carefully identified and the relative importance on academic performance and social adjustment determined.

3. Research in learning disabilities should be conducted with an awareness of what has been accomplished in disciplines outside the field of special education. For example, the knowledge available in psychology, guidance and counseling, and psychiatry should be tapped to help provide answers to problems that are not primarily educational or curriculum-related. The integration and application of knowledge from other fields will broaden our understanding of the problems faced by learning-disabled adolescents.

4. An ultimate goal of special education is to generate a smooth interface between learner characteristics and treatment variables. It is imperative, therefore, that research on learning-disability characteristics be conceptualized and conducted in the context of the secondary curriculum. Only when treatment variables and learner characteristics are treated concomitantly will the questions relating to each area be adequately answered.

5. The complexity of learning-disability characteristics calls for sophisticated research methodologies and sophisticated theoretical conceptualizations. The study of learning-disabled characteristics would be advanced if it were guided by a theory or framework that would provide a structure for analyzing research data and for generating systematic research questions. Senf (1972) has indicated the pressing need for such a framework in the study of abnormal functioning:

In order to understand abnormal functioning, it would be useful to have a theory substantiated by experiments which describes the course and functioning of normal behavior. Such a theory together with its supporting factual data would allow us to understand precisely where abnormality is centered. By examining the functioning of the person thought to be disabled in some way we would be able to decipher where his performance varies from that of the normally functioning individual. Such performance differences would imply within the context of the theory processes or systems which are functioning irregularly. . . . It should be clear why a theory is necessary in this endeavor and that a collection of unorganized facts will not suffice. Most basically, one need recognize that there are an endless number of data points that one could collect that would discriminate between any two samples of persons. Understanding deviant functioning . . . proceeds not simply by having a large collection of data but by having those data organized into a coherent framework. A framework allows some data to take on more importance in understanding the disability than others by specifying the manner in which the data are related to each other.   (p. 305)

6. The questions confronting the field may best be answered through the application of research methodologies that are capable of handling a large number of variables in a sophisticated fashion. The simple analysis of a limited number of factors in a correlational format, for example, will not provide answers sufficient to the problems.

7. Few researchers or authors have emphasized areas of strength in learning-disabled adolescents. Most characteristics are defined in terms of weakness and do not consider integrities that are available for compensating for the deficit or circumventing it. Research efforts should therefore shift from a concentrated emphasis on weakness to an exploration of strengths.

In conclusion, let us briefly turn our attention to the issue of educational services for learning-disabled adolescents. The past few years have witnessed a dramatic growth in interest in learning disabilities at the secondary level. Our eagerness to assist an age group that has been denied services for years has often resulted in hasty and sometimes short-sighted decisions. While pupils in need of help at the secondary level cannot wait for research to provide definitive answers on crucial issues, neither should they be expected to endure educational programs and service alternatives that have been conceived in limited knowledge and questionable assumptions.

Many secondary programs for learning-disabled students are merely an extension of the same service models used for elementary students. While some of these programs may be validly used with older students, they should not be applied in a blanket fashion. To make the same assumptions about secondary students as are made about elementary pupils is to ignore the critical changes that occur in the developmental process. Likewise, to lump all secondary students who are failing their curriculum into the same programs with the same goals is to deny the individuality of each student.

As handicapped students grow older, some of their disabilities may be reduced or become less distinguishable. On the other hand, maturation will not entirely eliminate all disabilities. In educational decision making we need to recognize and deal with the residual disabilities in terms of the student's present needs and future goals.

Consequently, programming at the secondary level should be greatly influenced by the salient characteristics of the learner. To this end, understanding and identifying psychoeducational characteristics of secondary-level learning-disabled students should have a high research priority. The results of such research would lead to a delineation of characteristics that would provide the basis for sound decision making in educational programming.

■ REFERENCES ■

Anderson, L. E. (Ed.). *Helping the adolescent with the hidden handicap.* Belmont, Calif.: Fearon Publishers/Lear Siegler, 1970.

Banks, O. *The sociology of education.* London: Batsford, 1971.

Banks, I., & Finlayson, D. *Success and failure in the secondary school: An interdisciplinary approach to school achievement.* London: Methuen & Co., 1973.

Boder, E. Developmental dyslexia: Prevailing diagnostic concepts and a new diagnostic approach. In H. R. Myklebust (Ed.), *Progress in learning disabilities* (Vol. 2). New York: Grune & Stratton, 1971.

Bradfield, R. Preparation for achievement. In L. E. Anderson (Ed.), *Helping the adolescent with the hidden handicap.* Belmont, Calif.: Fearon Publishers/Lear Siegler, 1970.

Bronfenbrenner, W. Some familiar antecedents of responsibility leadership in adolescents. In L. Petrullo & B. M. Bass (Eds.), *Leadership and interpersonal behavior.* New York: Holt, 1961.

Brutten, M., Richardson, S. O., & Mangel, C. *Something's wrong with my child.* New York: Harcourt Brace Jovanovich, 1973.

Bryant, N. D., & Kass, C. E. (Eds.). *Final report: Leadership training institute in learning disabilities* (Vol. 1). Tucson: University of Arizona, Department of Special Education, 1972.

Bryant, N. D., & McLoughlin, J. A. Subject variables: definition, incidence, characteristics, and correlates. In N. D. Bryant & C. E. Kass (Eds.), *Final report: Leadership training institute in learning disabilities* (Vol. 1.). Tucson: University of Arizona, Department of Special Education, 1972.

Budoff, M. Learning potential as a supplementary assessment procedure. In J. Hellmuth (Ed.), *Learning disorders* (Vol. 3). Seattle: Special Child Publications, 1968.

Cervantes, L. F. Family background, primary relationships, and the high school dropout. *Journal of Marriage and the Family,* 1965, 27, 218–223.

Clements, S. D. *Minimal brain dysfunction in children* (NINDS Monograph No. 3, U.S. Public Health Publication No. 1415). Washington, D.C.: U.S. Government Printing Office, 1966.

Compensatory education in early adolescence. Menlo Park, Calif.: Stanford Research Institute, 1974.

DeRuiter, J. D. *A Bayesian approach to the use of test data for the justification of learning disability in school-age children.* Unpublished doctoral dissertation, University of Arizona, 1973.

Deshler, D. D. *Learning disability in the high school student as demonstrated in monitoring of self-generated and externally-generated errors.* Unpublished doctoral dissertation, University of Arizona, 1974.

Deshler, D. D., & Alley, G. R. *Assessment of learning disabled adolescents.* Mansucript submitted for publication, 1975.

Deutch, C., & Schumer, F. *Brain-damaged children.* New York: Bruner/ Mazel, 1970.

Doehring, D. *Patterns of impairment in specific reading disability.* Bloomington: Indiana University Press, 1968.

Drake, C., & Cavanaugh, J. J. A. Teaching the high school dyslexic. In L. E. Anderson (Ed.), *Helping the adolescent with the hidden handicap.* Belmont, Calif.: Fearon Publishers/Lear Siegler, 1970.

Dyer, W. G. *The sensitive manipulator: the change agent who builds with others.* Provo, Utah: Brigham Young University Press, 1972.

Gordon, S. Reversing a negative self-image. In L. E. Anderson (Ed.), *Helping the adolescent with the hidden handicap.* Belmont, Calif.: Fearon Publishers/Lear Siegler, 1970.

Gordon, S. Psychological problems of adolescents with minimal brain dysfunction. In D. Kronick (Ed.), *Learning disabilities: Its implications to a responsible society.* Chicago: Developmental Learning Materials, 1969.

Griffin, M. How does he feel? In E. Schloss (Ed.), *The educator's enigma: The adolescent with learning disabilities.* San Rafael, Calif.: Academic Therapy Publications, 1971.

Hagin, R. How do we find him? In E. Schloss (Ed.), *The educator's enigma: The adolescent with learning disabilities.* San Rafael, Calif.: Academic Therapy Publications, 1971.

Havertape, J. F. *Problem solving in the learning disabled high school student.* Unpublished doctoral dissertation, University of Arizona, 1976.

Hollon, P. H. Poor school performance as a symptom of masked depression in children and adolescents. *American Journal of Psychotherapy,* 1970, *25,* 258–263.

Hudson, F. G. *Emerging roles in learning disabilities.* Presentation at Learning Disabilities Symposium, Fort Hayes, Kansas, 1974.

Jacobson, F. N. Learning disabilities and juvenile delinquency: A demonstrated relationship. In R. E. Weber (Ed.), *Handbook on learning disabilities.* Englewood Cliffs, N.J.: Prentice-Hall, 1974.

Karlsen, B., Madden R., & Gardner, E. F. *Stanford diagnostic reading test.* New York: Harcourt, Brace, and World, 1966.

Kass, C. E. Construction of a model of learning disability with attention to system-theoretic approaches. *Proceedings of the International Federation of Learning Disabilities.* Speech presented at the first meeting of the International Federation of Learning Disabilities, Amsterdam, The Netherlands, 1974.

Lubach, W. N. *Comparing normal and learning disabled students on a test of past tense verbs.* Unpublished master's thesis, University of Kansas, 1975.

Mauser, A. J. Learning disabilities and delinquent youth. *Academic Therapy,* 1974,*6,* 389–402.

Menkes, M. M., Rowe, J. S., & Menkes, J. H. A twenty-five year follow-up study on the hyperkinetic child with minimal brain dysfunction. *Pediatrics,* 1967, *39,* 303–399.

Morrow, W. R., & Wilson, R. C. Family relationships of bright high achieving and underachieving high school boys. *Child Development,* 1967, *32,* 501–509.

Myers, P. I., & Hammill, D. D. *Methods for learning disorders.* New York: Wiley, 1969.

Myklebust, H. R. *The development and disorders of written language: picture story language test.* New York: Grune & Stratton, 1965.

Myklebust, H. R. *Development and disorders of written language: Studies of normal and exceptional children.* New York: Grune & Stratton, 1973.

Myklebust, H. R., & Boshes, B. *Minimal brain damage in children* (Final Report, Contract No. 180-65-142, Neurological and Sensory Disease Control Program). Washington, D.C.: Department of Health, Education and Welfare, 1969.

Rogan, L. L., & Lukens, J. E. Education, administration and classroom procedures. In N. G. Haring (Ed.), *Minimal brain dysfunction in children* (NINDS Monograph No. 2 U.S. Public Health Publication No. 2015). Washington, D.C.: U.S. Government Printing Office, 1969.

Roman, M. *Reaching delinquents through reading.* Springfield, Ill.: Charles C Thomas, 1957.

Rosenthal, J. H. Self-esteem in dyslexic children. *Academic Therapy,* 1973, 9, 27–39.

Russell, R. W. The dilemma of the handicapped adolescent. In R. E. Weber (Ed.), *Handbook on learning disabilities.* Englewood Cliffs, N.J.: Prentice-Hall, 1974.

Schulman, J. L., Kaspar, J. C., & Throne, F. M. *Brain damage and behavior: A clinical-experimental study.* Springfield, Ill.: Charles C Thomas, 1965.

Senf, G. M. An information-integration theory and its application to normal reading acquisition and reading ability. In N. D. Bryant and C. E. Kass (Eds.), *Final report: leadership training institute in learning disabilities* (Vol. 2). Washington, D.C.: Office of Education, 1972.

Siegel, E. *The exceptional child grows up.* New York: E. P. Dutton, 1974.

Silver, L. B. Emotional and social problems of children with developmental disabilities. In R. E. Weber (Ed.), *Handbook on learning disabilities.* Englewood Cliffs, N.J.: Prentice-Hall, 1974.

Stenger, M. K. *Frequency of learning disabilities in adjudicated delinquents.* Unpublished master's thesis, University of Missouri at Kansas City, 1975.

Strother, C. R. Who is he? In E. Schloss (Ed.), *The educator's enigma: The adolescent with learning disabilities.* San Rafael, Calif.: Academic Therapy Publications, 1971.

Werry, J. W. Developmental hyperactivity. *Pediatric Clinics of North America,* 1968, 15, 581–599.

Werry, J. W., Weiss, G., Douglas, V., & Martin, J. Studies on the hyperactive child: The effect of chlorpromazine upon behavior and learning. *Journal of American Academy of Child Psychiatry,* 1966, 5, 292–312.

Whimbey, A. You can learn to raise your IQ score. *Psychology Today,* January 1976, pp. 27–29; 84–85.

Wilcox, E. Identifying characteristics of NH adolescents. In L. E. Anderson (Ed.), *Helping the adolescent with the hidden handicap.* Belmont, Calif.: Fearon Publishers/Lear Siegel, 1970.

Wilt, M. E. The teaching of listening and why. In V. Anderson et al. (Eds.), *Reading in the language arts.* New York: Macmillan, 1964.

Wissink, J. F. *A procedure for the identification of children with learning disabilities.* Unpublished doctoral dissertation, University of Arizona, 1972.

CHAPTER 4

CURRICULUM
DEVELOPMENT
RESOURCES

VIRGINIA L. BROWN

Because of the numerous differences between elementary and secondary education, learning-disabilities programs that were designed for elementary students cannot simply be superimposed onto secondary school curricula. They must be based on the widely divergent student needs and school structures found at the secondary level. The first part of this chapter reviews the distinguishing features of secondary education and focuses on the requirements of learning-disabled students at the secondary level. The remainder of the chapter lists and discusses the multitude of resources available to educators for setting up suitable curricula and developing instructional methods.

■ UNSTRUCTURED LIVES IN STRUCTURED ENVIRONMENTS ■

DISTINGUISHING CHARACTERISTICS OF SECONDARY STUDENTS
Planners of programs for secondary students should first consider the normal changes that accompany adolescent growth and development. Then the "strange" (but normal) behaviors typical of an adolescent will not be interpreted as signs of abnormality. It is just as important to understand students as developing adolescents as it is to consider them as "learning-disabled." Further, if a specific learning disability is indeed interfering with normal growth and development, individualized attention to the interference should have high priority.

Characteristics that distinguish the secondary-level student from the elementary include the following:

1. The increased behavioral independence of secondary students raises many considerations in secondary curriculum planning. Older students will not be as amenable to doing what is asked or required; they are unlikely to appreciate being identified with any special program or teacher; and less parental pressure can be brought to bear on their behavior. Secondary students should, therefore, participate heavily in the design of their own programs.

AUTHOR'S NOTE: Experiences relevant to the preparation of the material that appears in this chapter came primarily from my two years of program development with the Specialized Educational Services Division of the Madison (Wisconsin) Public Schools. I am especially grateful for the assistance of Mrs. Ruth Loomis, SES Coordinator; of Dr. Donald Hafeman, Director of the East Area; and of Dr. Clint Barter, then Principal of Memorial High School and now Superintendent at Brown Deer, Wisconsin.

2. The increased mobility of secondary students carries several implications. Basically, it permits a broader range of applications for skills and a generalization of skills to situations outside of school; this suggests that program designers must expand their conceptions of a student's "life-space." On the negative side, it may also mean a greater likelihood of repeated absenteeism and the resulting havoc in program continuity.

3. The increase in unsupervised time available to the student during the school day may be boon or bane. With the attractiveness of other uses of time, getting to classes on time may be a problem for some students.

4. Secondary students are forced to make occupational and life decisions at a time when they are least prepared to do so.

5. The distractions and social pressures faced by all students during adolescence are likely to be compounded for learning-disabled students. Remedial classwork is not likely to be one of their highest priorities.

6. There is likely to be a lessening of parental involvement in school and in the student's everyday life at the same time that there is increased parental concern about achievement and post-school planning.

7. Secondary students' longer accumulation of life experiences makes each student more unique as she or he becomes older, so programs at the secondary level should consider the "total person" with particular care. Learning-disabled students may by this time have an ingrained sense of failure; thus the turnabout or accommodation of their failures is more difficult.

8. The emotional and behavioral problems often accompanying learning disabilities become more pronounced in adolescents. Secondary educators may be forced to address these emotional problems before attempting academic remediation.

THE ORGANIZATION OF SECONDARY SCHOOLS

When learning-disabled students progress from elementary to secondary school, they encounter a new situation. Secondary-level conditions that affect their educational programming include these:

1. Credit and grade requirements must often be negotiated for the individual student. Special education personnel must accommodate state education requirements to special education programs and students.

2. In school districts using computer scheduling, learning-disabled students will have to be hand-scheduled.

3. Because of the larger number of students in secondary settings, school personnel are limited in considering individual needs.

4. With larger numbers of staff members, a student must learn a variety of response patterns to many kinds of adults.

5. The larger physical size of secondary schools makes mobility and the meeting of scheduling demands difficult for some students.

6. The heterogeneity of value systems in large, comprehensive high schools suggests both greater opportunity for broadening the outlook and the need for attention to "curriculum" elements such as values clarification.

7. There are usually limited opportunities for alternate educational subsystems within the total secondary system because too many secondary schools are inflexible in dealing with the handicapped.

8. For students with exceptional abilities, the curricular options are increased. For students with exceptional disabilities, the options are decreased. More options should be available for both.

9. The competitiveness of some activities such as physical education makes participation in these activities difficult for students who find competition difficult. How much de-emphasis on competition is possible or desirable is a controversial question. In some cases it is possible to de-emphasize competition; for example, in physical education many programs are moving toward education for lifetime sports such as boating, golfing, tennis, fishing, and hiking.

10. The organizational options within any one secondary school are often limited by current educational philosophy and by community interests. For example, educators may still be organizing and scheduling courses by grade levels despite a general trend toward nongraded education.

11. Because many learning-disabled students are nearing the end of their educational careers, educators may adopt an attitude of "why bother?" or "let's get going on a crash program."

12. The departmental administrative organization of the high school is foreign to most elementary school personnel. Learning-disabilities teachers may literally become outsiders with no departmental home or protections. The secondary learning-disabilities teacher must deal with this organizational reality.

13. The administrative problems of staff allocation and money for materials and supplies are very real. The complexity of these matters at the secondary level is much greater than in the elementary schools. Whenever students are mainstreamed and are also in special education programs, some equitable arrangements must be made between the two divisions.

14. Accommodating instructions, demonstrations, and assignment expectations for a wide range of students in heterogeneously organized classes that meet briefly each day is a very real problem for teachers. Learning-disabilities teachers must realize the scope and the nature of unanswered instructional questions in secondary education so that they do not feel personally responsible for the resolution of all problems. There is, however, an obligation to recognize and to work cooperatively with colleagues to improve long-standing problems.

In addition to the characteristics that differentiate elementary and secondary programs, several system variables are of interest in determining curriculum and materials needs. Some school districts have plans that allow for program modifications as learning-disabled students move from one level to another. These districts are likely to articulate services and curriculum throughout the elementary, middle, and secondary complexes, with preschool and postsecondary programs integrated within this framework. Longitudinal planning and monitoring are possible under these circumstances. When secondary programs operate independent of services and curriculum at other levels, service and curriculum continuity is disrupted.

Program planners in learning disabilities should not let their decisions be limited by what is currently available in curriculum, methods, materials, or tests. Instead, the program should be based upon as honest an appraisal as possible of student and community needs. The selection or development of curricula will then follow from intention rather than from chance. The development of anything like "A Curriculum for Learning-Disabled Secondary Students" would be unfortunate indeed.

■ CURRICULUM AND METHODOLOGY RESOURCES ■
FOR THE SECONDARY SCHOOL

There is so much information available on secondary education as well as on special education that any comprehensive listing of curricula, materials, and techniques is impossible. I will consider here, then, only the major areas of concern for secondary learning-disabilities teachers.

Some of these suggestions, which may seem basic to the experienced practitioner, are necessary for beginners, who are often not familiar with fundamental procedures. Perhaps this chapter will also serve to introduce experienced practitioners to new areas to explore or will remind them of old areas neglected because of the press of other concerns. In either case, educators should spend time exploring the resources available to them in order to develop well-rounded learning-disabilities programs.

Analysis of method is a diagnostic necessity if one seeks to locate and identify either a student's specific difficulties or problems with the method of teaching that is being employed. Further, the learning-disabilities teacher as well as the mainstream teacher will find many suggestions, charts, evaluation forms, and so on, valuable in designing instruction specifically for the adolescent population. Seldom does the older student appreciate being taught by "elementary" methods administered by an "elementary" teacher. The appendix to this chapter lists six secondary education and related special-methods texts, yielding more than fifty techniques or considerations. The secondary methods books usually include examples, values and limitations, planning sheets, and evaluation formats for each technique. Public and university libraries have additional resources.

Teachers of the learning-disabled should monitor the journals. They will find elaborations and applications of secondary methods, along with descriptions of emerging techniques. The journals cited in the Appendix to this chapter do not all deal with secondary education specifically, but all of them occasionally contain articles designed either to help teachers understand issues, problems, trends, and alternatives in secondary education or to provide them with ideas for creative, motivational instruction. Special features of many of the journals should be noted. They usually contain reviews of books, films, filmstrips, and kits; and some highlight Educational Resources Information Center (ERIC) document resources reviews. Advertisements in many journals tell about current products of interest to readers. Idea exchanges may serve to enrich teaching practices.

BASIC SKILLS REMEDIATION RESOURCES

Teachers of the learning disabled usually work to develop students' basic skills while satisfying content-area requirements. If, however, the student is severely disabled in basic skills, clinical methodology on a one-to-one basis may be called for. Descriptions of clinical techniques for students labeled as learning-disabled are primarily targeted to elementary students. In some instances, though, the methodology is equally useful for older students. Bryant (1971), Fernald (1943), and Gillingham and Stillman (1960) present techniques intended for one-to-one use in working with relatively severe learning problems. Stauffer (1970) describes the language-experience approach to reading instruction to show its usefulness for older students in clinical situations.

This chapter assumes that secondary education is substantively different from elementary education and that the usual notions of what constitutes "basic skills" must change. In their orientation to the secondary school, teachers of the learning-disabled should consider the special needs of their students in several different areas.

READING Standardized tests such as those found in Reading Tests for the Secondary Grades (Blanton, Farr, & Tuinman, 1972) are useful for administrative accountability and for research but are not of value for instruction. Less formal and more relevant assessment ideas must be used with learning-disabled students.

The secondary teacher concerned with basic reading ability should be very careful about saying that a student *cannot* read because of test- or school-related behaviors. It may instead be a question of discovering what the student *does* read—maybe movie, fashion, love, dragster, sex, or cycle magazines; maps; recipes; comics; or record jackets.

Tests dealing with syntax and semantics are likely to be of greater value than "diagnostic" tests of splinter skills. A reading test that may be suitable for the learning-disabled is the Reading Miscue Inventory (Goodman & Burke, 1972). In miscue analysis a reader's deviations from the printed text are analyzed in terms of their interference

81

with, or facilitation of, meaning. The methodology and concepts of miscue analysis are especially useful in determining the difficulty that students have with concepts in each content area. Some other new methods in secondary reading are similar to miscue analysis in their emphasis, in the obtaining of meaning, on conceptual and reasoning skills rather than on knowledge of component reading subskills.

Teachers who prefer a remedial reading lab will find an excellent resource in Brogden's book on the noncommitted learner (1970). Included here are references to the numerous high-interest, low-vocabulary materials. Many content-area professional associations are concerned with reading, and a monitoring of their journals will yield articles such as "How Can We Help Kids Read Science Textbooks?" (Gage, 1974).

Some texts in secondary reading show examples of modified pages from content-area textbooks so that the teacher may use the same text-modification ideas with local materials. Aukerman (1972) and Shepherd (1973) are also valuable references on secondary reading.

Burmeister (1974) and Herber (1970) organize their books along instructional- and cognitive-level considerations rather than by content areas. Herber focuses upon "reasoning" and provides numerous examples of written exercises designed to show how the organization and structure of such exercises can promote more thoughtful responses about the content area. Samples of formal "Reading and Reasoning Guides" are also provided. Burmeister's chapters deal with topics such as the teaching of concepts through vocabulary; interpreting and applying ideas; and analyzing, synthesizing, and evaluating ideas. Abundant examples of applications are provided throughout her text selections.

ARRANGEMENTS FOR COMPENSATORY SERVICES FOR SEVERELY DISABLED READERS Some students may have reading problems so severe that reading is not a medium of choice for their instruction. Special arrangements must be made for these students. A library for the blind and partially sighted may serve as a source of instructional material for them. The learning disabilities teacher should check the local library headquarters for information on such library resources.

Knowing how to get information from nontextual sources is also very important for the learning-disabled adolescent. Visual literacy, for example, is not limited to skill with words. The International Visual

Literacy Association (IVLA), an affiliate of the Association for Educational Communications and Technology (AECT), offers teaching suggestions that might be usefully employed by teachers of the learning-disabled in carrying out instruction without relying on written language.

Learning-disabled students may also benefit from having reading material they cannot manage recorded on records or tapes. Teachers or a teacher-parent-community group can organize recording services. The material may require the learning-disabilities teacher to insert explanations along the way or to accompany the recording with graphs, charts, maps, and the like. Jones (1975) describes a basic procedure for preparing teacher-made tapes for an individual lesson.

In some states, driver's license tests are allowed to be read to the examinee if a teacher provides corroboration of need. The state or local licensing agency can provide information about local practice. Students to whom tests are to be read aloud must be taught how to study and to respond differentially to various kinds of oral tests in much the same way as for written tests.

HANDWRITING   It may be necessary to spend a great deal of time motivating students to "write better." Courses in graphoanalysis or calligraphy may stimulate older students to improve their handwriting. Consideration should also be given to selecting and allowing students to concentrate on a single writing system. Block capitals are an especially relevant style to choose for today's computerized society. A student whose handwriting is intractable may need to be taught to type. Some teachers teach speed writing and shorthand to assist the student who writes poorly with note taking.

The secondary teacher should also understand that writing style may be an important personality attribute to older students, especially to girls. Legibility rather than "school style" should be the primary criterion of acceptability.

SPELLING   Spelling programs should be determined from the spelling demands of the content area and from social needs. Lists—even the basic ones—are of little value. Dolch-like words should be taught in context in dictation or practice. For example, *on* goes with phrases like "on and on," "right on!" and "on account of." Older students who are poor spellers can learn how to obtain the assistance of fellow students in checking their work and then make the spelling corrections themselves.

MATHEMATICS Rarely does a drill approach to basic math skills interest the older student. Nor by this time are drill papers appropriate; they simply do not work. In addition, learning-disabilities clinicians are unanimous in their dismay at rote learning in math, and few texts advocate such an approach. If computation is of great concern, a pocket calculator should be used. Most contemporary math programs teach the use of calculators.

Ashlock's book on error patterns in computation (1972) may be used by many students themselves to discover problem areas. This semi-programmed approach to math computation is a rarity in its emphasis upon process before speed and accuracy.

One of the most useful references for objectives, materials, and techniques that stress an activity approach to learning is found in the Laycock and Watson source book, *The Fabric of Mathematics* (1971). The activities, materials, techniques, and references are level-coded into five difficulty levels that roughly correspond to the degree of language behavior and sophistication (including reading) involved.

RESOURCES FROM LOCAL SCHOOL DISTRICTS

Many school districts develop useful materials for improving instruction, especially where there are departments of secondary education curriculum and instruction, or research and development. Many of these products are useful in pre-service or in-service education. Two relevant examples available from the Madison (Wisconsin) public schools are the learning packet *Readability: Matching the Reader with Print* (Nettleton & Sapone, no date), and *A Theoretical Model for Assessment of Adolescents: The Ecological/Behavioral Approach* (Laten & Katz, 1975).

PROFESSIONAL ASSOCIATIONS AS A RESOURCE

Professional associations usually offer a variety of publications, workshops, and information services for both members and nonmembers. Most organizations will supply brochures of their publications and services. Local councils of many of these associations can provide information on local services for specific problems.

A sixteen-page annotated guide to agencies and organizations concerned with exceptional children appears in the April 1969 issue of *Exceptional Children* (pp. 647–662). The annotations list each organization's purpose, membership requirements, publications, and sponsorship of conferences. There are also cross-lists according to service functions such as consultation, direct services, and so on.

Professional associations usually provide printed material on nearly all phases of instruction—content, methodology, evaluation of materials, evaluation of learning, and instructional management. Names and addresses of some of the major associations are contained in the Appendix to this chapter.

RESOURCES FOR PARENTS OF LEARNING-DISABLED STUDENTS

Parents of students labeled as learning-disabled will frequently need information, support, or specific teaching. Most parent-related resources are geared to the elementary level, but some techniques are adaptable to the problems experienced in the secondary-age student/parent relationships. The Association for Children with Learning Disabilities (ACLD) provides information, conferences, and personal contacts. Additional suggestions for printed resources are found in the Appendix to this chapter.

RESOURCES ON STUDY SKILLS AND TEST TAKING

Independent study is a major academic activity at the secondary level. A teacher usually assumes that students have learned to study at any level below the one in which they are presently enrolled. For secondary-level learning-disabled students this assumption is not always valid. The teaching of study skills often must be a major component of the learning-disabilities curriculum. Sometimes English departments offer study skills labs as a part of their ongoing programs. Even so, the student in the learning-disabilities program may need additional personalized assistance in order to take advantage of such a lab.

Colleges and universities often have study skills labs with various kits and media resources. Many college bookstores have a wide selection of books and pamphlets dealing with the how-to's of study and test taking. These may need to be taped and/or discussed with students individually. Study aids for specific subjects are also available at university bookstores. Many libraries issue publications dealing with special information location needs, for example, "Book Review Sources." The use of public libraries and reference sections will need to be taught on site and *with purpose*. Behavior rehearsal or role playing are often good techniques to use for "asking for help" training. The previously noted books on secondary education methodology and on reading in the content areas will also have sections on study skills, especially the ubiquitous SQ3R (skim, question, read, recite, review) methodology.

The learning-disabilities teacher will, perhaps, need to spend time teaching some students how to "operate" in various classes with a wide range of teacher behaviors. There are ethical problems in teaching students to modify the behavior of teachers; but for learning-disabled students (who may not learn this "normal" behavior incidentally), this technique should be considered. The student who can figure out what pleases the teacher, but does not choose to do so, is in a very different position from the student who just does not know what is happening. The learning-disabilities teacher should be familiar with the range of competencies and expectations of the content-area teachers to help the students understand their teachers better.

Several representative publications in study skills are annotated in the Appendix to this chapter. All need modification for presentation or work with students and are not suitable for independent use.

RESOURCES FROM OTHER AREAS OF EXCEPTIONALITY

Areas of exceptionality other than learning disabilities offer information, publications, and services of potential value in a learning-disabilities program.

DEAF AND HEARING-IMPAIRED   Because language is at the heart of many learning disorders, some of the techniques and materials of value in working with the deaf and hearing-impaired are also useful in learning-disabilities classes. One example of a relevant product is *The Language of Directions: A Programmed Workbook* (Rush, 1970), in which

86

commonly used "school work" directions are taught. This kind of material can serve teachers as a prototype in their development of similar products for secondary curricula.

MENTAL RETARDATION   One example of curriculum development activity that is directly applicable to learning disabilities at the secondary level in terms of methodology—and to some extent content—is the continuing curriculum project of Brown and his colleagues. Their validated techniques are contained in the series *Toward the Development and Implementation of an Empirically Based Public School Program for Trainable Mentally Retarded and Severely Emotionally Disturbed Students* (1971 to date).

BEHAVIOR DISORDERS AND PERSONAL PROBLEMS OF THE STUDENT   Students who experience or present severe behavior disorders do not belong in most learning-disabilities programs. It is not unusual, however, for students labeled as learning-disabled to have concomitant behavior or personal problems. To deal with them, secondary learning-disabilities teachers will need to have a natural or acquired repertoire of techniques. It is impossible to emphasize too strongly that learning-disabilities teachers at the secondary level should have had enough experience with adolescents so that they are familiar with developmental characteristics of this age group. Then teachers are not as likely to view normally fluctuating behaviors as permanent problem behaviors.

BEHAVIOR MODIFICATION   By the time the student is in a secondary education program, the use of behavior modification should certainly involve the student in the planning or managing of his or her own program. Sometimes students are taught the basic principles of behavior modification through resources such as Homme (1969), Malott (1972), Thoresen and Mahoney (1974), and Watson and Tharp (1972).

VALUES CLARIFICATION   There are many books dealing with techniques for helping students to clarify their own values and to understand better the values of others. Much of a teacher's work lies with the conflict of values among student, home, school, and society. It should be kept in mind that values clarification is a process rather than a judgment, and it bears no responsibility for outcomes. Raths, Harmin, and Simon

(1966) and Simon, Howe, and Kirschenbaum (1972) are classic works in this area. Additional material can be found in *Values Education Sourcebook* (Superka et al., 1976).

MORAL EDUCATION   The development of criteria with which to judge values is a controversial aspect of education, even though it is mandated in some states (California is one). Exploring moral and ethical standards and positions from extreme cultural relativity on the one hand to extreme personal relativity on the other is primarily the business of moral education. This subject is important for helping teenage students in a rapidly changing society. Galbraith and Jones (1976), Kohlberg (1973), and Wilson (1972) provide background material for the teacher.

COUNSELING   The learning-disabilities teacher in the secondary school is not expected to become a counselor for emotionally disturbed students. Yet, because of contact opportunities and confidence (when it is there), the learning-disabilities teacher should have some idea of how to help explore behavioral and personal problems. Practical suggestions are found in Krumboltz and Thoresen (1969) and in Rose (1972). Brammer (1973) deals with the entire question of the "helping" process.

GIFTED   Students who are labeled as learning-disabled run the risk of being removed from stimulating and creativity-inducing environments. But techniques for the gifted should no longer be prescribed just for those in classrooms for the gifted. They can be used for the development of every person's creative talents. Some introductory resources in this area are the materials of Covington, Crutchfield, Davis, and Olton (1974), Gallagher (1975), and Suchman (1962).

COOPERATIVE EXTENSION SERVICE RESOURCES

Cooperative Extension Service (CES) agencies such as 4-H (usually in the yellow pages under "county agricultural agents") provide a ready source of materials and units on a wide variety of topics such as small-motor repair, consumer education, and the development of a personal lifestyle. Remember that 4-H is not just a rural organization; it provides services in urban areas as well.

ADULT EDUCATION RESOURCES

Several organizations deal exclusively with various aspects of adult education, often with problems and practices in basic education. Their publications may be monitored for access to relevant materials, programs, and techniques.

Barnes and Hendrickson, through the Center for Adult Education at Ohio State University, provide an excellent *Review and Appraisal of Adult Literacy Materials and Programs* (1965) that is still relevant to contemporary programs. Especially helpful are the section on methodology for analyzing ABE (Adult Basic Education) materials and the listing of analyzed materials and their sources. Brooke's *Adult Basic Education* (1972) is an excellent resource book of readings about ABE programs, techniques, and materials in the United States and Canada. Griffith and Hayes (1970) present a series of symposium papers with a research orientation. Included are several chapters dealing with the evaluation of materials such as *Programmed Reading for Adults* (Buchanan, 1966) and *The Mott Basic Language Skills Program* (Chapman & Schulz, 1964).

Laubach and Laubach (1960) have provided the classic description of their world literacy method, *The Each One Teach One Way*. The book is divided into two parts: the first deals with teaching illiterates how to read; the second, with the problems of writing for "new literates." The bibliography and sources of information appended to the book are especially valuable.

Minkoff's annotated bibliography for teaching reading, writing, and mathematics (1967) remains a worthwhile source document.

The resources described briefly above are merely indicative of the continuing interest in adult basic education. Readers who go into the literature more thoroughly than I have done here will note that, with the exception of the work of programmed-materials authors, a consistent theme of reports on literacy programs is the need for tailoring materials to the population at hand rather than using commercially prepared materials or programs.

RESOURCES ON LIFE SKILLS

No special mention has been made of career or vocational education, sex education, and preparation for self-management of living skills. Many school districts have these programs readily available or at least a wealth of materials available on such subjects. Some of these areas, such as consumer education, may be used as introductions to basic skills, while others should be taught in and of themselves. Teachers should make certain that learning-disabled students are not denied access to these curriculum areas.

Except for the most seriously impaired, learning-disabled students in postelementary school do not need specialized techniques and materials that set them observably apart from their peers and reinforce the special label. Instead, the major activity needed is that of teacher development, for no curriculum or materials can ever really compensate for a teacher who is poorly prepared and/or uninterested in students and their problems. When we consider the very wide range and variety of possibilities to explore, use, and adapt from areas outside learning disabilities, the possibilities for the future are not only challenging but provocative and exciting as well.

■ REFERENCES ■

Ashlock, R. B. *Error patterns in computation: A semi-programmed approach.* Columbus, Ohio: Charles E. Merrill, 1972.

Aukerman, R. C. *Reading in the secondary school classroom.* New York: McGraw-Hill, 1972.

Barnes, R. F., & Hendrickson, A. *Review and appraisal of adult literacy materials and programs.* Columbus: Ohio State University Center for Adult Education, 1965.

Blanton, W., Farr, R., & Tuinman, J. J. (Eds.). *Reading tests for the secondary grades: A review and evaluation.* Newark, Del.: International Reading Association, 1972.

Brammer, L. M. *The helping relationship: Process and skills.* Englewood Cliffs, N.J.: Prentice-Hall, 1973.

Brogden, J. D. *Developing communication skills in noncommitted learners.* West Nyack, N.Y.: Parker Publishing Co., 1970.

Brooke, W. M. (Ed.). *Adult basic education: A resource book of readings.* Toronto: New Press, 1972.

Brown, L., et al. *Toward the development and implementation of an empirically based public school program for trainable mentally retarded and severely emotionally disturbed students.* Madison, Wis.: Madison Public Schools, Department of Specialized Educational Services, 1971 to date.

Bryant, N. D. *Trial remediation: learning sight words.* Unpublished manuscript, Columbia University, Teachers College, 1971.

Buchanan, C. *Programmed reading for adults.* New York: McGraw-Hill, 1966.

Burmeister, L. E. *Reading strategies for secondary school teachers.* Reading, Mass.: Addison-Wesley, 1974.

Chapman, B. E., & Schulz, L. *The Mott basic language skills program.* Chicago: Allied Educational Council, 1964.

Covington, M. V., Crutchfield, R. S., Davies, L., & Olton, R. M., Jr. *The productive thinking program: A course in learning to think.* Columbus, Ohio: Charles E. Merrill, 1974.

Fernald, G. *Remedial techniques in basic school subjects.* New York: McGraw-Hill, 1943.

Gage, T. How can we help kids read science textbooks? *The Science Teacher,* 1974, *41*, 37–40.

Galbraith, R. E., & Jones, T. M. *Moral reasoning: A teaching handbook for adapting Kohlberg to the classroom.* Anoka, Minn.: Greenhaven Press, 1976.

Gallagher, J. J. *Teaching the gifted child* (2nd ed.). Boston: Allyn and Bacon, 1975.

Gillingham, A., & Stillman, B. *Remedial training for children with specific disability in reading, spelling, and penmanship* (7th ed.). Cambridge, Mass.: Educators Publishing Service, 1960.

Goodman, Y. M., & Burke, C. L. *Reading miscue inventory.* New York: Macmillan, 1972.

Griffith, W. S., & Hayes, A. P. (Eds.). *Adult basic education: The state of the art.* Chicago: University of Chicago Department of Education, 1970.

A guide to agencies and organizations concerned with exceptional children. *Exceptional Children,* 1969, *35*, 647–662.

Herber, H. L. *Teaching reading in content areas.* Englewood Cliffs, N.J.: Prentice-Hall, 1970.

Homme, L. *How to use contingency contracting in the classroom.* Champaign, Ill.: Research Press, 1969.

Jones, J. A. Teacher-made lesson tapes. *Teacher,* 1975, *92*(5), 108–109.

Kohlberg, L. Continuities in childhood and adult moral development revisited. In P. Palter & K. W. Schaie (Eds.), *Life-span development psychology.* New York: Academic Press, 1973.

Krumboltz, J. D., & Thoresen, C. G. *Behavioral counseling: Cases and techniques*. New York: Holt, Rinehart and Winston, 1969.

Laten, S., & Katz, G. *A theoretical model for assessment of adolescents: The ecological/behavioral approach*. Madison, Wis.: Madison Public Schools, Division of Specialized Educational Services, 1975.

Laubach, F. C., & Laubach, R. S. *Toward world literacy: The each one teach one way*. Syracuse, N.Y.: Syracuse University Press, 1960.

Laycock, M., & Watson, G. *The fabric of mathematics (K-9)*. Hayward, Calif.: Activity Resources Co., 1971.

Malott, R. W. *Contingency management in education and other equally exciting places OR I've got blisters on my soul and other equally exciting places* (2nd ed.). Kalamazoo, Mich.: Behaviordelia, 1972.

Minkoff, D. *Adult basic education curriculum materials for teaching: An annotated bibliography of teaching reading, writing, and mathematics*. Newark, N.J.: Newark State College, Adult Education Resource Center, 1967.

Nettleton, A., & Sapone, C. *Readability: Matching the reader with print*. Madison, Wis.: The Madison Public Schools Department of Curriculum Development, no date.

Raths, L. E., Harmin, M., & Simon, S. B. *Values and teaching: Working with values in the classroom*. Columbus, Ohio: Charles E. Merrill, 1966.

Rose, S. *Treating children in groups*. San Francisco: Jossey-Bass, 1972.

Rush, M. L. *The language of directions—A programmed workbook*. Washington, D.C.: Alexander Graham Bell Association for the Deaf, 1970.

Shepherd, D. L. *Comprehensive school reading methods*. Columbus, Ohio: Charles E. Merrill, 1973.

Simon, S. B., Howe, L. W., & Kirschenbaum, H. *Values clarification: A handbook of practical strategies for teachers and students*. New York: Hart Publishing Co., 1972.

Stauffer, R. G. *The language-experience approach to the teaching of reading*. New York: Harper & Row, 1970.

Suchman, J. R. *The elementary school training program in scientific inquiry*. Urbana: University of Illinois, 1962.

Superka, D. P., Ahrens, C., Hedstrom, J. E., Ford, L. J., & Johnson, P. L. *Values education sourcebook: Conceptual approaches, materials analyses, and an annotated bibliography*. Boulder, Colo.: Social Science Education Consortium, 1976.

Thoresen, C., & Mahoney, M. J. *Behavioral self-control.* New York: Holt, Rinehart and Winston, 1974.

Watson, D. L., & Tharp, R. G. *Self-directed behavior: Self-modification for personal adjustment.* Monterey, Calif.: Brooks/Cole Publishing Co., 1972.

Wilson, J. *Practical methods of moral education.* London: Heinemann Educational, 1972.

SELECTED TEXTS ON SECONDARY EDUCATION AND SPECIAL METHODS

Bent, R. K., & Unruh, A. *Secondary school curriculum*. Lexington, Mass.: D. C. Heath, 1969.

An overview curriculum book designed to show the complexities of secondary curriculum development. The age of this book shows how little has changed in many high schools and yet, paradoxically, how rapidly "future thinking" is occurring.

Hoover, K. H. *The professional teacher's handbook: A guide for improving instruction in today's secondary schools*. Boston: Allyn and Bacon, 1973.

Kim, E. C., & Kellough, R. D. *A resource guide for secondary school teaching: Planning for competence*. New York: Macmillan, 1974.

Samalonis, B. L. *Methods and materials for today's high schools*. New York: Van Nostrand Reinhold, 1970.

All three of the above texts deal with the how-to's of instructional planning and evaluation. The many worksheets and guides that are found in each will help teachers to check out their skills and to learn new ones.

Joyce, B., & Weil, M. *Models of teaching*. Englewood Cliffs, N.J.: Prentice-Hall, 1972.

Provides models of instruction. The applied premise of this book is that matches can be made between teaching styles and learning styles and, further, that flexibility of teaching style is helpful in creating alternatives for a variety of learners.

Gordon, A. K. *Games for growth*. Palo Alto, Calif.: Science Associates, College Division, 1970.

An introduction to the design, use, and evaluation of laboratory learning experiences, games, or simulations.

JOURNALS TO MONITOR FOR INFORMATION AND IDEAS

American Vocational Journal (secondary), Vocational Association, Inc., 1510 H Street NW, Washington, D.C. 20005.

The Arithmetic Teacher (elementary, but with ideas for older students), National Council of Teachers of Mathematics, 1906 Association Drive, Reston, Virginia 22091.

Audiovisual Instruction (creative media uses and programs), Association for Educational Communications and Technology, 1201 16th Street NW, Washington, D.C. 20036.

Arts and Activities (ideas for K–12), 8150 North Central Park Avenue, Skokie, Illinois 60076.

The College Board Review (issues and trends in secondary education; transition to college), College Entrance Exam Board, 888 Seventh Avenue, New York, N.Y. 10019.

Compact (trends in school law, finance, and the like), Education Commission of the States, Suite 822, Lincoln Tower, 1860 Lincoln, Denver, Colorado 80203.

Education (innovative programs and practices at all levels), Project Innovation, 1402 West Capital Drive, Milwaukee, Wisconsin 53206.

Educational Leadership (contemporary programs, issues, problems), Association for Supervision and Curriculum Development, 1201 16th Street NW, Washington, D.C. 20036.

Elementary English (ideas applicable for older students), National Council of Teachers of English, 1111 Kenyon Road, Urbana, Illinois 61801.

Educational Technology (theme issues such as "individualized education"), Educational Technology Publications, Inc., 140 Sylvan Avenue, Englewood Cliffs, New Jersey 07632.

The Gifted Child Quarterly (ideas and trends), National Association for Gifted Children, 8080 Springvalley Drive, Cincinnati, Ohio 45236.

The High School Journal (current programs, issues, and trends), University of North Carolina Press, University of North Carolina, Bynum Hall, Chapel Hill, North Carolina 27514.

Improving College and University Teaching (many ideas useful for secondary level), Oregon State University Press, 101 Waldo Hall, Corvallis, Oregon 97331.

Journal of Applied Behavior Analysis (all methodology), University of Kansas, Department of Human Development, Lawrence, Kansas 66044.

The Journal of Negro Education (issues incident to the education of blacks), Howard University, Bureau of Educational Research, Washington, D.C. 20001.

Journal of Reading (secondary, college, and adult levels), International Reading Association, 800 Barksdale Road, Newark, Delaware 19711.

Journal of Reading Behavior (all research; all levels), National Reading Conference, Appalachian State University, Boone, North Carolina 18607.

Learning: The Magazine for Creative Teaching (unusual ideas; issues), Education Today Company, Inc., 530 University Ave., Palo Alto, California 94301.

Mathematics Teacher (general secondary resources), National Council of Teachers of Mathematics, 1906 Association Drive, Reston, Virginia 22091.

National Association of Secondary Principals: Bulletin (influences), 1904 Association Drive, Reston, Virginia 22091.

North Central Association Quarterly (current trends in secondary education), Association of Colleges and Secondary Schools, 5454 South Shore Drive, Chicago, Illinois 60615.

New Outlook for the Blind (many ideas relevant to the problems of learning-disabled students), American Foundation for the Blind, 15 West 16th Street, New York, N.Y. 10011.

Phi Delta Kappan (issues, trends, new programs), Phi Delta Kappa, Eighth Street and Union Avenue, Bloomington, Indiana 47401.

Plays: The Drama Magazine for Young People (new sources each month), Plays, Inc., 8 Arlington Street, Boston, Massachusetts 02116.

Reading Improvement (innovative ideas for teaching), Project Innovation, 1402 West Capital Drive, Milwaukee, Wisconsin 53206.

Reading Research Quarterly (research; in-depth studies), International Reading Association, 800 Barksdale Road, Newark, Delaware 19711.

The Reading Teacher (elementary, but with useful ideas for secondary), International Reading Association, 800 Barksdale Road, Newark, Delaware 19711.

The School Counselor (ideas, issues, trends), American Personnel and Guidance Association, 1607 New Hampshire Avenue NW, Washington, D.C. 20009.

School Science and Mathematics (classroom and school applications), School Science and Mathematics Association, Inc., Box 1614, Indiana University of Pennsylvania, Indiana, Pennsylvania 15701.

Science Curriculum Improvement Study (SCIS) Newsletter (practical), University of California, Science Curriculum Improvement Study, Lawrence Hall of Science, Berkeley, California 97410.

The Science Teacher (classroom ideas of contemporary relevance), National Science Teachers Association, 1201 16th Street NW, Washington, D.C. 20036.

Small Group Behavior (therapy and treatment), Sage Publications, Inc., 275 South Beverly Drive, Beverly Hills, California 90212.

Social Education (social studies ideas), National Council for Social Studies, 1201 16th Street NW, Washington, D.C. 10036.

Theory into Practice (innovative practices; controversial issues), Ohio State University, College of Education, 149 Arps, 1945 North High Street, Columbus, Ohio 43210.

Urban Education (politics; motivation ideas), Warren Button, Ed., Sage Publications, Inc., 275 South Beverly Drive, Beverly Hills, California 90212.

ASSOCIATIONS CONCERNED WITH THE IMPROVEMENT OF SECONDARY EDUCATION

International Reading Association, 800 Barksdale Road, Newark, Delaware 19711.

National Association of Secondary School Principals, 1904 Association Drive, Reston, Virginia 22091.

National Council for the Social Studies, 1201 16th Street NW, Washington, D.C. 20036.

National Council of Teachers of English, 1111 Kenyon Road, Urbana, Illinois 61801.

National Council of Teachers of Mathematics, 1906 Association Drive, Reston, Virginia 22091.

National Science Teachers' Association, 1742 Connecticut Avenue NW, Washington, D.C. 20009.

North Central Association of Colleges and Secondary Schools, 5454 South Shore Drive, Chicago, Illinois 60615.

RESOURCES ADAPTABLE FROM ADULT EDUCATION

Adult Education Association, 1225 19th Street NW, Washington, D.C. 20036.

Council for Basic Education, 725 Fifteenth Street NW, Washington, D.C. 20005.

National Association for Public Continuing and Adult Education (formerly the National Association for Public School Adult Education), 1201 16th Street NW, Washington, D.C. 20036. (Provides excellent material for working with nontraditional older students.)

RESOURCES FOR PARENTS

Association for Children with Learning Disabilities, 2200 Brownsville Road, Pittsburgh, Pennsylvania 15210.

Brownstone, J. E., & Dye, C. J. *Communication workshop for parents of adolescents: Leader's guide* and *Communication workshop for parents of adolescents: Parent's guide.* Champaign, Ill.: Research Press, 1973.

Council for Exceptional Children Information Center, 1920 Association Drive, Reston, Virginia 20091.

Madsen, C. K., & Madsen, C. H., Jr. *Parents/children/discipline: A positive approach.* Boston: Allyn and Bacon, 1972.

Patterson, G., & Gullion, M. E. *Living with children: New methods for parents and teachers.* Champaign, Ill.: Research Press, 1968. (also in Spanish edition)

Tharp, R. G., & Wetzel, R. J. *Behavior modification in the natural environment.* New York: Academic Press, 1969.

The exceptional parent: Children with disabilities/practical guidance. P.O. Box 964, Manchester, New Hampshire 03105. ($10.00 per year)

STUDY SKILLS

Christ, F. L. *Studying a textbook.* Chicago: Science Research Associates, 1966.

The exercises of this SQ3R approach to textbook study will prove useful, but going through them all may be tedious.

Millman, J., & Pauk, W. *How to take tests.* New York: McGraw-Hill, 1969.

This book is excellent for its comprehensiveness, clarity, and emphasis on preparation or study skills. The material is readily adaptable to secondary education. Emphasis is placed on intellectual, emotional, and physical preparation as well as on use of student time.

Morgan, C. T., & Deese, J. *How to study* (2nd ed.). New York: McGraw-Hill, 1969.

This was written for college students but is useful for almost every level. Self-evaluation, use of time, getting help, and living outside of school are topics of special interest. Traditional chapters on taking exams, on reading, and on writing papers are supplemented with special tips for major content areas. The book has many suggestions for analyzing a class situation and for understanding teacher behaviors.

Robinson, F. *Effective study.* New York: Harper and Row, 1971.

This book provides a detailed analysis of the SQ3R methodology.

Smith, S. W., Shores, L., & Brittain, R. *Best methods of study* (4th ed.). New York: Barnes & Noble, 1970.

Test preparation, use of resources, and personal management of study are some of the topics. There is a wide range of subject matter, from vocational subjects to the fine arts. Included is a brief section on teachers' expectations.

Todd, A. *Finding facts fast: How to find out what you want to know immediately.* New York: William Morrow, 1972.

A concise reference guide to information location resources, this book is useful to both teachers and students.

Zifferblatt, S. M. *Improving study and homework behaviors.* Champaign, Ill.: Research Press, 1970.

This semiprogrammed text could also be used for parent education activities. It is a behaviorist contingency-contracting approach to the management of independent study and homework.

CHAPTER 5

INSTRUCTIONAL STRATEGIES: A CLASSIFICATION SCHEMA

JANET W. LERNER

Many different instructional strategies and remedial approaches are currently being used (or are suggested for use) with adolescents who are failing in academic areas because of learning disabilities. These instructional strategies are known variously as *remediation, clinical teaching, academic therapy, academic intervention, tutoring,* and *teaching methods.* While some authorities may perceive shades of differences in their meaning, in this chapter all these terms are used interchangeably and are assumed to have the same meaning. The purpose of the chapter is to classify current approaches to remediation and to assess their applicability in programs for learning-disabled students at the secondary level.

In any discipline a necessary first step is to organize the known information in the field in a systematic fashion. Making a taxonomy that classifies teaching approaches is one way of sorting out the diverse approaches to learning disabilities and of understanding the remedial implications of each. Figure 5-1 is a taxonomic model that divides remediation into three classes: analysis of the student, analysis of the subject matter to be learned, and analysis of the environmental conditions under which the student learns. Within this model, each type of analysis is subdivided into specific categories of remediation; in all, there are nine categories. Each category differs in its applicability and appropriateness for remedial teaching of learning-disabled adolescents.

■ ANALYSIS OF THE STUDENT ■

The first three types of remedial approach—cognitive processing, sequential stages of development, and test related—concentrate on analysis of students and how they function.

THE COGNITIVE-PROCESSING APPROACH

The approach to remediation most readily associated with the field of learning disabilities is that of cognitive processing, or the ways in which a person processes information. In order to assess students' strengths and weaknesses, special educators study their visual and auditory processing skills, memory functions, and language abilities. Teaching

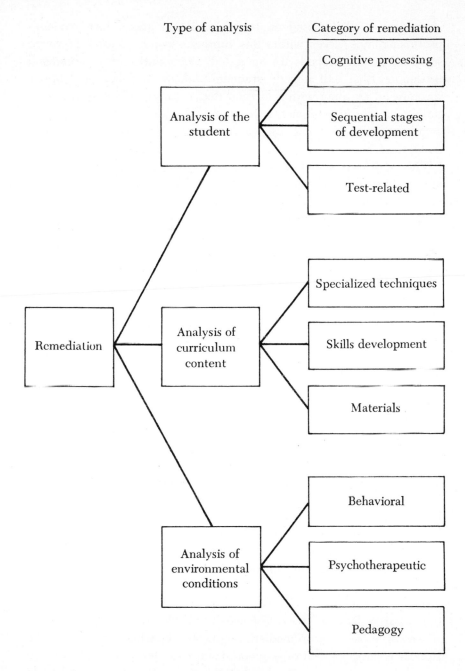

Figure 5-1   A classification of remediation

strategies are then based on this information about each student's processing style. Even within this approach to remediation, however, several different methods are suggested. Some authorities recommend procedures that will remedy students' deficits in processing; others recommend teaching with a method that uses pupils' strengths (aptitude-treatment interaction); still other authorities suggest doing both simultaneously—building up weak areas while teaching through strengths.

This approach, which may seem to provide a fresh, logical, and appealing view of learning-disabled students, is not a new one. Discussions of visual, auditory, tactile, and kinesthetic abilities appeared in the writings of Monroe (1932) and Fernald (1943) thirty to forty years ago. Though the cognitive-processing approach is currently popular and widely accepted, research evidence to substantiate its efficacy is still lacking (Mann & Phillips, 1971; Cohen, 1967; Hammill, Goodman, & Wiederholt, 1974; Hammill & Larsen, 1974a and 1974b). Another criticism of the cognitive-processing approach is that many teaching methods cannot—as this approach demands—be judged essentially visual or auditory. (For example, the phonics approach to the teaching of reading requires integrating visual and auditory skills, as do the so-called look-say methods.) There is also the question of the best age for processing instruction. Most of the tests and instruction for processing are geared for preschool or elementary school populations. By the time that students reach adolescence, many of their processing abilities have already matured, and attempts to develop these abilities further are no longer useful. At this point, rather than work on processing abilities as isolated and discrete functions, teachers should, whenever possible, incorporate processing instruction into their teaching of academic skills. Chapter 6 in this book further discusses the limits of the processing approach as an instruction strategy for adolescents. Despite serious limitations, the cognitive-processing approach is an important framework in the field of learning disabilities.

THE SEQUENTIAL-STAGES-OF-DEVELOPMENT APPROACH

A second approach to remediation—another in which analysis of the student is basic—is that of sequential stages of development. This approach focuses on the hierarchical stages of development of the normal growing child. One model, for example, refers to these stages of the maturation process as "sensation, perception, memory, symbolization, conceptualization" (Johnson & Myklebust, 1967). Piaget provides another schematic description of child development: sensorimotor period, preoperation period, concrete operations stage, and the formal operations stage (Flavell, 1973). Getman (1965) presents yet another hierarchical series of stages.

Such models presume that the development in each of the stages is sequential; that is, successful completion of each previous stage is a prerequisite to successful achievement at the next level. Diagnosis consists of determining the stage at which a pupil is functioning—the lowest level that a student has not successfully completed. Remediation consists of helping students to complete growth at the unfinished phase of development and then helping them go on to the next level. For example, a perceptually handicapped student has not completed growth at the perceptual stage of development; remediation would thus require training in perceptual skills. The constant assumption is that further growth and learning are dependent on the achievement at an earlier stage.

Since most sequential-developmental models specify development at the preschool and primary levels, the sequential-stages-of-development approach to remediation is not pertinent to adolescents. In addition, research to substantiate this method of remediation is lacking (Goodman & Hammill, 1973). Critics also point to the gap between training in the sequential stages of motor development and the demands of academic learning.

TEST-RELATED APPROACHES

Another approach to remediation that emphasizes analysis of the student is the test-related approach. The theory here is that a particular diagnostic instrument pinpoints areas that need remediation. The model upon which the test was based is accepted as the model of learning disabilities. An examiner might give the Illinois Test of Psycholinguistic Abilities (ITPA), assuming that the test model effectively categorizes the ways in which the student functions psycholinguistically (Kirk, McCarthy, & Kirk, 1968). Many materials have been specifically designed to remediate deficits revealed by the ITPA. For example, Bush and Giles (1969) provide exercises similar to the test items, and commercial materials include the MWM Program (Minskoff, Wiseman,

& Minskoff, 1972) and the Goal Language Development Game (Karnes, 1972). In the Frostig Developmental Test of Visual Perception and its accompanying teaching materials (Frostig, 1964; Frostig & Horne, 1964; Frostig et al., 1972), the approach is similar. After the test is given and scored, the results are used to select a remediation procedure.

As the ITPA and Frostig's DTVP are designed for younger students, not adolescents, their use with secondary students exceeds the intention of the test developers. Moreover, research to substantiate the value of the test-related approach—even for younger students—is lacking. This remedial approach does help students improve in the specific skill being tested and remediated, but the carry-over to other learning is not known (Hammill & Wiederholt, 1973). Teachers planning to use test data as the basis for remediation must be aware of the shortcomings of the test and should judge its appropriateness for use with adolescents.

■ ANALYSIS OF THE CURRICULUM CONTENT ■

The specialized-techniques, skills-development, and materials approaches to remediation analyze the subject matter or the content to be learned, rather than analyzing the pupil. The method of remediation is the same for all students, no matter how different their learning styles may be.

THE SPECIALIZED-TECHNIQUES APPROACH

One approach to remediation that analyzes content is that of specialized techniques. Unlike the developmental methods typically used in the regular classroom, these techniques are considered highly specialized and highly differentiated ways of attacking specific learning problems. The developer of the teaching procedures involved often requires their exclusive use and abandonment of other techniques. Some examples are the Fernald, Gillingham, Fitzgerald, VAKT, and organic methods.

There are several criticisms of the specialized-techniques approach. Upon close examination we often find that these "unique" methods are not so different from methods that have been used throughout the years.

The remedial treatment in these approaches is the same for all students, no matter what the specific problem or the age of the student. There is little research showing that a specific specialized technique is, indeed, superior to other remedial and developmental methods.

THE SKILLS-DEVELOPMENT APPROACH

Another view of remediation that focuses on content is that of skills development. In this method a hierarchy of skills of the subject area (reading, arithmetic, spelling, and so on) is postulated. The remedial specialist attempts to determine how far the student has progressed and thus where in the hierarchy the teaching should begin. The assumption is that, by mastering each of the subskills of the subject, the student will master the subject. In reading, for example, the ability to read is analyzed in terms of subskills of reading. Word attack skills are viewed as a set of subskills that can again be subdivided into an ordered sequence of subskills. Because growth is assumed to proceed through a sequence of skills, each phase of developmental growth is likened to climbing rungs on a ladder; a learner who misses some rungs may fall off altogether.

The criterion-referenced materials that are now appearing on the market (as both testing and teaching materials) are representative of the skills-development approach to teaching. Their authors put forth a sequence of reading skills. If the student's test for each skill is not satisfactory, teaching is provided specifically for that skill.

The skills-development approach is one that can readily be used with learning-disabled adolescents. It not only permits teachers to focus on specific subskills but also allows the students themselves to become involved in the analysis of their skills, see for themselves where they are deficient, and thus be motivated to develop or correct their areas of weakness. The focus is on the task to be learned rather than on the student who is to learn it.

This approach, while it has its advantages, also leaves certain issues unresolved. Thompson and Dziuban (1973) question the existence of an empirically derived hierarchy of reading skills. They question whether the ordered sequence of skills set forth by the authors of the material is the best sequence for the particular student needing help. Teachers have pointed out the increased paperwork and record keeping required by some of the criterion-referenced materials. They also report that students who are able to pass criterion tests for a specific subskill cannot transfer this subskill to other reading situations.

THE MATERIALS APPROACH

Publishers' materials are the basis of yet another category of remediation concerned with the content rather than with the student. In this case the materials guide and direct the procedures of remediation. The basic decision is which material to use; once this decision is made, the materials themselves become the further decision makers. For example, if a basal reader series is selected for use in remediation, the material can guide the skills sequence, provide appropriate practice activities, suggest instructor's questions, and give step-by-step instructional procedures. In many ways this is one of the easiest methods to use because it minimizes decision making for the teacher. (For example, the materials might offer instructions such as these: "After completing the story on pages 20–25, ask the questions on page 33 of this manual; give the practice skills on page 34; follow this with the activities on pages 15 and 16 in the workbook.")

Good remedial therapy or clinical teaching, however, requires constant decision making. Indeed, the ability to make appropriate judgments and decisions is considered one of the most essential competencies of the clinical teacher. When the teacher depends on particular materials, the materials themselves become the remedial procedures; they become the master rather than the servant of the clinician. Over-reliance on a materials approach may lead to irrelevant instruction. Durkin (1974) warns that teachers must clarify their own role insofar as materials are concerned. By depending on materials, she asserts, teachers become an assistant to materials.

It is important that the teacher have an abundance of materials to select from and that the materials be used in the way the teacher deems appropriate. While there has been a scarcity of material for adolescents (most materials have been designed for elementary-age pupils), currently many materials that are geared for the adolescent are coming onto the market. Teachers of adolescents should search out these materials, try them out, and evaluate them, for they need to view materials as tools—important tools—to be used to help individuals learn.

■ ANALYSIS OF ENVIRONMENTAL CONDITIONS ■
OF LEARNING

The final set of remedial approaches looks at various elements of the environment surrounding learning rather than at the student or at the content of the curriculum. This category of remediation includes the behavioral approach, the psychotherapeutic approach, and the pedagogical approach.

THE BEHAVIORAL APPROACH

A growing movement in the remediation of learning problems focuses on changing the student's behavior. The approach is usually referred to as behavior modification, but a recent branch of the movement is called precision teaching.

Unlike the categories discussed earlier (which analyze the student, the content to be learned, or the materials or techniques to be used), this approach focuses on the conditions or environment of learning. What is studied is a specific learning behavior itself, along with the events that precede and follow this target behavior. Based on principles of reinforcement theory, the technique is used to remediate students by eliminating undesirable behaviors and establishing specific desirable behaviors.

Users of the behavioral approach are not concerned with the causes of a pupil's learning problems or the methods a student adopts to process information, but rather with manipulating the environment to bring about the desired behavior. In this approach identification of the problem and the ability to manipulate the behaviors involved are sufficient; there is no need to look further for underlying explanations (Poteet, 1973).

The behavioral approach to teaching appears to be as successful with adolescents as with younger pupils. Nonetheless, it has its critics. Many educators find its concepts and goals to be limiting, confining, and contrary to their ideas of freedom and learning. Goodman (1974), for example, has the following to say about behavior modification:

We've got to tell the operant conditioners and the contingency reinforcers that kids can learn like pigeons but pigeons can't learn like kids and that learning theories that try to reduce learning to read to bite-size pellets that pigeons can swallow are inappropriate and theoretically wrong and ultimately harmful to at least some kids. We've got to assert that if kids learn to read with these pigeon picking programs, that's a tribute to the language learning competence of kids which makes it possible to overcome the absurdities of programs like *Distar* and *BRL* and learn to read anyway. Most children can learn in spite of such programs which fragment reading into sequences of measurable irrelevant trivia. But enough children suffer that I would like to see signs displayed all over the walls of the exhibit areas of professional conferences of groups like IRA and NCTE which say, "Caution: Instructional materials displayed here may be injurious to the mental health of your pupils."

PSYCHOTHERAPEUTIC REMEDIATION

The remedial method that concentrates on the feelings of the student and his or her relationship with the therapist is called the psychotherapeutic approach to remediation. The psychodynamics of remediation are too often forgotten in the labyrinth of materials, techniques, methods, modalities, and baseline data. Failing students are unhappy in the learning situation; their frustrations, poor ego development, and feelings of inadequacy all lead to continued failure and lack of learning. The psychotherapeutic approach tries to reverse the situation by building positive attitudes and by establishing a healthy psychodynamic relationship between teacher and student.

The psychodynamics of failure dictate that even if a pupil is well adjusted on entering school, continued failure in school learning is practically certain to have unfavorable effects on personality. As the pupil becomes an adolescent and enters secondary school, feelings of failure, frustration, and oversensitivity tend to increase. Then, too, emotional problems are almost always in evidence. Reactions take the form of withdrawal, anxiety, conscious refusal to learn, overt hostility, negative reaction to learning, resistance to independence, discouragement, fear that success is dangerous, distractibility, absorption in a private world, and indifference (Harris, 1970). In one study almost one-fourth of the individuals under eighteen were referred for psychiatric evaluation because of academic difficulties (Nichol, 1974).

From this perspective the tasks of remediation are rebuilding students' egos, giving students the confidence and assurance they lack, and letting them know that, as the teacher, you understand their problems and are confident that they can learn and succeed.

110

Like the other approaches we have been looking at, the psycho-therapeutic approach to remediation has its critics. Evidence is lacking as to whether a psychotherapeutic approach alone is sufficient. The critics fear that overemphasis on the psychotherapeutic approach will mean a neglect of teaching. In fact, some cynics suggest that the sole result of such an approach is the creation of "happy failures," that is, students who have learned to be content with their failure to learn. In discussing the limits of psychotherapeutic treatment of students with learning disabilities, McCarthy (1971) notes: "After several decades of often fruitless effort at manipulating the child's attitude toward learning it became apparent ... that motivation, could at best produce a child who was comfortable, albeit euphoric, with nonlearning."

REMEDIATION THROUGH PEDAGOGY

The last category of remediation to be presented is pedagogy. According to Cohen (1971), the major cause of reading failure is "dyspedagogia," lack of good teaching. It seems to follow that pedagogy, or good teaching, can be considered a method of remediation.

Several research studies, in fact, have concluded that the most important variable in a person's learning is the teacher (Bond & Dykstra, 1967; Chall & Feldmann, 1966; Harris et al., 1968). What some writers suggest is replacing the term *learning disability* with the term *teaching disability*, shifting the focus from something deviant or pathological within the student to the inadequacies of the teaching environment, including the teacher. Further, Bateman (1974) questions whether labels such as *learning disabilities* or *minimal brain dysfunction* do not serve as a sophisticated excuse for poor teaching or even nonteaching. According to Cutts (1975), the goal in producing teachers should be not to discover "teacher-proof" materials but rather to develop "materials-proof" teachers.

Finding good teachers for adolescents is of critical import. These teachers not only must understand the technicalities of pedagogy but must understand and relate to adolescents as well. While there is ready agreement that the teacher is a crucial component, there is not such accord as to what the essential ingredients of the good teacher are. What is the essential attribute? Is it kindness, empathy, the ability to structure the class, creativity, enthusiasm, neatness, order, ability to individualize, punctuality, consistency, knowledge of the field, love of children, diagnostic skills, familiarity with the materials, or some other characteristic? Until we get a clear answer as to what qualities we are looking for, the plea for good teachers is nebulous.

■ A SYSTEMS APPROACH TO REMEDIATION ■

This chapter has presented a model of remediation consisting of three types of analysis and nine different categories of remediation. In any teaching situation the methods are unlikely to be as distinctly separate as presented here; teachers' instructional strategies may fit into two or more categories as they shift from one approach to another. The purpose of the analysis, then, was not so much to recommend a single approach to remediation as to (1) classify the remedial approaches that are suggested and used, and (2) point out the implications of each approach for use with adolescent students.

Research efforts to substantiate the efficacy of one specific remedial approach have not resulted in findings that clearly support any specific category. Each remedial category has merit, yet none has strong supportive evidence. Each has valid arguments, yet each is vulnerable to criticism.

As no one category can be relied on as *the* way to provide remediation, overdependence on only one approach should be avoided. After a five-year follow-up study of learning-disabled students, Koppitz (1973) concluded that

learning disabilities cannot be corrected or "cured" by any specific teaching method or training technique. It is imperative that teachers have a wide range of instructional materials and techniques at their disposal and that they are imaginative and flexible enough to adapt these to the specific needs of their pupils.

Minskoff (1973), also perceiving the learning-disabled as a heterogeneous population, proposes, therefore, that teachers be able to construct and utilize a great variety of teaching methods, materials, and approaches. Similarly, concern about "the ideal teaching program" is expressed by Keogh (1975), who emphasizes that the heterogeneity of learning-disabled students requires a variety of teaching options.

Perhaps thinking of remediation in terms of each category alone is simplistic. What we need is a model of remediation that takes into account the interacting effects of each category. Each remedial approach can make a contribution to the total system of clinical teaching. Classification is only the initial step; the development of a systems approach to remedial teaching should be the next task.

■ REFERENCES ■

Bateman, B. D. Educational implications of minimal brain dysfunction. *Reading Teacher*, 1974, 27, 662–668.

Bond, L., & Dykstra, R. The cooperative research program in first grade reading instruction. *Reading Research Quarterly*, 1967, 2, 1–142.

Bush, W. J., & Giles, M. T. *Aids to psycholinguistic teaching*. Columbus, Ohio: Charles E. Merrill, 1969.

Chall, J., & Feldmann, S. First grade reading: An analysis of the interactions of professed methods, teaching implementation, and child background. *Reading Teacher*, 1966, 19, 569–575.

Cohen, S. A. Studies in visual perception and reading in disadvantaged children. *Journal of Learning Disabilities*, 1967, 2, 8–13.

Cohen, S. A. Dyspedagogia as a cause of reading retardation in learning disorders. In B. Bateman (Ed.), *Learning disorders* (Vol. 4, Reading). Seattle: Special Child Publications, 1971.

Cutts, W. Does the teacher really matter? *The Reading Teacher*, 1975, 28, 449–452.

Durkin, D. Some questions about questionable instructional material. *The Reading Teacher*, 1974, 8, 13–21.

Fernald, G. *Remedial techniques in basic school subjects*. New York: McGraw-Hill, 1943.

Flavell, J. H. *The developmental psychology of Jean Piaget*. Princeton, N.J.: Van Nostrand, 1973.

Frostig, M. *Frostig developmental test of visual perception*. Palo Alto, Calif.: Consulting Psychologists Press, 1964.

Frostig, M., & Horne, D. *The Frostig program for the development of visual perception*. Chicago: Follett, 1964.

Frostig, M., Miller, A., & Horne, D. *Pictures and patterns* (Rev. ed.). Chicago: Follett, 1972.

Getman, G. M. The visuomotor complex in the acquisition of learning skills. In J. Hellmuth (Ed.), *Learning disorders* (Vol. 1). Seattle: Special Child Publications, 1965.

Goodman, K. Effective teachers of reading know language and children. *Elementary English,* 1974, *51,* 823–828.

Goodman, L., & Hammill, D. The effectiveness of Kephart-Getman activities in developing perceptual-motor and cognitive skills. *Focus on Exceptional Children,* 1973, *4,* 1–9.

Hammill, D., Goodman, L., & Wiederholt, J. L. Visual-motor processes: Can we train them? *The Reading Teacher,* 1974, *27,* 469–480.

Hammill, D. D., & Larsen, S. C. The effectiveness of psycholinguistic training. *Exceptional Children,* 1974, *41,* 5–15. (a)

Hammill, D. D., & Larsen, S. C. The relationship of selected auditory perceptual skills and reading disability. *Journal of Learning Disabilities,* 1974, *7,* 219–326. (b)

Hammill, D. D., & Wiederholt, J. L. Review of the Frostig visual perception test and the related training program. In L. Mann & D. A. Sabatino (Eds.), *The first review of special education.* New York: Grune & Stratton, 1973.

Harris, A. *How to increase reading ability* (5th ed.). New York: David McKay, 1970.

Harris, A., et al. *A continuation of the CRAFT project* (USOE No. 5-0570-2-12-1). New York: Selected Academic Readings (1 W. 39th Street), 1968.

Johnson, D., & Myklebust, H. *Learning disabilities.* New York: Grune & Stratton, 1967.

Karnes, M. *Goal language development game.* Springfield, Mass.: Milton-Bradley, 1972.

Keogh, B. Replies of leading professionals. *Journal of Learning Disabilities,* 1975, *5,* 322–325.

Kirk, S., McCarthy, J., & Kirk, W. *The Illinois test of psycholinguistic abilities.* Urbana: University of Illinois Press, 1968.

Koppitz, E. M. Special class pupils with learning disabilities: A five-year follow-up study. *Academic Therapy,* 13 (Winter, 1972–1973), 17–26.

Lerner, J. W. *Children with learning disabilities: Theories, diagnosis, and teaching strategies* (2nd ed.). Boston: Houghton Mifflin, 1976.

Mann, L., & Phillips, W. Fractional practices in special education. In D. Hammill & N. Bartel (Eds.), *Educational perspectives in learning disabilities.* New York: Wiley, 1971.

McCarthy, J. Learning disabilities: Where have we been? Where are we going? In D. Hammill & N. Bartel (Eds.), *Educational perspectives in learning disabilities*. New York: Wiley, 1971.

Minskoff, E. Creating and evaluating remediation for the learning disabled. *Focus on Exceptional Children*, 1973, 5, 1–11.

Minskoff, E., Wiseman, D., & Minskoff, J. *The MWM program of development of language abilities*. Ridgefield, N.J.: Educational Performance Associates, 1972.

Monroe, M. *Children who cannot read*. Chicago: University of Chicago Press, 1932.

Nichol, H. Children with learning disabilities referred to psychiatrists: A follow-up study. *Journal of Learning Disabilities*, 1974, 7, 118–122.

Poteet, J. A. *Behavior modification: A practical guide for teachers*. Minneapolis: Burgess Publishing Co., 1973.

Thompson, R. A., & Dziuban, C. Criterion-referenced reading tests in perspective. *Reading Teacher*, 1973, 37, 292–294.

CHAPTER 6

REMEDIATION OF ABILITY DEFICITS: SOME MAJOR QUESTIONS

JAMES E. YSSELDYKE

School pyschologists, special educators, and regular classroom teachers have, during the last several years, labeled a certain group of elementary-age pupils as learning-disabled. While considerable attention was being directed to identification of, and educational programming for, this group, the students so labeled were getting older. We now witness an increasing concern regarding the education of learning-disabled pupils in the secondary school.

Opinions differ sharply regarding strategies for identifying and educating learning-disabled pupils, but common to nearly all definitions of learning disability has been this contention: The condition is characterized by deficits, deficiencies, or disabilities in one or more of the psychological processes or abilities believed relevant to the acquisition of academic skills.

An obvious emphasis on process disorders is apparent in the more commonly accepted definition formulated by the National Advisory Committee on Handicapped Children (1968), which is quoted in Chapter 1 of this book.

The contention that the learning-disabled demonstrate process or ability deficits or disorders has led to wholesale efforts to remediate those processes. We have witnessed, along with curricular emphasis, the development of numerous psychometric devices designed to delineate ability strengths and weaknesses. Elementary education for the learning-disabled has been characterized by ability assessment and training (Ysseldyke & Salvia, 1974).

Most attempts to alleviate or ameliorate ability deficits have been at the preschool and elementary level. For both theoretical and practical reasons, few studies report the results of attempts to remediate ability deficits with learning-disabled secondary pupils. While ability training with younger pupils is questioned by some, even those who support it state that such practices will be ineffective for secondary-age youngsters. Their arguments are based largely upon the theory that abilities relevant to learning have matured by age nine to fourteen. Wepman, Cruickshank, Deutsch, Morency, and Strother (1975), for example, state:

For the child above nine years of age, intervention will need to be thought of as mainly compensatory rather than corrective. Where perceptual problems of discrimination, memory, sequencing, closure, or spatial orientation still exist, direct remediation is unlikely to be effective, since basic processing ability is by this age as developed as it ever will be. (p. 314)

Ability deficits must be identified before they can be remediated. However, most ability measures are inappropriate for use with adolescents. The Illinois Test of Psycholinguistic Abilities is designed for use with children between two and ten years of age, the Koppitz version of the Bender Visual Motor Gestalt Test for ages five to ten, and the Frostig Developmental Test of Visual Perception until age eight.

All of the preceding should suggest that the issue of remediating the ability deficits of adolescents raises several fundamental questions. If ability remediation is to be viable, something called a "learning ability" has to be known to exist in the first place. If we are to talk about the extent to which an individual pupil demonstrates specific strengths and weaknesses in abilities, we must be able to assess abilities validly. To engage in ability training with adolescents, we must be able to demonstrate that the abilities continue to develop into adolescence, that they function in the acquisition of academic skills, and that they *can* be remediated. This chapter addresses these basic questions.

■ DO ABILITIES EXIST? ■

The failure of some pupils to acquire academic skills has been attributed to a variety of ability deficits. Observed differences in the extent to which students profit from instruction have been attributed, in part, to differences in the way they process information.

When certain individuals fail to demonstrate profit, and such failure cannot be attributed readily to overall developmental rate, emotional disturbance, sensory impairment or environmental deprivation, then differences in performance are attributed to differences in the maturation, development, or nurturance of what have been called learning abilities. Kass and Myklebust (1969) say that essential learning abilities are "those currently referred to in behavioral science as involving perception, integration and expression either verbal or non-verbal."

Abilities cited as causative of, or contributive to, differences in educational performance include a variety of cognitive abilities (Bortner, 1971; Marietta, 1970), perceptual processes (Buktenica, 1971; Crawford, 1966; Frostig & Orpet, 1969; Jander, 1971; Koppitz, 1970; McQuarrie, 1967; and Sabatino, 1969), language or psycholinguistic abilities (Kass, 1966; Keenan, 1968; Kirk, 1966; and Kirk & Kirk, 1971), and attentional processes (Eisenburg, 1966, and Oettinger, 1971). In most instances, learning disabilities have been attributed either to specific process disabilities or to combinations of disabilities.

Researchers have expended considerable effort, mostly in work with elementary-age children, in attempts to delineate the psychological and developmental processes essential to learning. In some instances, educators have relied heavily on psychological and developmental theory in describing processes relevant to education. For example, Kirk used Osgood's communication model in the study of psycholinguistic disabilities in children. In other cases, educators have relied on research designed to delineate learning characteristics of mentally retarded or brain-injured children (research such as the earlier investigations of Goldstein & Sheerer and Werner & Strauss) to identify process dysfunction as a cause of learning disabilities. In nearly all cases, however, the identification of specific deficits or disabilities occurs after the student has failed. In addition, tests constructed for use with adults (the Graham Kendall and the Bender Visual Motor Gestalt Test, for example) or tests constructed with no theoretical basis often were administered to groups of students in attempts to identify deficits in those who demonstrated learning difficulties. Abilities that could be identified by tests were called educationally relevant. In this sense, the study of learning disabilities has been psychoeducational and psychometric. The field was defined by the existence of tests or subtests said to measure specific characteristics. And, as more tests have become available, the abilities that they have been designed to measure have been more and more finely fractionated. Deficits are test-identified and indeed test-named. They are defined in terms of "accepted diagnostic procedures in psychology and education" (Kass & Myklebust, 1969).

Most empirical evidence for the existence of abilities and ability deficits is derived from a body of descriptive, comparative, and correlational research. After observing pupils experiencing difficulty in learning, educators administered batteries of tests in efforts to describe the learning characteristics of these students. McLeod (1965), for example, reported 260 behavioral and learning characteristics associated with failure in learning to read. Similarly, Coleman and Sandhu (1967) used tests to describe 364 children referred to a university clinic for learning disorders. Thorum and Riley (1971), using the ITPA, described the psycholinguistic abilities of Navajo schoolchildren; and Knights and Hinton (1969) described the clinical and psychological test characteristics associated with "minimal cerebral dysfunction."

Psychological and educational tests have been administered to criterion groups of students in a comparative effort to identify the characteristics that significantly discriminate between groups. Kass (1966) administered the ITPA to "good" and "poor" readers in an attempt to identify the psycholinguistic correlates of reading difficulty. Similarly, Cromer and Wiener (1966) investigated idiosyncratic response patterns in "good" and "poor" readers. Gallagher (1957) compared the test performance of brain-injured and non-brain-injured mentally retarded persons, while Hutchinson and Clark (1968) reported differences in auditory and visual discrimination skills between normal and articulation defective pupils.

A third body of descriptive research attempts to predict the success of students in academic situations. De Hirsch (1966), for example, administered thirty-seven tests to thirty boys and twenty-three girls in an effort to identify those tests or test-identified characteristics that best predict success in reading.

Other investigations have also been post hoc as opposed to predictive. Numerous studies (which I summarized in 1973) have correlated students' performance on process or ability measures with scores on standardized achievement tests.

Finally, several studies have employed factor-analytic designs to identify patterns of abilities or disabilities in pupils who are experiencing academic difficulty. Leton (1972) factor-analyzed the ITPA and WISC scores earned by learning-disabled students, while Ayres (1965) reported patterns of perceptual-motor dysfunction in pupils on the basis of their performance on a battery of tests. Sabatino (1968) used twenty-three measures to assess the information-processing behaviors of forty-five learning-disabled boys, aged seven to twelve. On the basis of intercorrelations among the various subtests, he reported that perceptual disorders may occur as single disabilities or as auditory-visual-integrative "perceptual errors." Varimax rotation of the correlation matrix (a factor analysis using twenty-three measures with forty-five children) revealed four major categories of learning disability. Sabatino and Hayden (1970) used a similar battery with 243 "learning-disabled" students divided on the basis of age (over 9-6 and younger than 9-6). They factor-analyzed the two resulting correlation matrices, identifying different factors for the two groups. Sabatino and Hayden stated that their results "supported the generally held developmental hypothesis that six to nine years is the maximum growth period for perceptual functional performance" and that after age ten integrated language skills became of prime importance.

Evidence that ability deficits are the cause of learning disabilities is at best incomplete and hypothetical. Many test-identified and test-named abilities have been shown to describe populations of atypical learners, to discriminate between specific criterion groups, to predict academic failure, and to relate to academic success or failure. The evidence is, however, simple correlational evidence. Educators have violated a fundamental statistical principle in assuming that correlation implies causation. Psychological and developmental abilities that correlate with academic success have been viewed as *causative* of success or failure. The empirical support for the existence of abilities is based on testimonial arguments by experts and on the results of descriptive research fraught with serious methodological errors and, in the majority of cases, incorrect interpretation.

Mann (1971a) has taken strong issue with those who advocate process or ability assessment and training. He states:

What does not exist cannot be trained. Abilities are best considered referent terms that help to categorize the ways in which people behave and that may provide useful leads in evaluation and practice. However, "abilities," and specifically test-identified "abilities," are increasingly and alarmingly coming to be regarded as real entities—processes and causative factors—by many of us who deal with them, and, as a consequence, much of our effort is being misdirected into training *them* instead of the children who have learning problems.   (p. 323)

We have not demonstrated that processes and/or abilities exist, yet we continue to identify learning-disabled students as demonstrating process and/or ability deficits. We operate as though such deficits were real and observable.

■ CAN ABILITIES BE MEASURED? ■

Learning-disabled pupils are seen as demonstrating ability deficits as determined by disparities in performance on psychoeducational tests.

The definition is easy, but putting the definition into operation is a difficult matter. To demonstrate a disparity, one must first be able to measure the disparate ability. No one specifies tests to be used in identifying ability deficits, and no one appears willing to make a commitment regarding the degree of disparity necessary to speak of deficits.

Kass and Myklebust (1969) define significant deficits "in terms of accepted diagnostic procedures in psychology and education." Yet neither they nor other psychologists and educators ever specify "accepted diagnostic procedures." The result is that "accepted diagnostic procedures" are defined in terms of their acceptance to the individual psychologist. This is at best a haphazard practice.

Bateman's (1965) definition of learning-disabled students as those who "manifest an educationally significant discrepancy between their estimated intellectual potential and actual level of performance related to basic disorders in the learning processes" is a vague specification of what is meant by a significant deficit. Just what is an "educationally significant discrepancy"? Do we again leave this to "professional judgment"?

Reliance upon deficit scores in the identification and diagnostic evaluation of learning-disabled pupils is an extremely haphazard practice. Salvia and Clark (1973), taking into account the reliabilities of specific aptitude and achievement tests, and using basic statistical formulas to compute the reliabilities of deficit scores, have illustrated the fact that such practices often result in misidentification.

Most attempts to identify process deficits or disabilities use norm-referenced tests. The tests are used to identify those who are significantly deviant in one or more processes and who therefore warrant special attention. Yet, despite the existence of normative uniformities in development, it is possible to identify both wide variations within the range of normality and innumerable individual patterns of development.

Ausubel (1957) has commented on attempts to identify deviation from normal development by stating:

Developmental norms are valuable because they provide a standard or frame of reference for evaluating and interpreting the status or current behavior of an individual. They can be misused if the range of variability is overlooked; if expectations for *all* children are geared to group averages; if substantial parallelism is expected between component rates of growth; if they are unwarrantedly applied to individuals who could not be included in the sampling population; and if individual guidance is predicated upon normative comparisons alone to the exclusion of information regarding individual patterning. (p. 112)

Salvia and I (Ysseldyke & Salvia, 1974, 1975) have illustrated that current ability measures lack the necessary reliability and validity to be used in making programmatic decisions regarding students or to identify diagnostic strengths and weaknesses. Mann (1970, 1971b) and Mann and Phillips (1967) have repeatedly argued against fractional practices in special education. They believe that we do not yet have measurement precise enough for engaging in such practices.

We have been unable to precisely, reliably, and validly assess specific processes or abilities at the elementary level. At the secondary level, few tests exist that allow us to do so. Though such empirical support is absent, the market is currently flooded with how-to books and articles on diagnostic-prescriptive teaching—the making of differential curricular decisions for handicapped pupils on the basis of the results of psychoeducational assessment (Bateman, 1967, 1968; Carter & McGinnis, 1970; Dechant, 1968, Ensminger, 1970; Frostig, 1967a, 1967b; Grzynkowicz & Sturch, 1969; Kirk & Kirk, 1971; Roswell & Natchez, 1964; Valett, 1969; and Wilson, 1971).

■ DO ABILITIES DEVELOP INTO ADOLESCENCE? ■

To justify ability remediation at the secondary level, it will be necessary to show that those abilities continue to develop into adolescence. Growth in different abilities tapers off at different ages, depending on the particular abilities being considered *and* the devices used to measure them. Fluctuations in rate of growth may be caused by (1) factors relevant to the standardization, reliability, and validity of specific measuring instruments or to situational variability associated with test administrations, (2) significant changes in environment, or (3) idiosyncratic irregularities in the process of growth that occur even in a relatively constant environment (Ausubel, 1967). Test comparisons show that performance on specific intellectual instruments tapers off at different ages. Students' performance on the Blind Learning Aptitude Test (Newland, 1969), a test that primarily assesses fundamental psychological processes necessary to learning, tapers off at about age eleven. Performance on the Army Alpha and the Concept Maturity Tests, tests that sample primarily the products of learning, continues to increase until about age fifty (Bayley, 1955; Owens, 1953).

Most data concerning the development of abilities come from research on the development of intellectual abilities. Guilford (1967) states: "The typical growth curve is one of negative acceleration, in which averages for age groups cease to gain further at various ages in the late teens." Guilford qualified this observation, though, by stating: "The fact that the average reaches a maximum level at a certain age does not mean that all members of the population stop growing at that age. Some probably keep on developing while others decline, and a balance is reflected in the means" (p. 419).

The fact that different abilities reach maturity, *on the average,* at different ages was illustrated by Thurstone and Ackerman (1929). They reported that the average child reaches 80 percent maturity in specific abilities at the following ages:*

Perceptual speed	12
Space	14
Reasoning	14
Memory	16
Numerical facility	16
Verbal comprehension	18
Word fluency	Later than 20

Current research from developmental psychology indicates that intellectual abilities mature, on the average, at different ages and that there is a considerable variability for specific individuals.

■ ARE ABILITIES USED IN THE SAME WAY? ■

Learning-disability theorists typically believe that ability maturation in elementary students is a necessary condition for academic success. They state that the pupil who demonstrates ability deficits or disorders

* Data are from *The Nature of Human Intelligence* by J. P. Guilford. Copyright © 1967 by McGraw-Hill, Inc. Used with permission of McGraw-Hill Book Company.

can expect to have learning difficulties. The pupil is presumed to use fundamental processes or abilities to acquire academic skills. A question relevant to the remedial education of secondary students is whether those processes or abilities are used in a similar way at the secondary level.

The difference between an elementary and secondary student is that the latter has a much longer learning history. Gagné (1968) speaks of the cumulative-learning hypothesis. Estes (1970) states:

Except perhaps in infancy, a great part of the variance in rates of learning between individuals must be attributable to differences in the results of past learning. Observed rates of learning in most situations, we now realize, depend to a major extent upon habits or strategies of selective attending, seeking of information, coding and recoding of stimulus information, rehearsing, and the like, and the manner in which these are organized. Individual differences in these habit systems may indirectly reflect differences in capacities, but they must also be strongly determined by variation in motivational systems and in previous opportunities to learn. (p. 31)

New learning at any age is dependent on the recombining of previously acquired discriminations, behavior sequences, principles, and concepts. In secondary-level learning these factors play a more complex role, primarily because of differences in learning history.

Remedial efforts with adolescents frequently fail to take into account the learning history of the student. A student who experiences difficulty at the secondary level (especially difficulties presumed to consist of processing difficulties) usually has a long history of academic failure. Pupils who experience considerable difficulty learning to read, for example, may well experience considerable negative conditioning to visual/verbal stimuli. The negative conditioning may, quite understandably, generalize to include the agent who dispenses such stimuli, the classroom teacher. Yet remedial efforts are largely visual/verbal in nature and administered by the teacher.

We simply do not know to what extent abilities, if they exist and develop into adolescence, have the same relationship to learning that they purportedly do in the younger years.

■ CAN PROCESSES BE REMEDIATED? ■

Because of the absence of psychometric instruments for delineation of processes in secondary-age youngsters, there have been few attempts to remediate processes at the secondary level. Examination of our track record with elementary pupils, however, does not provide impressive support for process remediation.

As I reported in 1973, most research on diagnostic-prescriptive teaching has employed either gain-score or aptitude-treatment interaction designs. A fundamental weakness in both designs led to the conclusion that there is little empirical support for diagnostic-prescriptive teaching. More recently, Salvia and I (Ysseldyke & Salvia, 1975) explored the methodological problems in aptitude-treatment research. To date there is little empirical support for the contention that instruction can, or should, be differentiated on the basis of specific pupil aptitudes.

■ SHOULD ABILITIES BE REMEDIATED? ■

The answer to this question is a qualified no. Current assessment devices lack the necessary precision and sophistication to be used to fractionate abilities in students. Remedial education is directed to remediation of something. If we cannot adequately identify what it is that we wish to remediate, how can we provide remedial instruction?

Attempts to remediate abilities have come about as a result of our having defined learning-disabled pupils as demonstrating ability deficits. Such deficits are *presumed* deficits, and their identification is based on the results of psychoeducational evaluations. Yet tests cannot sufficiently delineate abilities. The results of descriptive and correlational research have somehow led us to believe that correlates of academic difficulty are indeed *causes* of such difficulties. Remedial efforts have employed evaluative designs replete with methodological weaknesses and inadequate controls. Indeed, the entire developmental history of ability remediation has been characterized by numerous logical fallacies.

127

■ SO WHAT? ■

I cannot end by merely pointing out that there is little empirical support for ability remediation, ability training, or whatever we choose to call it. I firmly believe that it is incumbent upon special educators to use, and insist upon the use of, validated educational programs with handicapped youngsters. Ability training programs are, to date, experimental at best, and the use of unvalidated experimental programs in the public schools is quite clearly experimentation with human subjects. As such, it requires strict compliance with the American Psychological Association's ethical standards regarding research with human subjects.

Thus far, this chapter has largely equated the practice of diagnostic-prescriptive teaching with ability training. The intent of this chapter was to review problems in the use of ability training programs with adolescents. There *are* alternatives to ability training. Salvia and I (Ysseldyke & Salvia, 1974) discussed task analysis and specific skill training as an alternate to ability assessment and ability training efforts. Bagnato and I (Ysseldyke & Bagnato, 1976) described the work-sample approach to assessment and job-task analysis specifically for exceptional adolescents. Whatever the goal of secondary education for exceptional students (these are seldom articulated clearly), instructional analysis, learning-task analysis, and job-task analysis are preferable to ability assessment and training.

Major proponents of the task-analysis approach (Bijou, Peterson, Harris, Allen, & Johnson, 1969; Gold, 1968a; Mann, 1971; Reynolds, 1975) reject the use of norm-referenced tests designed to assess processes and abilities; rather, task analysis focuses on skill development.

Task analysis is a broad term used to denote two subactivities. Consisting of both content analysis and learning-task analysis (Gagné, 1974), it is especially useful when the goal is teaching of academic skills. Task analysis consists of breaking down a complex terminal behavior into its component parts (enabling behaviors), teaching those enabling behaviors that a pupil does not yet demonstrate, and integrating those behaviors into the terminal objective. It involves both content analysis (categorization of the components of existing curricular content) and learning-task analysis, defined by Gagné (1974) as "identifying and classifying the performances that are the outcomes of learning, and also those subordinate performances that are prerequisite to such learning." Task analysis is more than simple identification of learner weaknesses.

For over a decade, the work-sample approach to training and evaluating the skill development of exceptional adolescents (primarily the mentally retarded) has been advocated by many professionals but has not been put into operation widely (DiMichael, 1960; Gold, 1968b; Ladas, 1961; Sinick, 1962; TOWER, 1967). The approach is most useful when vocational training is the goal. Work samples are actually tasks that approximate real-life job circumstances more closely than do tests. Work samples, representative of later job situations, are standardized. Individuals functioning in the simulated environment gain experience in realistic, prevocational situations. According to TOWER,

the work sample technique focuses upon the assessment of concrete work skills related to specific job families. . . . Interest, behavior, attitude are assessed by careful observation of the client in the work setting. . . . Suitable criteria for speed and quality, equipment and tools, and the time required to complete a specific task have been developed on the basis of detailed task analysis. . . . The client first explores his capacities and skills in a variety of tasks and then approaches a series of tests or "evaluations," within a specific job family for which he has evidenced both aptitude and interest, that range from simple to complex. (pp. 30–31)

In essence, through careful organization and task analysis, the work-sample technique becomes a criterion-referenced procedure that imbeds assessment within the process of instructional programming, training, and placement. The crucial factor is the similarity between the sampled and predicted behavior. "The potential value of the work sample approach then, is to develop standardized methods of reporting behavior in a situation that is commensurate with the kind of work the client is likely to be doing" (Gold, 1968b, p. 109).

Task analysis and the work-sample approach are not panaceas. However, there is considerably more empirical support for these procedures than for ability assessment and training. At this time, I believe, special educators need to follow two lines of attack. First, task-analysis and work-sample approaches should characterize our efforts until we have empirical support for other alternatives. Second, we need to direct our efforts to scientific research designed to identify—reliably and validly—those processes or abilities that may be relevant to learning, and to establish empirical links between observed differences in students and the relative effectiveness of different instructional strategies, materials, techniques, and programs.

■ REFERENCES ■

Ausubel, D. P. *Theory and problems of child development.* New York: Grune & Stratton, 1957.

Ayres, J. Patterns of perceptual-motor dysfunction in children: A factor analytic study. *Perceptual and Motor Skills,* 1965, *20,* 335–368.

Bateman, B. An educator's view of a diagnostic approach to learning disorders. In J. Hellmuth (Ed.), *Learning disorders* (Vol. 1). Seattle: Special Child Publications, 1965.

Bateman, B. Three approaches to diagnosis and educational planning for children with learning disabilities. *Academic Therapy Quarterly,* 1967, *3,* 11–16.

Bateman, B. *Interpretation of the 1961 Illinois Test of Psycholinguistic Abilities.* Seattle: Special Child Publications, 1968.

Bayley, N. On the growth of intelligence. *American Psychologist,* 1955, *10,* 805–818.

Bijou, S. W. What psychology has to offer education—Now. *Journal of Applied Behavior Analysis,* 1970, *3,* 65–71.

Bijou, S. W., Peterson, R. F., Harris, F. R., Allen, D. W., & Johnson, M. S. Methodology for experimental studies of young children in natural settings. *The Psychological Record,* 1969, *19,* 177–210.

Bortner, M. Phrenology, localization, and learning disabilities. *Journal of Special Education,* 1971, *5,* 23–29.

Buktenica, N. A. Identification of potential learning disorders. *Journal of Learning Disabilities,* 1971, *4,* 379–383.

Carter, H., & McGinnis, D. *Diagnosis and treatment of the disabled reader.* New York: Macmillan, 1970.

Coleman, J., & Sandhu, M. A descriptive-relational study of 364 children referred to a university clinic for learning disorders. *Psychological Reports,* 1967, *20,* 1091–1105.

Crawford, J. *Children with subtle perceptual motor difficulties.* Pittsburgh: Stanwix House, 1966.

Cromer, W., & Wiener, M. Idiosyncratic response patterns among good and poor readers. *Journal of Consulting Psychology,* 1966, *30,* 1–10.

Dechant, E. *Diagnosis and remediation of reading disability.* West Nyack, N.Y.: Parker Publishing Company, 1968.

de Hirsch, K. *Predicting reading failure.* New York: Harper & Row, 1966.

DiMichael, S. G. Vocational diagnosis and counseling of the retarded in sheltered workshops. *American Journal of Mental Deficiency,* 1960, *64,* 652–657.

Eisenburg, L. The management of the hyperkinetic child. *Developmental Medicine of Child Neurology,* 1966, 8, 593–598.

Ensminger, E. A proposed model for selecting, modifying, or developing instructional materials for handicapped children. *Focus on Exceptional Children,* 1970, *1,* 1–9.

Estes, W. K. *Learning theory and mental development.* New York: Academic Press, 1970.

Frostig, M. Testing as a basis for educational therapy. *Journal of Special Education,* 1967, *2,* 15–34. (a)

Frostig, M. *The relationship of diagnosis to remediation in learning problems.* San Francisco: Rosenburg Foundation, 1967. (b)

Frostig, M., & Orpet, R. E. Four approaches to diagnosis of perceptual disturbances in reading disability. *British Journal of Disorders of Communication,* 1969, *4,* 41–45.

Gagné, R. M. Contributions of learning to human development. *Psychological Review,* 1968, *75,* 177–191.

Gagné, R. M. Task analysis—its relation to content analysis. *Educational Psychologist,* 1974, *11,* 11–18.

Gallagher, J. J. A comparison of brain-injured and non-brain-injured mentally retarded children on several psychological variables. *Monograph of the Society for Research in Child Development,* 1957, *22,* 65.

Gold, M. W. The acquisition of a complex assembly task by retarded adolescents. Urbana: University of Illinois Childrens' Research Center, 1968. (a) (Mimeograph)

Gold, M. W. Research on the vocational habilitation of the retarded: The present, the future. In N. R. Ellis (Ed.), *International review of research in mental retardation* (Vol. 3). New York: Academic Press, 1968. (b)

Grzynkowicz, W., & Sturch, J. *Readings in diagnosis for prescriptive teaching.* New York: Selected Academic Readings, 1969.

Guilford, J. P. *The nature of human intelligence.* New York: McGraw-Hill, 1967.

Hutchinson, B., & Clark, D. Auditory and visual discrimination skills of normal and articulation-defective children. *Perceptual and Motor Skills,* 1968, *26,* 259–265.

Jander, B. C. Learning disabilities: Evaluation and programming. *Optometric Weekly,* 1971, *62,* 872–876.

Kass, C. E. Psycholinguistic disabilities of children with reading problems. *Exceptional Children,* 1966, 32, 533–539.

Kass, C., & Myklebust, H. Learning disabilities: An educational definition. *Journal of Learning Disabilities,* 1969,2, 377–379.

Keenan, J. S. The nature of receptive and expressive impairments in aphasia. *Journal of Speech and Hearing Disorders,* 1968, 33, 20–25.

Kirk, S. A. *The diagnosis and remediation of psycholinguistic disabilities.* Urbana: University of Illinois, Institute for Research on Exceptional Children, 1966.

Kirk, S. A., & Kirk, W. D. *Psycholinguistic learning disabilities: Diagnosis and remediation.* Urbana: University of Illinois Press, 1971.

Knights, R. M., & Hinton, G. G. Minimal brain dysfunction: Clinical and psychological test characteristics. *Academic Therapy Quarterly,* 1969, 4, 265–273.

Koppitz, E. M. Brain damage, reading disability and the Bender Gestalt Test. *Journal of Learning Disabilities,* 1970, 3, 429–433.

Ladas, P. G. Worksample learning rates of the mentally retarded trainee as indicators of production in a work-training center. *Personnel and Guidance Journal,* 1961, 39, 396–402.

Leton, D. A factor analysis of ITPA and WISC scores of learning disabled pupils. *Psychology in the Schools,* 1972, 9, 31–36.

Mann, L. Are we fractionating too much? *Academic Therapy,* 1970, 5, 85–91.

Mann, L. Perceptual training revisited: The training of nothing at all. *Rehabilitation Literature,* 1971, 32, 322–327, 335. (a)

Mann, L. Psychometric phrenology and the new faculty psychology: The case against ability assessment and training. *Journal of Special Education,* 1971, 5, 3–14. (b)

Mann, L., & Phillips, W. A. Fractional practices in special education: A critique. *Exceptional Children,* 1967, 33, 311–319.

Marietta, D. E. The role of cognitive regulators in learning disabled teenagers. *Academic Therapy Quarterly,* 1970, 5, 177–186.

McLeod, J. *Some psychological and psycholinguistic aspects of severe reading disability.* Unpublished doctoral dissertation, University of Queensland, 1965.

McQuarrie, C. W. The Winter Haven program. *Academic Therapy Quarterly,* 1967, 2, 66–72.

National Advisory Committee on Handicapped Children. *Special education for handicapped children. First annual report.* Washington, D.C.: U.S. Department of Health, Education and Welfare, 1968.

Newland, T. E. *Manual: The blind learning aptitude test.* Louisville, Ky.: American Printing House for the Blind, 1969.

Oettinger, L. Learning disorders: Hyperkinesis and the use of drugs in children. *Rehabilitation Literature,* 1971, 32, 162–167.

Owens, W. A. Age and mental abilities: A longitudinal study. *Genetic Psychological Monographs,* 1953, 48, 3–54.

Reynolds, M. C. Trends in special education: Implications for measurement. In W. Hively & M. C. Reynolds (Eds.), *Domain-referenced testing in special education.* Minneapolis: University of Minnesota, Leadership Training Institute/Special Education, 1975.

Roswell, F., & Natchez, G. *Reading disability: Diagnosis and treatment.* New York: Basic Books, 1964.

Sabatino, D. A. Information processing behaviors associated with learning disabilities. *Journal of Learning Disabilities,* 1968, 1, 440–450.

Sabatino, D. A. The construction and assessment of an experimental test of auditory perception. *Exceptional Children,* 1969, 36, 729–737.

Sabatino, D. A., & Hayden, D. L. Variation in information processing behaviors as related to chronological age differences for children failing elementary grades. *Journal of Learning Disabilities,* 1970, 3, 404–412.

Salvia, J., & Clark, J. Use of deficits to identify the learning disabled. *Exceptional Children,* 1973, 39, 305–308.

Sinick, D. Client evaluation: Work task approach. *Rehabilitation Record,* 1962, 3, 6–8.

Thorum, A. R., & Riley, G. D. A pilot study of the psycholinguistic abilities of Navajo school children. *California State Federation CEC Journal,* 1971, 20, 43–45.

Thurstone, L. L., & Ackerman, L. The mental growth curve for the Binet tests. *Journal of Educational Psychology,* 1929, 20, 569–583.

TOWER: Testing orientation and work evaluation. New York: Rehabilitation Institute for the Crippled and Disabled, 1967.

Valett, R. E. *Programming learning disabilities.* Palo Alto, Calif.: Fearon Publishers, 1969.

Wepman, J. M., Cruickshank, W. M., Deutsch, C. P., Morency, A., & Strother, C. R. Learning disabilities. In N. Hobbs (Ed.), *Issues in the classification of children* (Vol. 1). San Francisco: Jossey-Bass, 1975.

Wilson, J. A. *Diagnosis of learning difficulties.* New York: McGraw-Hill, 1971.

Ysseldyke, J. E. Diagnostic-prescriptive teaching: The search for aptitude-treatment interactions. In L. Mann & D. A. Sabatino (Eds.), *The first review of special education.* Philadelphia: JSE Press, 1973.

Ysseldyke, J. E., & Bagnato, S. Assessment of exceptional students at the secondary level: A pragmatic perspective. *The High School Journal,* 1976, *59,* 282–289.

Ysseldyke, J. E., & Salvia, J. Diagnostic-prescriptive teaching: Two models. *Exceptional Children,* 1974, *41,* 181–185.

Ysseldyke, J. E., & Salvia, J. Methodological problems in aptitude treatment interaction research with intact groups. University Park, Pennsylvania: Mimeograph, 1975.

CHAPTER 7

LANGUAGE AND SPEECH DIFFICULTIES

MERRILL C. SITKO
PATRICIA H. GILLESPIE

This chapter is an interpretive review of researchers' work on the speech and language characteristics of learning-disabled adolescents. We should note at the outset that our review of the literature of psychology and education convinces us that there is still not enough research on this subject. Our focus is on the following areas: (1) definitions of language, (2) assessment of language and speech, (3) language and speech characteristics of learning-disabled adolescents, (4) intervention strategies, and (5) implications for further research and programming. In addition to reporting other researchers' findings, we also present our own ideas on these matters.

■ DEFINITIONS OF LANGUAGE ■

Language is defined in many ways by many investigators with varying degrees of precision. These definitions are, in part, dependent on the investigators' disciplines. For instance, Carroll (1953) defines language from a linguistic point of view as "a structured system of arbitrary vocal sounds which is used, or can be used, in interpersonal communication by an aggregation of human beings, and which rather exhaustively catalogs the things, events, and processes in the human environment."

In this instance Carroll sees language as an internalized system or code that the individual has acquired and is able to use in verbal communication. This emphasis on coding is also present in other linguistic definitions of language, for example, that of Ervin-Tripp (1966). Speech, on the other hand, is the behavioral manifestation of language—that is, communication or overt verbal performance.

Much of the current research and theorizing in language comprehension and production depends on recent work in psycholinguistics. The transformational-generative point of view is represented by Chomsky (1957, 1965), who sees language as an abstract system of knowledge in which sound and meaning are associated grammatically in a specific and complex manner. According to Chomsky and his associates (McNeill, 1970; Slobin, 1971), when individuals acquire a language they learn an elaborate system of syntactic, semantic, and phonological rules. These rules establish the basic competence or abstract linguistic knowledge that underlies the generative nature of language performance. Finally, from an applied linguistic point of view, language is a social tool or means of communication used by people to carry on the affairs of society (Dever, in preparation).*

Learning theorists such as Skinner (1957) and Staats and Staats (1968) apply S-R operant conditioning principles to language and language acquisition. According to Skinner, specific verbal or linguistic behaviors are acquired or learned through a combination of operant conditioning and response generalization. Similarly, Staats and Staats employ such behavioristic principles as association formation and stimulus-and-response generalization in their account of language acquisition. In this view, language is actually a form of operant behavior that requires immediate reinforcement for its maintenance. However, notions of simple learning models such as Skinner's and mediated learning models (Mowrer, 1954; Osgood, 1957) do not fully account for language acquisition (Chomsky, 1959, 1968; Fodor, 1966). Wardhaugh (1972) and Newcomer and Hammill (1976) have written excellent comparisons of linguistics-oriented and learning-oriented theories of language acquisition.

It is important to stress the distinction between speech and language. Carroll (1967) states that when we are referring to speech, "we are, or should be, referring to the actual behavior of ... individuals in using language, the amount of talking, the conditions under which talking is elicited, and so forth." Again, speech is the behavioral manifestation of language.

Marge (1972) distinguishes the four main components of language behavior: listening, speaking, reading, and writing. He, like others, emphasizes that language is composed of phonological, morphological, syntactic, and semantic components that one must acquire in order to understand and speak a language. All these components are found in studies of the language and speech difficulties of learning-disabled adolescents.

■ ASSESSMENT OF LANGUAGE DISABILITIES ■

Precise assessment in terms of developmental levels of language is a prerequisite to the development of language intervention strategies.

---

* For a comprehensive review of the literature, see Fillenbaum, 1971; McNeill, 1966; Menyuk, 1971; Olson, 1970; Slobin, 1972.

Yet language assessment for the learning-disabled and mildly retarded is still rather primitive. In an intensive review of the language literature dealing with the retarded, Sitko and Semmel (1973) found a lack of effective assessment of the language competence and language performance of retarded and disadvantaged students. Rosenberg (1970) emphasized that the normal and the handicapped need assessment devices based on the most current research in the language sciences. He feels that developers of language tests do not consider everything currently known about language and language development; for example, he severely criticizes the ITPA for not incorporating recent work in developmental psycholinguistics. Moreover, other evaluations of the ITPA indicate severe weaknesses in its rationale, validity, and reliability (Cazden, 1971; Dever, 1971; Hammill & Larsen, 1974; Mehrabian, 1970; Newcomer & Hammill, 1976; Sedlack & Weener, 1973; Severson & Guest, 1970; Van Hattum, 1969; Weener, Barritt, & Semmel, 1967; Ysseldyke & Salvia, 1974). McCarthy (1975) criticizes the ITPA—normed on children aged three through ten—as an inappropriate tool for assessing and researching language difficulties in adolescents. Newcomer and Hammill (1976) found little support for the continued use of either the ITPA-related diagnostic procedures or its related remedial materials.

Irwin, Moore, and Ramps (1972) noted that evaluations of language disorders are incomplete. Specifically, they say that a direct measure of deep structure (in transformational terms) is beyond our clinical ability and that certain language measures are more precise than others. Dever (1971) argues that current methods of testing language development in students do little to provide a methodology for the clinician, special teacher, or resource teacher.

Adequate assessment of language development (Lee, 1974) stops too early in the sequence of development to be of much use in evaluations of secondary students (Dever, in preparation). Few instruments are available for measuring and classifying the dramatic changes in syntax, semantics, and phonological skills that children experience after age five. Reliable, valid, and educationally relevant measures of adolescents' language competencies do not exist.

If we wish to develop effective remedial or developmental language training programs, we must first be able to assess accurately the nature of the adolescent's language problem. Unfortunately, in approaching

138

learning disabilities, we have become too normative and product-oriented rather than criterion-, task-, and process-oriented.

■ **LANGUAGE CHARACTERISTICS OF ADOLESCENT** ■
LEARNING-DISABLED STUDENTS

The literature of language and speech characteristics of learning-disabled adolescents raises several critical issues:

1. A precise operational definition of learning disabilities has not been established (Gearheart, 1973; McDonald, 1968; Lerner, 1971; Myers & Hammill, 1969; USPHS, 1969; Wepman et al, 1975; Wiederholt, 1974).

2. Criteria for selecting individuals for descriptive studies dealing with language vary greatly (Adelman, 1971; Bortner & Birch, 1969; O'Grady, 1974; Orlando, 1973; Wepman et al., 1975).

3. Investigators differ widely in orientation and definitions of language and language behaviors (Carroll, 1953; Chomsky, 1957, 1965; Ervin-Tripp, 1966; McNeill, 1970; Newcomer & Hammill, 1976; Sitko & Semmel, 1973; Slobin, 1971; Skinner, 1957; Staats & Staats, 1968).

4. Many language characteristics ascribed to the learning-disabled are based on clinical observations rather than on empirical evidence (Marge, 1972).

5. Only minimal research exists concerning speech and language characteristics of the adolescent learning-disabled.

6. The many gaps and methodological weaknesses make generalization from the studies on children to the adolescent extremely difficult (Marge, 1972; Wepman et al., 1975; Wiederholt, 1974).

Since very little of the research in learning disabilities has dealt with older students, we will briefly review in this chapter some of the studies of younger pupils, despite the problem of generalization just mentioned. The sections that follow categorize this research into studies of speech characteristics, general language difficulties, and information processing. Research studies relating to reading problems and reading as a language-processing activity are covered in Chapter 8.

SPEECH DISORDERS AND LEARNING DISABILITIES

Speech difficulties have been included among the characteristics of the learning-disabled. Specifically, immature speech patterns, mild speech irregularities, problems of articulation, and general intelligibility cluttering—a rapid, jerky, stumbling speech with marked omissions and substitutions to a degree approaching jargonic speech (Harris, 1970)—have been noted in some learning-disabled students. Johnson (1973) describes some pupils with psychoneurological learning disorders as having difficulties with the motor patterns for speaking. This is characterized as *dyspraxia* (poor lip and tongue mobility), although no evidence of paralysis or structural problems exists. According to Johnson and Myklebust (1967), the apraxic has the adequate lip and tongue movements but does not "know how or where to place his tongue." They also describe apraxic speech disorders among adolescents, along with necessary intervention strategies for correcting the difficulties. Myers and Hammill (1969) note from clinical experiences that many of these pupils "show evidence of poor lip and tongue mobility and coordination."

De Hirsch (1963) describes learning-disabled adolescents who exhibit speech irregularities, cluttering, and minor articulation inaccuracies as part of their total language disability. Jansky (1969) writes of a severely dyslexic adolescent who had been referred for speech evaluation at the age of six and who still possessed poor motor speech patterns. Members of the boy's family exhibited hesitations, disorganizations, blocking, and stuttering into their adolescent and adult life. Both de Hirsch and Jansky describe such adolescents as "plastic"—having an inability to stabilize various types of configurations (Bender, 1953).

Most of the speech difficulties observed in learning-disabled adolescents are clinical and descriptive. Although mild speech irregularities are described by a few investigators, the incidence and nature of speech problems have been virtually neglected.

GENERAL LANGUAGE DIFFICULTIES

Studies dealing with the language of learning-disabled students reflect a wide variety of interpretations and assessments of language. The following categories reflect the language research found in the literature: oral language, including reception, integration, and production; written expression; and information processing.

ORAL LANGUAGE Numerous investigators, theorists, and clinicians have addressed the difficulties that learning-disabled students have in the receptive, integrative, and expressive aspects of oral language.

Semel and Wiig (1975a) summarized the findings of a series of studies investigating comprehension of critical word sequences and syntactic structures, knowledge and comprehension of English morphology, comprehension of linguistic concepts requiring logical operations, and immediate recall of semantically and syntactically varied sentences in learning-disabled students. They found that:

1. Learning-disabled students have distinct limitations in acquisition and comprehension of syntax. This supports related research findings that a large number of learning-disabled students are significantly deficient in receptive and expressive syntactic abilities. Moreover, learning-disabled pupils exhibit quantitative deficits in the ability to process and synthesize critical verbal elements. Delays in the acquisition of syntactic rules are not significantly reduced with age (that is, between seven and eleven years). Error patterns are most discriminating on sentences of higher grammatical complexity such as question sentences, sentences with demonstratives and "why" forms, possessive relationships, and relationships with direct and indirect objects.

2. Learning-disabled students exhibit quantitative delays in the acquisition of morphology when compared with achieving age peers. In particular, these students reveal the greatest relative differences for third-person singular, possessives, and adjectival inflections.

3. Learning-disabled students exhibit significant deficits in the comprehension of linguistic concepts in which logical relationships are expressed between two or more verbal elements. They demonstrate the greatest number of errors in comprehending familial relationships, followed (in order of decreasing problems) by spatial relationships, temporal relationships between sequential events, passive relationships, and comparative relationships. Moreover, comprehension of familial relationships by learning-disabled students tends to be at "sensorimotor" or "preoperational" levels.

141

4. Learning-disabled students continue to experience comprehension deficits in these linguistic concepts into adolescence.

5. Learning-disabled students show impairments of abstraction, generalization, simultaneous analysis, and synthesis, along with delays in logical growth.

6. Sentence length and structure are significant variables in learning-disabled students' recall of sentences.

7. Significant variables in sentence recall by learning-disabled adolescents are semantic consistency and syntactic complexity. The data on sentence recall suggest limitations in short-term memory in learning-disabled adolescents. The data further imply that deep structure and semantic interpretations (represented in long-term memory) facilitate auditory processing and recall. The authors conclude that several research areas of auditory language process deficits associated with learning disabilities need further investigation, particularly those areas related to comprehension of prepositions and prepositional phrases, negations, adjectives, and modifier-strings.

Wiig and Semel (1975) report a scarcity of investigations into the nature and extent of deficits in productive language associated with learning disabilities. Learning-disabled students have been found to exhibit oral language problems characterized by deficits in oral syntax, name- and word-finding difficulties, and deficits in "verbal fluency" (Bannatyne, 1971; Johnson & Myklebust, 1967; Kass, 1962; Lerner, 1971; Rabinovitch, 1959).

In their 1975 study of language production of thirty-two learning-disabled students aged twelve to sixteen, Wiig and Semel administered an experimental test battery containing the following subtests: verbal opposites (Detroit Test of Learning Aptitudes), visual confrontation naming (Boston VA Test), fluency of controlled association (adapted from the Boston VA Test), and sentence production (Minnesota Test for Differential Diagnosis of Aphasia). In addition, conversational speech characteristics were rated on the Rating Scale Profile of the Boston VA Test. Comparisons of performances on the subtests indicated that the academically achieving adolescents performed significantly better than did the learning-disabled adolescents on all but two of the subtests—sentence production and fluency of controlled association.

142

A comparison of ratings showed that the learning-disabled adolescents scored close to normal on speech characteristics other than phrase length and grammatical form. Wiig and Semel also found that:

1. On the verbal opposites subtest, which required accurate naming of antonyms in response to stimulus words, the learning-disabled adolescents demonstrated significantly less ability than their normal peers in retrieving accurate verbal opposites and a lower verbal retrieval speed for opposites.

2. On the confrontation naming subtest, requiring retrieval of verbal labels in response to pictorial presentations of objects, letters, geometric forms, actions, numbers, and colors, the learning-disabled adolescents did significantly less well in the accuracy and speed with which they labeled the pictorial presentations. Wiig and Semel further report similar deficits in the accuracy and speed with which younger dyslexic children name pictured objects.

3. The controlled association subtests required retrieval and naming of category class members. Differences between the two groups evidently resulted from reduced semantic categorization by the learning-disabled adolescents. The finding appeared not to contradict previous reports that learning-disabled children develop linguistic categorization rules at expected ages (see Bartel, Grill, & Bartel, 1973).

4. On the sentence production test, requiring a grammatical sentence to be formulated using various stimulus words, the learning-disabled adolescents formulated their sentences less quickly and accurately than the academically achieving group. In addition, they were poorer at defining words. Their responses lacked abstract, general aspects of the concepts.

The Wiig and Semel findings suggest "a relationship between productive language deficits in learning disabilities and delays in the development of specific aspects of cognition and convergent and divergent production of semantic units and reductions in the retrieval of verbal labels and syntactic structures." Wiig and Semel further report that their findings support previous observations of problems in oral language experienced by pupils with learning disabilities. On this basis they conclude that productive-language deficits associated with learning disabilities may persist into adolescence and may relate to earlier observed difficulties in language processing. The authors indicate a need for (1) early screening and identification of productive-language deficits and (2) emphasis on training learning-disabled pupils in language production abilities.

WRITTEN EXPRESSION Marked impairment in spelling and in all forms of written expression is consistently found by those working with students categorized as dyslexic, neurologically impaired, brain-injured, and specifically learning-disabled (Boder, 1971; de Hirsch, 1963; Lerner, 1971; Myers & Hammill, 1969; Myklebust, 1973; McLeod, 1965; Orton, 1937; Saunders, 1962).

According to Myklebust, the learning of written language is a developmental process that continues through adolescence. Johnson and Myklebust describe writing as a form of expressive language and a complex process involving the highest forms of language. They attribute difficulties of written language to such deficits in auditory comprehension as auditory discrimination problems, oral syntax disorders, reauditorization deficits, reading difficulties, and disturbances in visual-motor integration.

Myklebust (1965) uses his Picture Story Language Test for studying characteristics of the written language of the learning-disabled. Myklebust (1973) also used the test to study characteristics of the written language of students whom he categorized as dyslexic and learning-disabled. The dyslexic population consisted of sixty-six seven- to eighteen-year-old students, 83 percent of whom had positive findings on EEG and neurological evaluations. A normal control was also chosen from the urban public schools. The dyslexics experienced major difficulty in written expression on the categories of story length and syntax. Normal children achieved adult level syntax at age eleven; the dyslexics, not until age fifteen. Myklebust also found positive correlations between auditory processes and written language.

Boder (1971) and de Hirsch (1963) describe writing problems of the learning-disabled. According to Boder, certain spelling patterns can be used to identify dyslexia. To describe severe spelling and handwriting problems of dyslexics, she uses the term *dysgraphia,* a term used by others as well. De Hirsch describes some dyslexic adolescents as exhibiting bizarre spelling patterns due to inability to retain the internal design of printed words and to carry the gestalt of a word into another setting. Poor visual and auditory memory and discrimination are given as causes of spelling difficulties in adolescents.

Since the introduction of the phenomenon *strephosymbolia*— twisted symbols—by Orton, the literature is replete with descriptions of learning-disabled students' reversals and rotations in written expression. Most often, severe spelling problems are cited as symptoms of other language and perceptual difficulties, that is, auditory receptive problems, visual-motor integration difficulties, sound-blending ability, auditory-visual integration, and memory. Except, perhaps, for Myklebust's study of 1973, little systematic analysis of problems and processes involved in written expression has been conducted with the adolescent learning-disabled.

INFORMATION PROCESSING AND LANGUAGE BEHAVIOR

One promising approach to investigating language problems of learning-disabled adolescents is based on work in psycholinguistics and cognitive psychology, particularly information theory. Researchers in these fields are concerned specifically with issues relating to selecting, storing, processing, and retrieving relevant information in a learner's environment. They frequently stress the limited capacity of the human information-processing system and the importance of subjective organization and efficient high-level cognitive and linguistic processes or strategies for recoding stimulus input in maximizing the amount of relevant information that can be received, processed, and remembered (Ausubel, 1968; Broadbent, 1958; Bruner, Goodnow, & Austin, 1956; Bruner, Oliver, & Greenfield, 1966; Hagen, 1972; Hunt, 1966; Mandler, 1967; McNeill, 1970; Miller, 1956; Miller, Galanter & Pribram, 1960; Neisser, 1967; Newell & Simon, 1972; Olson, 1970; Piaget, 1951, 1955, 1966; Slobin, 1971; Taba, 1966; Tulving, 1962; Tulving & Donaldson, 1972; Vygotsky, 1962; White, 1965). In fact, school learning and social adaptation in general depend greatly on the learner's ability to decode, interpret, and encode stimulus input accurately. A learner is an active organizer of information, equipped with a repertory of organizational processes that facilitate selection of the responses appropriate to the particular learning situation and exclusion of irrelevant information.

Research related to the language of learning-disabled adolescents has focused mainly on the performance aspect of language behavior—

that is, descriptive aspects of the student's speech and the psychological variables affecting it. As efficient information processing is very important in human learning and memory, it is possible that memory and other deficits—including reading deficits attributed to learning-disabled students—are partially the result of faulty or inefficient processing and organization of linguistic stimuli.

From a psycholinguistic point of view, we need to determine if the linguistic problems associated with learning disabilities come from performance variables (short-term memory deficits, attentional deficits, social-cultural-situational factors, motivation, and so on) or from competence variables (lack of knowledge of specific grammatical, phonological, and semantic relationships or rules), or perhaps from the interaction of both competence and performance variables.

Most definitions of learning disabilities make some reference to difficulties in information processing. Unfortunately, the nature of the relationship between information processing and language and speech difficulties in the learning-disabled is not clear. Measures for assessing information processing are still in a primitive state. For instance, in the area of reading, Orlando (1973) states: "The measures used to assess 'information-processing deficits' are the same measures that have been used for years by school psychologists to identify general visual and auditory problems, without regard to specific reading skill behaviors of the child."

Information-processing skills of learning-disabled students have generally been assessed by standardized instruments of auditory and visual-motor perception. These include the Wepman Test of Auditory Discrimination (Wepman, 1958), the ITPA, the Visual Motor Gestalt Test (Bender, 1938), and the Developmental Test of Visual Perception (Frostig & Horne, 1964). Recently the usefulness of these tests and their related programs in determining, assessing, and enhancing critical processing skills in language and reading has been seriously questioned (for example, Camp, 1973; Cohen, 1969; Hammill & Larsen, 1974a, 1974b; Hammill & Wiederholt, 1973; Newcomer & Hammill, 1976; Orlando, 1973; Samuels, 1973; Sedlak & Weener, 1973; Ysseldyke, 1973). These authors provide excellent reviews of the mass of literature related to learning-disabled subjects' decoding, integration, and encoding of auditory and visual stimuli.

Unfortunately, past studies of the information processing of learning-disabled subjects have yielded diverse and conflicting findings. As a

146

result, our understanding of the basic processes underlying language problems of learning-disabled adolescents is extremely limited, as is our confidence in prescribing efficient language remediation and training programs.

In our view there is a scarcity of investigations exploring the nature and extent of language-processing strategies and language deficits in learning-disabled adolescents. For instance, there is some indication that the ability to process and organize linguistic information may be strongly related to reading variables. Despite the importance of efficient information processing in learning and memory, researchers have paid relatively little attention to the language and cognitive strategies observed among learning-disabled students in various learning situations. Chalfant and Scheffelin (1969) note the need for comprehensive research on both receptive and expressive language disorders or difficulties related to central-processing dysfunctions. Moreover, Keough and Donlon (1972) conclude that assessments of the ways that pupils approach and attempt to solve learning tasks, the kinds of information they use, the ways they organize this information, and the speed with which they use it may provide critical information for development of remedial programs. Only recently have researchers in learning disabilities begun to focus on language-processing strategies of learning-disabled children and adolescents (Bartel, Grill, & Bartel, 1973; Semel & Wiig, 1975a, 1975b; Wiig & Semel, 1973, 1974, 1975).

In their excellent investigation of language-production deficits in adolescents with learning disabilities, Wiig and Semel (1975) conclude that the deficits observed in their population of learning-disabled adolescents may be related to previously observed difficulties in language processing associated with learning disabilities. They suggest that observed deficits in the accuracy and speed of convergent and divergent production of semantic units, confrontation naming, and sentence formulation may reflect such receptive-language problems in learning disabilities as reduced comprehension of linguistic structures and linguistic concepts requiring logical operations. Semel and Wiig (1975a) conclude that future investigations in learning disabilities should consider "the relationships between visual perception, linguistic and cognitive processing, and 'channel capacity' and 'chunking' characteristics of learning disabled youngsters."

Freston and Drew (1974) investigated the verbal performance of learning-disabled students as a function of organization of input. They explored the effects of organized versus unorganized material on the free recall performance of learning-disabled students from seven to seventeen years old. The sample was randomly subdivided into groups receiving either organized or unorganized verbal material. Materials consisted of twelve tests of five stimulus words each. Organized lists were composed of four conceptual categories from stimuli of high, intermediate, and low difficulty as determined by frequency of occurrence in English-language usage. This resulted in a low-, intermediate-, and high-difficulty list for each conceptual category. The twelve unorganized lists were formed from identical stimulus items of high, intermediate, and low difficulty, with the conceptual categories randomized.

The words in each list were given orally at the rate of one per second. Subjects had a thirty-second free recall period following each of the twelve lists. Results indicated that the degree of organization of the material did not significantly influence performance. Subjects did, however, react to differences in the material's difficulty, giving more correct responses on material of low difficulty than on material of intermediate and high difficulty.

The data failed to support previous work with subjects of normal intelligence (Drew & Altman, 1970) and with educable mentally retarded adolescents (Gerjuoy & Spitz, 1966; Gerjuoy & Alvarez, 1969) that suggests a facilitative influence of organized material. Freston and Drew hypothesize that their learning-disabled subjects recalled unorganized material as effectively as organized material because the subjects were not sensitive to the conceptual framework used to group the stimulus words and hence did not codify the material efficiently. The authors feel that factors such as attending, codification, storage, and recall should be studied in depth in subsequent investigations.

Several other investigators have stressed that memory and attentional processes are closely related to language proficiency and deficit (Birch, 1964; Graham, 1968; Hallahan & Cruickshank, 1973; Johnson & Myklebust, 1967; Samuels, 1973; Senf & Freundl, 1971).

Tarver and Hallahan (1974) reviewed the findings of twenty-one experimental studies of attention deficits in students who represented a variety of learning disabilities and who ranged from kindergarten age to sixteen years, three months, old. The authors made the following conclusions:

1. Students with learning disabilities, including "underachievers" and students with reading disabilities, exhibit more distractibility than do controls on tasks of figure-ground perception involving embedded contexts and on tests of incidental versus central learning. On the other hand, they are not differentially distracted by other types of distractors including flashing lights or extraneous color cues.

2. Hyperactivity of learning-disabled students may be situation-specific, with high levels of activity exhibited in more structured situations.

3. Students with learning disabilities tend to be more impulsive (less reflective) as a group than are normal controls.

Correlational evidence suggests that measures of impulsivity-reflectivity and central learning and incidental learning are related. "Impulsivity and inability to ignore irrelevant information indicate deficiencies in control of attention." Students with learning disabilities, particularly hyperactive ones, are deficient in the ability to maintain attention for prolonged periods of time. Tarver and Hallahan further indicate that WISC subtest patterns may be of some value in differential diagnosis of attentional processes in learning disabilities. Nevertheless, they note that although a WISC subpattern may be characteristic of groups of disabled readers, it is not characteristic of individuals. Moreover, they indicate that particular subtests of standardized instruments like the WISC do not lend themselves to disclosing discrete and specific aspects of the student's psychological functioning.

Samuels (1973) found several shortcomings in the research on causes of reading difficulty. He believes that invalid research results and conclusions have resulted. Much of the research has been on variables, with little or no direct connection with basic *processes* involved in learning. Samuels particularly criticizes "comparing good and poor readers on variables which had no direct connection with the learning process, using matched-group designs, unreliability of prediction formulas, reading-achievement and IQ tests, piecemeal research, and using students with a history of reading failure."

Samuels emphasizes that to overcome the problem of piecemeal research, the basic processes involved in verbal learning should be investigated in a systematic and comprehensive manner. He says that the research literature provides evidence for several basic processes in

149

associational learning that are also involved in learning to read. These processes include attentional processes, distinctive-feature learning, visual and auditory memory, auditory discrimination, and meditational processes.

Specifically, Samuels' review indicates that physiological correlates (such as galvanic skin response and heart rate) are related to learning; that low-achieving students, including poor readers, tend to be more distractible than high-achieving students; and that at the upper elementary level, a positive relationship exists between attention and achievement. There is also evidence that whole-word methods of teaching reading in combination with highly discriminable words and the use of such incidental cues as color-coding words lead to rapid initial learning but to poor transfer.

Samuels indicates that questions concerning where learners focus attention, what cues they select, and whether focal attention is directed at a relevant dimension of the stimulus complex have important implications for reading. He further reports that research on visual memory and reading associates poor reading performance with inferior visual memory. Moreover, the superior visual memory of good readers appears to result from their ability to identify distinctive features and to encode them verbally with relatively greater accuracy and consistency.

Samuels presents an information-processing model of associational learning as a method for studying variables or factors associated with differences in reading achievement (and hence, learning disabilities). This model is based on conceptualizations from cognitive psychology and contains components considered basic to the verbal-learning process: attention, visual and auditory discrimination, auditory and visual memory, short- and long-term memory, and mediation. In addition, a viable research design is provided for investigating and relating the various components of the model.

A particularly important application of an information-processing approach to language functioning relates to teaching reading and constructing reading materials for learning-disabled adolescents. In fact, there is evidence that the ability to process and organize linguistic information may be strongly related to the nature of the reading process and to reading difficulties of poor readers (Bower, 1970; Goodman, 1965, 1968, 1969; Kolers, 1969, Lefevre, 1964; Neisser, 1967; Ryan & Semmel, 1969; Sitko & Semmel, 1973; Smith, 1971). Reading researchers in learning disabilities have, unfortunately, paid little attention to the possible relationship between reading behavior and information processing in learning and memory. Much of the reading instruction and research with learning-disabled students has been based on graphic features and perceptual features of language, rather than on language structure and language processing.

In summarizing the various models for reading based on the active participation of the reader, Ryan and Semmel emphasize the importance of efficient and hierarchical language-processing strategies in both beginning and mature reading. They conclude that reading can be viewed as a "constructive active process in which the reader uses his cognitive and linguistic knowledge to reproduce a probable utterance from a careful sampling of cues. S/He then matches that prediction for appropriateness."

Ryan and Semmel present considerable evidence suggesting that reading is a cue-sampling process rather than one requiring absolute discrimination of detail. The authors further emphasize that reading material should be written both to maximize the reader's opportunity to develop efficient habits of forming and testing hypotheses and to allow the reader to use linguistic context (semantic and syntactic relationships) to determine word perception and comprehension. Moreover, the disabled reader should be encouraged by the teacher to apply appropriate high-order language strategies. Such strategies are already available from oral language usage. Emphasis should be on "conceptual" rather than "perceptual" aspects of reading and on relations rather than single words.

Some of the difficulty that learning-disabled adolescents have in reading comprehension and in other areas of reading probably results from a basic weakness in their ability to process and organize reading materials efficiently and hierarchically. In fact, evidence with the mildly retarded indicates that retarded students' difficulty in reading comprehension comes from a basic inability to organize verbal input efficiently for storage and retrieval during the act of reading (Bilsky & Evans, 1970; Blanton, 1974; Evans, 1970).

Our review of the literature suggests that many language strategies exhibited by learning-disabled subjects are deficient and reflect primitive and inefficient levels of cognitive and linguistic information processing. It seems logical to suggest that language training techniques involving learning-disabled subjects should include the modification of inefficient language strategies to more hierarchical, rule-governed

151

strategies. In essence, learning-disabled students should be taught to organize linguistic information efficiently.

■ INTERVENTION FOR LANGUAGE DIFFICULTIES ■

Adequate development of instructional strategies in language (excluding speech disorders) for learning-disabled adolescents is lacking. In addition, the results of research in various instructional approaches have been conflicting, and the studies themselves have been criticized for improper design (Wiederholt, 1974). The efficacy of training specific language skills (for example, those constructs of language exemplified by research and training with the ITPA) has not been sufficiently established. Nor has the relationship between training in language skills and school achievement been thoroughly examined (Hammill & Larsen 1974a; Newcomer & Hammill, 1976; Sedlak & Weener, 1973). Hence, a discussion of instructional strategies in language for learning-disabled adolescents is clouded by the issues previously discussed in this chapter. Moreover, learning-disabled adolescents may have such additional difficulties as socioemotional problems (Gordon, 1970) and severe reading and spelling retardation (de Hirsch, 1963), which confuse the training picture.

Educators frequently urge the development of early screening, identification, and intervention strategies for all language-impaired students (Marge, 1972). Marge discusses this issue:

The research and clinical evidence, moreover, is noticeably in favor of the efficacy of early intervention for all linguistically handicapped children. The "wait and see policy" invariably led to many unnecessary complications which enlarge the problem of providing an effective training program.

Marge also presents the opposing view held by Lenneberg (1966), who advocates postponing language training until pupils mature in language at their own rate. If language functioning is inadequate, special training is given at a later age. Lenneberg feels that later training is more beneficial because the student has more social experiences and is capable of understanding the purpose of instruction.

Early intervention in language problems is favored by most special educators. There are many language programs now available commercially for handicapped students, including the learning-disabled. Some are based on the ITPA—the Minskoff, Wiseman, and Minskoff (MWM) Program for Developing Language Abilities and the Goal Program (Karnes, 1973). Remedial activities for use after diagnosis with the ITPA have been developed by Bush and Giles (1969), Karnes (1968), and Rupert (1971). Other language programs are the Peabody Language Development Kits (Dunn & Smith, 1965, 1966, 1967; Dunn, Horton, & Smith, 1968), the Wilson Syntax Program (Wilson, 1972), and Distar (Englemann & Osborn, 1970). For a thorough review of language intervention programs, see Hammill and Bartel (1975).

THE NATURE OF LANGUAGE PROGRAMS

Marge places programs of language intervention in two broad categories: diagnostic approaches that assess the status of students' disabilities, attempt etiology and prognosis, and suggest appropriate procedures for modifying adolescents' linguistic behavior; and training methods that help adolescents attain language function appropriate to their age.

Many language programs in learning disabilities appear in the first category. Educators attempt to determine the etiology of students' language disorders (brain damage, perceptual impairment, and so forth); the cause then determines the nature of the training program. For example, a student found to be brain-damaged may be given a language program that includes supposed language-correlated activities in such categories as auditory and visual perception and perceptual-motor skills.

Marge (1972), however, has found that the determination of etiology may not be an effective means of developing language programs. When adolescents are placed in a category (for example, learning-disabled), planners of language programs may assume that these students have uniform language behaviors. As we noted earlier, learning-disabled adolescents typically display heterogeneity in learning behaviors.

A second approach to language disorders is to determine the exact nature of the linguistic behaviors. The ITPA and the programs based on its subtests represent attempts by Kirk and his associates to assess and program for the intra-individual differences of the student. The concept is admirable, but the theoretical constructs of the ITPA have been criticized for not including current findings in language (New-comer & Hammill, 1976; Sitko & Semmel, 1973). Further research in the field may yield data that will allow the programmer to ascertain the linguistic strategies of the adolescent and provide a variety of alternatives for intervention.

ADOLESCENTS AND LANGUAGE INTERVENTION

Although language intervention for learning-disabled adolescents at the secondary level has been proposed by several learning-disabilities specialists (Bailey, 1975; de Hirsch, 1963; Drake, 1970; Giles, 1975; Lyness, 1973; Wiig & Semel, 1975), the emphasis remains on early intervention. In addition, it is not certain whether language and perceptual skills can be acquired beyond a certain age (Bannatyne, 1971). Wepman et al. (1975) differentiate between intervention before and after age twelve. Before adolescence, the programs are developmental; after adolescence they are compensatory. According to Wepman et al., adolescent students should be taught to use their best skills in coping with the academic demands of secondary programs.

We feel that language programs for adolescents should be developed as thoroughly as language programs for elementary students. Although most children achieve a great deal of language maturity at age four, students with language problems need help into their midteens if their language disorder is severe (Menyuk, 1971). Several investigators report that the language development of students with language difficulties is not qualitatively different from that of normal students. Rather, they say that development is merely slowed (Fygetakis & Ingram, 1973; Sitko & Semmel, 1973; Wiig & Semel, 1975).

If learning-disabled adolescents are developmentally behind their peers, they should have a language program that adequately task-analyzes their linguistic skills. Recent investigators advocate task analysis as an efficient approach to improving language and other instruction with learning-disabled individuals (Bijou, 1970; Lloyd, 1975; Siegel, 1972; Ysseldyke & Salvia, 1974). Matching instructional strategies to the needs of the student should extend beyond formal test results. As stated, the efficacy of test-related programs in relation to academic gains has been questioned. In addition, test-related programs call for making instructional decisions based on testing that occurs outside the environment or curriculum found in the classroom.

Because of the variability of settings and needs, it is impossible to use an educational program appropriate for all interventions. Solutions to educational problems are most often situationally specific.

As an alternative to global assessment measurements, we propose using a decision-making task-analytic approach. Such an approach should consider the student, teacher, material, and situational variables. In task analysis, the educator analyzes the steps required to complete the task as well as the entry level of the student. Instruction begins where the student has been assessed to be on the skill continua. At present, nothing systematic is known about the interaction of the adolescent's language capabilities with the content being offered, the manner of presentation, motivational factors, and so forth.

More research is needed to determine the developmental stages of the language of adolescents. More research is needed on qualitative rather than quantitative differences in language processing between adolescents with adequate language skills and those with language difficulties.

Educational personnel must form teams to view educational programming as a problem-solving or decision-making process. The teacher should stand at the center of the process and, if programming is to be fully implemented, should engage in the decision making. A systematic approach to programming should be used. Because of the variability in settings and needs, it is impossible to predict an appropriate educational strategy without considering the total learning environment. Most often, solutions to problems are situationally dependent. Therefore, it is imperative that educational personnel—those, after all, who know best the specific learning situations in which their students are involved—be skilled in the process of decision making or problem solving. One diagnostic teaching approach recently formulated by us (Gillespie & Sitko, 1974, 1976) stresses the importance of training teachers to become themselves effective organizers of instruction and effective, pupil-oriented decision makers.

■ CONCLUSIONS ■

Because so little research is devoted to the language difficulties of the learning-disabled, educational personnel have little to guide them in developing individualized programs in speech and language. At best, the results of the research reviewed in this chapter may provide only hypotheses or "in the ballpark" hunches which can be used in finding solutions to a learning-disabled adolescent's language problems in the classroom. Little attention has been focused on how the environmental and organismic variables studied in basic research affect the complex types of language-oriented learning and processing found in the classroom. Reliable, valid, and educationally relevant measures of adolescents' language competencies do not exist.

We are left instead with many norm-referenced global measures of language aptitudes with modest predictive validity. Only a limited range of standardized instruments exists for the assessment of language, especially for adolescents. Many of these are based on doctrinaire, inadequately researched theories of learning disabilities. Moreover, there is a dearth of criterion-referenced instruments in language that are appropriate for the adolescent.

Comparison studies conducted to determine the language characteristics of learning-disabled adolescents typically group individuals in a certain manner. Categorizing in most cases leads to stereotyping, and group characteristics are ascribed to individuals (Reynolds & Balow, 1972). Often these ascribed language characteristics do not take into account the interaction among such variables as educational settings, teacher preparation, experiential background, social-cultural factors, and emotional adjustment. If programming is to be beneficial, the interaction of students with their total environment must be considered. More reliable language measures that reflect current linguistic developments and are normed or *specific* to adolescent populations should be constructed. In addition, assessment should be related to the purposes for which the adolescent has been referred. Language assessment should not be used to categorize or place the adolescent, but rather to enhance the adolescent's learning potential and achievement. The main concern should be precise individual, in situ criterion- and task-analytic assessment, followed by the selection of instructional alternatives that take into consideration both individual and situational factors.

For example, more attention must be given to inter- and intra-individual differences of learning-disabled adolescents. Even if we had rich resources in instrumentation, inter- and intra-learning variability among students with learning and language difficulties is so great that tests have limited value in instructional design. Although diagnostic tests have been constructed to isolate variability within individuals, this technique does not consider in situ assessment. Hence, one of the biggest challenges of a language-assessment program is to coordinate its objectives with the behavioral characteristics and linguistic needs of the learning-disabled student.

In general, there are few empirically oriented and methodologically sound investigations dealing with speech and language difficulties of learning-disabled adolescents. Furthermore, the many gaps in related language research make generalization practically impossible. The literature is unclear as to the exact nature of the linguistic problems of learning-disabled adolescents. Little progress has been made in the study of phonological, morphological, syntactic, and semantic development of language in these students.

Future language research should explore the exact nature and extent of basic language and/or cognitive-processing strategies and language deficits among learning-disabled adolescents in language-related academic situations. Evidence suggests that many of the language strategies exhibited by learning-disabled students are deficient and reflect primitive and inefficient levels of cognitive and linguistic information processing. Viable models similar to Samuels' information-processing model of associational learning are needed to stimulate and guide investigations of variables associated with individual differences in language behavior—including reading and writing—and language development. It is fruitless to prescribe language remediation and training programs for the learning-disabled until we have some understanding of the basic processes underlying their language and speech difficulties. Do their linguistic problems result from performance variables (short-term memory deficits, attentional deficits, social-cultural-situational factors, motivation), from competence variables (lack of knowledge of specific grammatical, phonological, and/or semantic relationships or rules), or from both competence and performance variables?

As was the case with language assessment and characteristics of language behavior, evidence of effective language programming for learning-disabled adolescents is lacking. Recently, more attention has focused on developing effective instructional strategies for learning-disabled adolescents who lack basic language skills. Special educators favor early screening, identification, and intervention. While interest in developing efficient instructional strategies in language disabilities is increasing, materials and programs not carefully validated with adolescents are circulating. Adapting or adopting assessment techniques and instructional strategies used (with questionable efficacy) with younger learning-disabled students is not the solution to programming for adolescents.

We discussed our own approach to language programming. This approach is based on in situ assessment of adolescents' linguistic strategies. It is a task-analytic approach to the development of linguistic skills that considers the interaction of teacher, pupil, material, and situational variables. In our view educational programming is a systematic problem-solving or decision-making process. Therefore, we believe, teachers who are *effectively* trained as organizers and decision makers will better meet the individual linguistic needs of learning-disabled students.

■ REFERENCES ■

Adelman, H. S. The not so specific learning disability population. *Exceptional Children*, 1971, 37, 528–533.

Adler, S. Dialectal differences and learning disorders. *Journal of Learning Disabilities*, 1972, 5, 344–350.

Ausubel, D. P. *Educational psychology: A cognitive view*. New York: Holt, Rinehart and Winston, 1968.

Bailey, E. J. *Academic activities for adolescents with learning disabilities*. Evergreen, Colo.: Learning Pathway, 1975.

Bannatyne, A. *Language, reading, and learning disabilities*. Springfield, Ill.: Charles C. Thomas, 1971.

Baratz, J. C., & Shuy, R. W. (Eds.). *Teaching black children to read*. Washington, D.C.: Center for Applied Linguistics, 1969.

Bartel, N. R., & Axelrod, J. Nonstandard English usage and reading ability in black junior high students. *Exceptional Children*, 1973, 39, 653–655.

Bartel, N. R., Grill, J. J., & Bartel, H. W. The syntactic-paradigmatic shift in learning disabled and normal children. *Journal of Learning Disabilities*, 1973, 6, 518–523.

Bartel, N. R., Grill, J. J., & Bryen, D. N. Language characteristics of black children: Implications for assessment. *Journal of School Psychology*, 1973, *11*, 351–364.

Bender, L. A visual motor gestalt test and its clinical use. *American Orthopsychiatric Association Research Monograph*, No. 3, 1938.

Bender, L. Childhood schizophrenia. *Psychiatric Quarterly*, 1953, *27*, 663–681.

Bijou, S. W. What psychology has to offer education—now. *Journal of Applied Behavior Analysis*, 1970, *3*, 65–71.

Bilsky, L., & Evans, R. A. Use of associative clustering technique in the study of reading disability: Effects of list organization. *American Journal of Mental Deficiency*, 1970, *74*, 771–776.

Birch, H. G. (Ed.). *Brain damage in children: The biological and social aspects.* Baltimore: Williams and Wilkins, 1964.

Blanton, L. P. *The relation of organizational abilities to the comprehension of connected discourse in educable mentally retarded and nonretarded children.* Unpublished doctoral dissertation, Indiana University, 1974.

Boder, E. Developmental dyslexia: Prevailing diagnostic concepts and a new diagnostic approach. In H. R. Myklebust (Ed.), *Progress in learning disabilities* (Vol. 2). New York: Grune & Stratton, 1971.

Bortner, M., & Birch, H. J. Brain damage an educational category? In M. Bartner (Ed.), *Evaluation and education of children with brain damage.* Springfield, Ill.: Charles C Thomas, 1969.

Bower, T. G. R. Reading by eye. In H. Levin & J. P. Williams (Eds.), *Basic studies on reading.* New York: Basic Books, 1970.

Broadbent, D. E. *Perception and communication.* London: Pergamon, 1958.

Bruner, J. S., Goodnow, J. J., & Austin, G. A. *A study of thinking.* New York: Wiley, 1956.

Bruner, J. S., Oliver, R. R., & Greenfield, P. M. *Studies in cognitive growth.* New York: Wiley, 1966.

Bryen, D. N. Special education and the linguistically different child. *Exceptional Children*, 1974, *40*, 589–599.

Bush, W. J., & Giles, M. T. *Aids to psycholinguistic teaching.* Columbus, Ohio: Charles E. Merrill, 1969.

Butterfield, E. C., & Belmont, J. M. The role of verbal processes in short-term memory. In R. L. Schiefelbusch (Ed.), *Language of the mentally retarded.* Baltimore: University Park Press, 1972.

159

Camp, B. W. Psychometric tests and learning in severely disabled readers. *Journal of Learning Disabilities,* 1973, *6,* 512–517.

Carroll, J. B. *The study of language: A survey of linguistics and related disciplines in America.* Cambridge, Mass.: Harvard University Press, 1953.

Carroll, J. B. Psycholinguistics in the study of mental retardation. In R. L. Schiefelbusch, R. H. Copeland, & J. O. Smith (Eds.), *Language and mental retardation.* New York: Holt, 1967.

Cawley, J. F., Goodstein, H. A., & Burrow, W. H. *The slow learner and the reading problem.* Springfield, Ill.: Charles C. Thomas, 1972.

Cazden, C. B. Evaluation of learning in preschool education: Early language development. In B. S. Bloom, J. T. Hastings, & G. F. Madaus (Eds.), *Handbook on formative and summative evaluation of student learning.* New York, McGraw-Hill, 1971.

Chalfant, J. C., & Scheffelin, M. A. *Central processing dysfunctions in children.* Bethesda, Md.: National Institute of Neurological Diseases and Stroke, 1969.

Chomsky, N. A. *Syntactic structures.* The Hague: Mouton, 1957.

Chomsky, N. A. A review of B. F. Skinner's "Verbal behavior." *Language,* 1959, *35,* 26–58.

Chomsky, N. A. *Aspects of the theory of syntax.* Cambridge, Mass.: MIT Press, 1965.

Chomsky, N. A. *Language and mind.* New York: Harcourt Brace Jovanovich, 1968.

Cohen, S. A. Studies in visual perception and reading in disadvantaged children. *Journal of Learning Disabilities,* 1969, *2,* 498–507.

de Hirsch, K. The concept of plasticity and language disabilities. Paper presented at the meeting of the American Orthopsychiatric Association, Washington, D.C., March 1963.

Dever, R. *A comment on the testing of language development in retarded children.* Bloomington: Indiana University, Center for Innovation in Teaching the Handicapped, 1971. (Technical Report 1.22)

Dever, R. *Applied linguistics and language-handicapped children.* Columbus, Ohio: Charles E. Merrill, forthcoming.

Drake, C., & Cavanaugh, J. J. A. Teaching the high school dyslexic. In L. E. Anderson (Ed.), *Helping the adolescent with the hidden handicap.* San Rafael, Calif.: Academy Therapy Publications, 1970.

Drew, C. J., & Altman, R. Effects of input organization and material difficulty on free recall. *Psychological Reports,* 1970, *27,* 335–337.

Dunn, L. M., & Smith, J. O. (Eds.). *Peabody language development kit. Level number 1.* Circle Pines, Minn.: American Guidance Service, 1965.

Dunn, L. M., & Smith, J. O. *Peabody language development kit. Level number 2.* Circle Pines, Minn.: American Guidance Service, 1966.

Dunn, L. M., & Smith, J. O. *Peabody language development kit. Level number 3.* Circle Pines, Minn.: American Guidance Service, 1967.

Dunn, L. M., Horton, R. B., & Smith, J. O. *Peabody language development kit: Level P.* Circle Pines, Minn.: American Guidance Service, 1968.

Ellis, N. R. Memory processes in retardates and normals. In N. R. Ellis (Ed.), *International review of research in mental retardation* (Vol. 5). New York: Academic Press, 1970.

Englemann, S., & Osborn, J. *Distar: An instructional system.* Chicago: Science Research Associates, 1970.

Ervin-Tripp, S. M. Language development. In L. W. Hoffman & M. L. Hoffman (Eds.), *Review of child development research* (Vol. 2). New York: Russell Sage Foundation, 1966.

Evans, R. A. Use of associative clustering technique in the study of reading disability: Effects of presentation mode. *American Journal of Mental Deficiency,* 1970, 74, 765–770.

Fillenbaum, S. Psycholinguistics. In P. Mussen & M. Rosenzweig (Eds.), *Annual review of psychology.* Palo Alto, Calif.: Annual Reviews, 1971.

Fodor, J. A. How to learn to talk: Some simple ways. In F. Smith & G. A. Miller (Eds.), *The genesis of language: A psycholinguistic approach.* Cambridge, Mass.: MIT Press, 1966.

Foster, R., Giddan, J. J., & Stark, J. *Assessment of children's language comprehension.* Palo Alto, Calif.: Consulting Psychologists Press, 1972.

Freston, C. W., & Drew, C. J. Verbal performance of learning disabled children as a function of input organization. *Journal of Learning Disabilities,* 1974, 7, 424–429.

Frostig, M., & Horne, D. *The Frostig program for the development of visual perception: Teachers guide.* Chicago: Follett, 1964.

Fygetakis, L. J., & Ingram, D. Language rehabilitation and programmed conditioning: A case study. *Journal of Learning Disabilities,* 1973, 6, 60–64.

Gearheart, B. W. *Learning disabilities: Educational strategies.* St. Louis: C. V. Mosley Co., 1973.

Gerjuoy, I. R., & Alvarez, J. V. Transfer of learning in associative clustering of retardates and normals. *American Journal of Mental Deficiency,* 1969, 73, 733–738.

Gerjuoy, I. R., & Spitz, H. H. Associative clustering in free recall: Intellectual and development variables. *American Journal of Mental Deficiency,* 1966, *70,* 918–927.

Giles, M. T. *Adolescent classroom screening.* Evergreen, Colo.: Learning Pathways, Inc., 1975.

Gillespie, P. H., & Johnson, L. *Teaching reading to the mildly retarded child.* Columbus, Ohio: Charles E. Merrill, 1974.

Gillespie, P. H., & Sitko, M. C. A decision-making model for training preservice teachers in diagnostic-prescriptive teaching. Bloomington: Indiana University, Center for Innovation in Teaching the Handicapped, 1974.

Gillespie, P. H., & Sitko, M. C. A decision-making model for training preservice teachers in diagnostic teaching. *Exceptional Children,* April 1976, 401–402.

Goodman, K. S. A linguistic study of cues and miscues in reading. *Elementary English Review,* 1965, *42,* 639–742.

Goodman, K. S. (Ed.), *The psycholinguistic nature of the reading process.* Detroit: Wayne State University, 1968.

Goodman, K. S. Words and morphemes in reading. In K. S. Goodman & J. T. Fleming (Eds.), *Psycholinguists and the teaching of reading.* Newark, Del.: International Reading Association, 1969.

Goodman K. S. Reading: A psycholinguistic guessing game. In K. S. Goodman (Ed.), *Individualized instruction: A reader.* New York: Holt, Rinehart & Winston, 1972.

Gordon, S. Reversing a negative self image. In L. E. Anderson (Ed.), *Helping the adolescent with the hidden handicap.* San Rafael, Calif.: Academic Therapy Publications, 1970.

Gottsleben, R. H., Busehini, G., & Tyack, D. Linguistically based training programs. *Journal of Learning Disabilities,* 1974, *7,* 197–203.

Graham, N. C. Memory span and language proficiency. *Journal of Learning Disabilities,* 1968, *1,* 644–648.

Hagen, J. W. Strategies for remembering. In S. Farnham-Diggory (Ed.), *Information processing in children.* New York: Academic Press, 1972.

Hallahan, D. P., & Cruickshank, W. M. *Psycho-educational foundations of learning disabilities.* Englewood Cliffs, N.J.: Prentice-Hall, 1973.

Hammill, D. D., & Bartel, N. R. *Teaching children with learning and behavior problems.* Boston: Allyn and Bacon, 1975.

Hammill D. D., & Larsen, S. C. The effectiveness of psycholinguistic training. *Exceptional Children,* 1974, *51,* 5–14. (a)

Hammill D. D., & Larsen, S. The relationship of selected auditory perceptual skills and reading ability. *Journal of Learning Disabilities,* 1974, 7, 429–435. (b)

Hammill, D. D., & Wiederholt, J. L. Review of the Frostig visual perception test and the related training program. In L. Mann & D. A. Sabatino (Eds.) *The first review of special education* (Vol. 1). Philadelphia: JSE Press, 1973.

Harris, A. J. *How to increase reading ability.* New York: David McKay, 1970.

Herrick, M. J. Disabled or disadvantaged: What's the difference? *Journal of Special Education,* 1973, 7, 381–386.

Hunt, E. B. *Concept learning: An information processing problem.* New York: Wiley, 1966.

Irwin, J. V., Moore, J. M., & Ramps, D. L. Nonmedical diagnosis and evaluation. In J. V. Irwin & M. Marge (Eds.), *Principles of childhood language disabilities.* Englewood Cliffs, N.J.: Prentice-Hall, 1972.

Jansky, J. A case of severe dyslexia with aphasic-like symptoms. In W. Otto & K. Koenke (Eds.), *Remedial teaching: Research and comment.* Boston: Houghton Mifflin, 1969.

Johnson, D. J. The language continuum in children with learning problems. In S. G. Sapir & A. C. Nitzburg (Eds.), *Readings in a developmental interaction approach.* New York: Brunner/Mazel Publishers, 1973.

Johnson, D. J., & Myklebust, H. *Learning disabilities: Educational principles and practices.* New York: Grune & Stratton, 1967.

Karnes, M. B. *Activities for developing psycholinguistic skills with pre-school culturally disadvantaged children.* Washington, D.C.: Council for Exceptional Children, 1968.

Karnes, M. *The goal program.* Springfield, Mass.: Milton Bradley, 1973.

Kass, C. E. *Some psychological correlates of severe reading disability.* Unpublished doctoral dissertation. University of Illinois, 1962.

Keough, B. K., & Donlon, G. Field dependence, impulsivity, and learning disabilities. *Journal of Learning Disabilities,* 1972, 5, 331–336.

Kirk, S. A. A behavioral diagnosis and remediation of learning disabilities. In *Proceedings of the conference on exploration into the problem of the perceptually handicapped child, first annual meeting,* Chicago, 1963.

Kolers, P. A. Reading is only incidentally visual. In K. S. Goodman & J. T. Fleming (Eds.), *Psycholinguistics and the teaching of reading.* Newark, Del.: International Reading Association, 1969.

Labov, W. Academic ignorance and black intelligence. *The Atlantic*, 1972, *229*, 59–67.

Lee, L. L. *Developmental sentence analysis*. Evanston, Ill.: Northwestern University Press, 1974.

Lee, L. L., & Canter, S. M. Developmental sentence scoring: A clinical procedure for estimating syntactic development in children's spontaneous speech. *Journal of Speech and Hearing Disorders*, 1971, *36*, 315–340.

Lefevre, C. A. *Linguistics and the teaching of reading*. New York: McGraw-Hill, 1964.

Lenneberg, E. H. The natural history of language. In F. Smith & G. Miller (Eds.), *The genesis of language*. Cambridge, Mass.: MIT Press, 1966.

Lerner, J. W. *Children with learning disabilities*. Boston: Houghton Mifflin, 1971.

Lloyd, J. The pedagogical orientation: An argument for improving instruction. *Journal of Learning Disabilities*, 1975, *8*, 74–78.

Lyness, S. L. The last step in language development. *Academic Therapy*, *8*, 1973, 349–354.

Mackie, R. P. The handicapped benefit under compensatory education programs. *Exceptional Children*, 1968, *34*, 603–606.

Mandler, G. Verbal learning. In G. Mandler et al. (Eds.), *New directions in psychology (No. 3)*. New York: Holt, 1967.

Marge, M. The general problem of management and corrective education. In J. V. Irwin & M. Marge (Eds.), *Principles of childhood language disabilities*. Englewood Cliffs, N.J.: Prentice-Hall, 1972.

McCarthy, J. Report of Leadership Training Institute. Presented at ACLD, New York, February 1975.

McDonald, C. W. Problems concerning the classification and education of children with learning disabilities. *Learning disorders (Vol. 3)*. Seattle: Special Child Publications, 1968.

McLeod, J. Some psychological and psycholinguistic aspects of severe reading disability. Unpublished doctoral dissertation, University of Queensland (Australia), 1965.

McNeill, D. Developmental psycholinguistics. In F. Smith & G. A. Miller (Eds.), *The Genesis of language: A psycholinguistic approach*. Cambridge, Mass.: MIT Press, 1966.

McNeill, D. The development of language. In P. H. Mussen (Ed.), *Carmichael's manual of child psychology* (Vol. 1). New York: Wiley, 1970.

Mehrabian, A. Measures of vocabulary and grammatical skills for children up to age six. *Developmental Psychology,* 1970, *2,* 439–446.

Menyuk, P. *The acquisition and development of language.* Englewood Cliffs, N.J.: Prentice-Hall, 1971.

Miller, G. A. The magical number seven, plus or minus two: Some limits on our capacity for processing information. *Psychological Review,* 1956, *63,* 81–97.

Miller, G. A., Galanter, E., & Pribram, K. H. *Plans and the structure of behavior.* New York: Holt, 1960.

Mowrer, O. H. The psychologist looks at language. *American Psychologist,* 1954, 9, 660–694.

Myers, P. I., & Hammill, D. D. *Methods for learning disorders.* New York: Wiley, 1969.

Myklebust, H. R. *Development and disorders of written language.* New York: Grune & Stratton, 1965.

Myklebust, H. R. *Development and disorders of written language: Studies of normal and exceptional children* (Vol. 2). New York: Grune & Stratton, 1973.

Neisser, U. *Cognitive psychology.* New York: Appleton-Century-Crofts, 1967.

Newcomer, P. L., & Hammill, D. D. *Psycholinguistics in the schools.* Columbus, Ohio: Charles E. Merrill, 1976.

Newell, A., & Simon, H. A. *Human problem solving.* Englewood Cliffs, N.J.: Prentice-Hall, 1972.

O'Grady, D. J. Psycholinguistic abilities in learning disabled, emotionally disturbed, and normal children. *Journal of Special Education,* 1974, *8,* 157–166.

Olson, D. Language acquisition and cognitive development. In H. C. H. Haywood (Ed.), *Social-cultural aspects of mental retardation.* New York: Appleton-Century-Crofts, 1970.

Orlando, C. P. Review of the reading research in special education. In L. Mann & D. A. Sabatino (Eds.), *The first review of special education* (Vol. 1). Philadelphia: JSE Press, 1973.

Orton, S. *Reading, writing and speech problems in children.* New York: Norton, 1937.

Osgood, C. E. Motivational dynamics of language behavior. In M. Jones (Ed.), *Nebraska symposium on motivation.* Lincoln: University of Nebraska Press, 1957.

Piaget, J. *The child's conception of the world.* London: Routledge & Kegan Paul, 1951.

Piaget, J. Language and thought of the child. New York: International Universities Press, 1955.

Piaget, J. *Psychology of intelligence.* Totowa, N.J.: Littlefield, Adams, 1966.

Rabinovitch, R. D. Reading and learning disabilities. In S. Arieti (Ed.), *American handbook of psychiatry.* New York: Basic Books, 1959.

Redelheim, P. S. Learning-disabled or culturally disadvantaged. A separate piece? *Journal of Special Education,* 1973, 7, 399–407.

Reynolds, M. C., & Balow, B. Categories and variables in special education. *Exceptional Children,* 1972, 38, 357–366.

Rosenberg, S. Problems of language development in the retarded. In H. C. Haywood, *Social-cultural aspects of mental retardation.* New York: Appleton Century Crofts, 1970.

Rupert, H. A. *A sequentially compiled list of instructional materials for remediational use with the ITPA.* Washington, D.C.: Council for Exceptional Children, 1971.

Ryan, E. B., & Semmel, M. I. Reading as a constructive language process. *Reading Research Quarterly,* 1969, 5, 59–83.

Samuels, S. J. Success and failure in learning to read: A critique of the research. *Reading Research Quarterly,* 1973, 8, 200–239.

Saunders, R. E. Dyslexia: Its phenomenology in reading disability: Progress and research needs. In J. Money (Ed.), *Dyslexia.* Baltimore: Johns Hopkins Press, 1962.

Sedlak, R. A., & Weener, P. Review of research on the Illinois Test of Psycholinguistic Abilities. In L. Mann & D. A. Sabatino (Eds.), *The first review of special education* (Vol. 1). Philadelphia: JSE Press, 1973.

Semel, E. M., & Wiig, E. *Language processing deficits in learning disabled children and adolescents.* Paper presented at the Second International Scientific Conference on Learning Disabilities, Brussels, Belgium, January 1975. (a)

Semel, E. M., & Wiig, E. Comprehension of syntactic structures and critical verbal elements by children with learning disabilities. *Journal of Learning Disabilities,* 1975, 8, 46–51. (b)

Senf, G. M., & Freundl, P. C. Memory and attention factors in specific learning disabilities. *Journal of Learning Disabilities,* 1971, 4, 94–106.

Severson, R. A., & Guest, K. Toward the standardized assessment of the language of disadvantaged children. In F. Williams (Ed.), *Language and poverty.* Chicago: Markham, 1970.

Siegel, E. Task analysis and effective teaching. *Journal of Learning Disabilities,* 1972, *5,* 519–532.

Sitko, M. C., & Semmel, M. I. Language and language behavior of the mentally retarded. In L. Mann & D. A. Sabatino (Eds.), *The first review of special education* (Vol. 1). Philadelphia: JSE Press, 1973.

Skinner, B. F. *Verbal behavior.* New York: Appleton-Century-Crofts, 1957.

Slobin, D. I. *Psycholinguistics.* Glenview, Ill.: Scott, Foresman, 1971.

Slobin, D. I. Early grammatical development in several languages with special attention to Soviet research. In T. G. Bever & W. Weksel (Eds.), *The structure and psychology of language.* New York: Holt, Rinehart and Winston, 1972.

Smith, F. *Understanding reading: A psycholinguistic analysis of reading and learning to read.* New York: Holt, Rinehart and Winston, 1971.

Staats, A. W., & Staats, C. K. *Language, learning and cognition.* New York: Holt, Rinehart and Winston, 1968.

Taba, H. *Teaching strategies and cognitive functioning in elementary school children.* San Francisco: San Francisco State College, February 1966. (Cooperative Research No. 1404)

Tarver, S. C., & Hallahan, D. P. Attentional deficits in children with learning disabilities: A review. *Journal of Learning Disabilities,* 1974, *1,* 560–569.

Tulving, E. Subjective organization in free recall of "unrelated" words. *Psychological Review,* 1962, 69, 344–354.

Tulving, E., & Donaldson, W. (Eds.). *Organization of memory.* New York: Academic Press, 1972.

Tyack, D. The use of language samples in a clinical setting. *Journal of Learning Disabilities,* 1973, 6, 213–216.

U.S. Public Health Service. *Minimal brain dysfunction in children, Phase II.* Washington, D.C.: Government Printing Office, 1969.

Van Hattum, R. J. *New dimensions for the speech and hearing program in the school: Language and the retarded child.* Paper presented at the California State Department of Education, San Diego, November 1969.

Vygotsky, L. S. *Thought and language.* Cambridge, Mass.: MIT Press, 1962.

Wardhaugh, R. Theories of language acquisition in relation to beginning reading instruction. *Language Learning,* 1972, *21,* 1–26.

Weener, P., Barritt, L. S., & Semmel, M. I. A critical evaluation of the Illinois Test of Psycholinguistic Abilities. *Exceptional Children,* 1967, *33,* 373–380.

Wepman, J. M. Auditory discrimination test. Chicago: Language Research Associates, 1958.

Wepman, J. M., Cruickshank, W. M., Deutsch, C. P., Morency, A., & Strother, C. R. Learning disabilities. In N. Hobbs (Ed.), *Issues in the classification of children* (Vol. 1). San Francisco: Jossey-Bass, 1975.

White, S. W. Evidence for a hierarchical arrangement of learning processes. In L. P. Lipsitt & C. C. Spiker (Eds.), *Advances in child development and behavior* (Vol. 2). New York: Academic Press, 1965.

Wiederholt, J. L. Historical perspectives on the education of the learning disabled. In L. Mann & D. A. Sabatino (Eds.), *The second review of special education.* Philadelphia: JSE Press, 1974.

Wiig, E. H., & Semel, E. M. Comprehension of linguistic concepts requiring logical operations by learning disabled children. *Journal of Speech & Hearing Research,* 1973, *16,* 627–637.

Wiig, E. H., & Semel, E. M. Logico-grammatical sentence comprehension by adolescents with learning disabilities. *Perceptual Motor Skills,* 1974, *38,* 1331–1334.

Wiig, E. H., & Semel, E. M. *Language production deficits in learning disabled adolescents.* Paper presented at the Second International Scientific Conference on Learning Disabilities, Brussels, Belgium, January 1975.

Williams, F., & Wood, B. S. Negro children's speech: Some social class differences in word predictability. *Language and Speech,* 1970, *13,* 141–150.

Wilson, M. S. *The Wilson syntax program.* Cambridge, Mass.: Educators Publishing Service, 1972.

Ysseldyke, J. E. Diagnostic-prescriptive teaching: The search for aptitude-treatment interactions. In L. Mann & D. A. Sabatino (Eds.), *The first review of special education* (Vol. 1). Philadelphia: JSE Press, 1973.

Ysseldyke, J. E., & Salvia, J. Diagnostic-prescriptive teaching: Two models. *Exceptional Children,* 1974, *41,* 181–185.

CHAPTER 8

READING PROBLEMS

PATRICIA H. GILLESPIE
MERRILL C. SITKO

According to the literature, learning-disabled youngsters frequently have reading difficulties. Most often their reading problems have been characterized as symptoms of language or perceptual deficits, but reading difficulties have also been correlated with other symptoms sometimes found in the learning-disabled—symptoms such as memory problems.

As we consider in this chapter the reading characteristics of learning-disabled students, we should keep in mind certain persistent problems. Most of these will sound familiar to readers who have gone through this book chapter by chapter.

1. Though the reading achievements of learning-disabled elementary students receive much attention, those of learning-disabled adolescents are frequently neglected.

2. Criteria for the identification of learning-disabled students vary widely.

3. Investigators who have attempted to describe the reading characteristics of learning-disabled students often differ in their interpretation of the reading process.

4. Assessment instruments used to detect reading difficulties interpret the reading process differently, and they are of questionable validity and reliability.

5. The existing descriptions of reading characteristics of learning-disabled students are based mostly on clinical observations rather than on rigorous empirical evidence.

Differentiating the actual learning-disabled pupil (dyslexic, specific reading-disabled, and the like) from the student with a general reading difficulty has always been a problem for those involved in differential diagnosis and programming (Orlando, 1973). Not all reading failure has been attributed to specific learning disabilities.

Learning-disabled adolescents who exhibit severe reading disorders are often called dyslexic (Critchley, 1964; Johnson & Myklebust, 1965, 1967; Isom, 1969; Money, 1962; Samuels, 1973). Literally, the term *dyslexia* means the inability to cope with symbols or words. Among the characteristics ascribed to dyslexic adolescents are perceptual-motor problems, left-right confusion, memory problems, spelling difficulties, strephosymbolia (twisted symbols), and difficulties of heredity (Bannatyne, 1971; Hearns, 1969; Shedd, 1968).

170

There is no clear evidence that dyslexia, neurological impairment, and reading failure are directly related (Howard, 1969). Indeed, the issues are confused by the lack of a clear definition of the term *dyslexia*.

Satz and Sparrow (1970), in examining the problem of interpreting research studies on dyslexics, came to these conclusions:

> Much of our current confusion over this disorder is due to deficits in experimental design and methodology. Numerous studies have been based on heterogeneous clinic samples which comprise children from socially and educationally deprived areas, many of whom have neurologic abnormalities, sensory handicaps, emotional problems or even impaired intelligence. By definition, these studies are unrepresentative of developmental dyslexia.

■ READING MODELS ■

Because we feel that investigators of learning disabilities tend to neglect present theories in the reading field while trying to improve the reading of learning-disabled pupils, we are including a review of reading models. These differing interpretations are responsible for the multitude of approaches to reading education. Commenting on this situation, W. Blanton (1973) said:

> As a primary form of information processing in literate societies, reading is one of the more complex acts performed by man. Educators have been constantly challenged to explicate the reading process and to determine how reading skill is learned; and more recently, members of related disciplines have developed an interest in reading. Consequently, a great amount of information concerning reading has accumulated. One might expect that we have an adequate theory to explain how the complex process we call reading is either acquired or functions. This is not the case, however.

Williams (1973) classifies past and present theories of reading models as taxonomic models, psychometric models, psychological models, linguistic models, and information-processing models. Educators in learning disabilities have adopted several of these models. The taxonomic, psychometric, and psychological models are those most cited in clinical and empirical evidence of reading characteristics of learning-disabled adolescents.

TAXONOMIC MODELS

These models categorize reading skills according to word perception (pronunciation and meaning), comprehension, and assimilation of what is read. Many reading tests (for example, the Gray Oral Reading Test) and programs currently used with learning-disabled students reflect components of this model.

PSYCHOMETRIC MODELS

Psychometric models of reading attempt to identify variables and subvariables that contribute to deficiencies in reading comprehension. Williams said that the goal of this model was the determination of "the nature of the combination of the hierarchically organized subsystems that form a working system for attaining speed and power of reading." In this approach a set of variables thought to account for the reading deficiencies are selected from a theory or past research. A student's performance is then analyzed to determine which variables relate to the student's reading deficiency.

Much research has been conducted on variables such as language, auditory and visual discrimination, visual and auditory memory, auditory-visual integration, and intelligence and attention in order to determine the relationship between these variables and reading achievement (Birch & Belmont, 1964; Johnson & Myklebust, 1967; Kass, 1966; Money, 1962; Samuels, 1973; and Satz & Friel, 1974). In addition, patterns of performance of brain-injured and dyslexic children and youth on the WISC have been studied (Clements & Peters, 1962). The development of psychometric measures such as the ITPA and the Developmental Test of Visual Perception (Frostig & Horne, 1964) and the emphasis on perception, attention, memory, and other "reading correlates" comprise much of the research in reading and the learning-disabled.

Although many studies attempting to define correlates of reading do not use psychometric devices, they are similar to others in that they investigate variables and subvariables that may account for deficiencies in reading achievement. Such factors as experiential background, general health, visual and auditory defects, speech impairments, motor disturbances, intelligence, language skills, visual and auditory perception, perceptual-motor skills, and emotional and social adjustment have been related to reading achievement (Gillespie & Johnson, 1974).

172

Cited as possible causes or correlates of reading disability are poor memory (Kass, 1966); difficulty in integration of auditory and visual stimuli (Beery, 1967; Birch & Belmont, 1964); memory factors (Ellehammer, 1967; VandeVoort & Senf, 1973); attentional deficits (Lahaderne, 1968); sequencing difficulties (McLeod, 1967); language difficulties (Myklebust, 1973); and deficient information-organization processing (Senf, 1971).

Although much research has focused on causes of reading failure in children and adolescents, no results have been conclusive. Moreover, many studies of reading disability include variables that have little direct connection with the reading process per se. Samuels summarizes the shortcomings of the research:

Despite an impressive amount of research on causes of reading retardation, the bulk of the research fails to add up to much: (a) the research has been piecemeal in its approach rather than systematic; (b) the matched group designs generally used in these studies were inadequate; (c) the students were used for research after they had been identified as having a reading problem rather than before, thus masking what is cause and what is effect; (d) numerous studies have investigated variables which are not components of a learning model of reading acquisition; (e) diagnostic labels were used, implying that causes of the reading problem were known; and (f) sources of unreliability in achievement expectancy formulae, reading achievement tests, and intelligence tests have resulted in invalid research results and conclusions.

PSYCHOLOGICAL MODELS

Williams characterizes the psychological models as those that are influenced by psychologists interested in the reading process. She identifies these psychologists as Skinner (1957), Staats, Staats, Schultz, and Wolf (1962), and Gagné (1970) in the behavioral approaches category; Gibson (Gibson, Shurcliff, & Yonas, 1970) and Elkind (Elkind, Horn, & Schneider, 1965) in the cognitive category; and Venezky and Calfee (1970) in the information-processing category.

Briefly, behavioral psychologists view reading as operant learning with the reading response attached to specific textual cues. The strengthening of this association occurs via the mechanism of reinforcement (Bloom, 1973). Reinforcement includes discrimination training, in that specific verbal responses are reinforced as they occur with certain visual stimuli. Shaping is an integral part of the teaching of reading and writing in this approach.

Programmed reading and programmed tutoring incorporate these learning principles. Materials for special populations, including learning-disabled adolescents, use discrimination learning and reinforcement (Bijou and Associates, 1972; Fitzhugh & Fitzhugh, 1966; Woodcock, 1969; Woolman, 1966). The engineered classroom (Hewett, 1969) and environments established by Haring and Hauch (1969) have been used as vehicles for teaching learning-disabled children and youths to read.

According to Williams (1973), Gibson has developed an organized interpretation of reading that combines the elements of language (phonological, semantic, and syntactic) with the distinctive features of the graphic symbols. Students learn the shapes of the letters and use systematic scanning in an active process of comparing and selecting appropriate cues. In acquiring more cues, pupils inductively group them into larger units of information, which are then used in reading larger, more efficient units such as phrases. Rules of information are correspondents between graphemic and phonemic systems, rules of orthography (structural analysis), grammar, and meaning. Gibson recommends training in reading be within a rule-oriented framework.

Research in the distinctive features of letters offers much potential for the development of instructional strategies for problem readers. In a review of visual memory of poor and good readers, Samuels concludes that the superior visual memories of good readers result from their ability to attend to distinctive features and to encode them verbally. Gibson et al. (1962), Guralnick (1972), and Popp (1964) offer a means for analyzing the characteristics of letters that tend to confuse poor readers. Gibson's contribution to this area is unique because of her specificity of analysis of graphic forms.

Cognitive psychologist David Elkind (1967) uses a Piagetian approach in his developmental theory. Elkind emphasizes the perceptual components of reading that embody a logical operation—for example, the understanding of grammatical structures. As students mature, they are not dependent solely on the visual-perceptual aspects of reading. Elkind stresses sensory-motor methods in remediation that facilitate the internalized actions of perceptual activities.

In general, reading instruction for learning-disabled students has stressed the perceptual aspects of reading as well as sensory-motor training. Perhaps learning-disabled adolescents' apparent inability to perform visual-perceptual tasks can be explained in developmental terms: child attends to the perceptual rather than the cognitive tasks of reading, and perhaps this perceptual emphasis persists into the adolescent years of the learning-disabled pupil. A summary of Piaget's views of the development of mathematical concepts may hold true for the reading difficulties of some children and adolescents. According to Lovell (1966): "For Piaget, perceptions and associated images will not provide the concept of a group, because as we have seen, they are rigid, irreversible and cannot be arranged in various ways. Later, the child's thoughts will be more maneuverable or operational."

LINGUISTIC AND INFORMATION-PROCESSING MODELS

The information-processing models—called psychological models by Williams—are receiving much attention. Since many information models also include linguistic features, we are combining the information-processing and linguistic models for the purposes of this discussion.

Investigators in special education (Sabatino & Hayden, 1970; Van Meel, Vlek, & Bruijel, 1970) have come to relate information processing with reading, and tests such as the ITPA have been designed to incorporate measures of information processes. In addition, the ability of retarded students to organize verbal input for retrieval while reading has been explored by Bilsky and Evans (1970), L. Blanton (1974), and Evans (1970), and reviewed by L. Blanton, Sitko, and Gillespie (in press).

In their work in information processing, Venezky and Calfee (1970) describe input and output in terms of visual scanning: After scanning for large manageable units such as phrase boundaries, the pupil then decodes the phrase into smaller units. There is also an integration stage of syntactic semantic features. Similarly, Van Meel, Vlek, and Bruijel (1970) speculate that reading problems may result from incorrect, incomplete scanning procedures. They conclude that, as the complexity of visual discrimination tasks increases, the performance of learning-disabled students decreases.

Smith (1971) combines elements of language and information processing to explain the reading process. He describes the competent reader as one who tests features extending beyond the discrete visual features of the printed material. A reader need not attend to all the visual features; rather, the student must combine visual configuration and context. Syntactic and semantic redundancies in word sequences are used to find meaning. The reader moves directly from visual features to meaning, by simultaneously combining information from surface and deeper structures of the language with visual features of the words. This sampling of visual features allows the student to select the correct response, as syntax, or surface meaning, serves as a cue to the deep structure of the printed material.

Smith describes poor readers as those who are not able to use fully the syntactic and semantic redundancy of the material. They may require a maximum of visual information to obtain meaning from surface structure. This procedure may hinder comprehension and tax the pupils' short-term memories.

Ryan and Semmel (1969) emphasize the importance of language-processing strategies in reading. They contend that reading is a "constructive active process in which the reader uses his cognitive and linguistic knowledge to reproduce a probable utterance from a careful sampling of cues, then matches that prediction for appropriateness." Emphasis is on "conceptual" aspects of reading more than on units or single words.

The role of language processing in reading is described by Neisser (1967). Other aspects of linguistic features, including intonation (pitch, juncture, stress) of clauses and sentences, are stressed by Lefevre (1964).

Although K. S. Goodman is placed in the linguistic models category by Williams (1973), his views on reading are similar to those of information-processing theorists. For example, Goodman (1968) says that the reading process is a matter of recoding, decoding, and encoding. In recoding, the student merely "re-codes" graphic symbols into aural symbols. This does not mean that the student understands or "decodes" the graphic message. Encoding involves grasping meaning while reading orally. If students are deciphering the materials that they read silently, they must decode or obtain meaning and then encode meaning as oral output when asked to read orally.

K. S. Goodman (1972) calls reading a psycholinguistic guessing game that uses language cues selected from perceptual input. To read, a child must have language information that is encoded in graphic symbols. Goodman also designates "cue systems" that are necessary for the reader to understand written language. He considers "miscues" in oral reading important to the teacher because they provide information about the student's language skills. Cues may be based on (1) clues within written words; (2) the flow of the language in terms of operational (function) order, inflection or inflectional agreement, intonation or reference to what comes before or after the word in question; and (3) cues external to the language and the reader such as dialect and experiential and family background (1968). If error analysis of a student's reading miscues is qualitative rather than quantitative, the teacher can use oral reading as a means of assessing the language strategies that a student uses while reading.

The Reading Miscue Inventory developed by Goodman and Burke (1972) is one source for a qualitative analysis of a pupil's miscues. It can serve as a framework for the study of learning-disabled students' cueing systems. Levitt (1972) has conducted research on the qualitative differences of retarded children's reading responses as compared to those of competent readers. Similar research is needed in the field of learning disabilities.

In summary, although investigators have many interpretations of the reading process, an organized and integrated framework is appearing. According to W. Blanton (1973), future research will require a "commitment on the part of the reading researcher to long periods of investigation on carefully selected issues requiring up to ten years research to unravel."

■ ASSESSMENT IN READING ■

Investigators attempting to describe the reading attainment level and reading characteristics of learning-disabled students have many norm-referenced instruments from which to choose. (See Maurogenes, Winkley, Hanson, & Vacca, 1974, for a comprehensive list and description of reading tests on the secondary level.) There are, however, many shortcomings in reading tests. Several are criticized for their lack of validity and reliability for all levels of achievement (Lennon, 1967; Farr & Tuinman, 1972; Samuels, 1973). Others are questioned for not accounting for guess factors (Fry, 1971) and their lack of correlation with other reading tests; thus the diagnosis varies, depending on the test administered (Froese, 1971). Moreover, most of these tests adhere to a taxonomic model of reading in which the research reports the word recognition level, oral and silent reading level, listening comprehension, phonetic analysis, and measurement of reading rate, rather than reporting the strategies that the reader uses.

Scores from these reading tests are often used to identify students as learning-disabled. However, the many formulas that have been developed to determine the child's reading expectancy make this a questionable practice. Since a student's reading retardation depends upon the formula or procedure used (Reed, 1970; Simmons & Shapiro, 1968), a student may thus be classified learning-disabled in one study but not in another.

Recently, reading educators have developed criterion-referenced tests to assess reading skills. These tests are the outgrowth of a behavioristic task-analytic approach that emphasizes specific educational tasks (Bateman, 1966–1967; Prescott, 1971). Criterion-referenced tests do more than measure global skills as general reading level (Johnson & Kress, 1971); because the tests require specificity, students must make a careful analysis of tasks. Criterion-referenced testing is, however, not without flaws. According to Prescott (1971), one weak point of criterion-referenced assessment is the assumption that the skills to be measured can be placed in a hierarchy. This assumption creates a problem, since there is no clear empirical evidence that one uses a progression in learning to read.

Although criterion-referenced testing is more accurate than standardized tests (which measure a child's ability only in relation to that of another child), it still requires a "base of reference." Placing a test at a certain level implies that a specific response is expected from the child. Since the "correct" response is one that is considered "typical" for a certain age or capacity, norming is still involved. Nonetheless, criterion-referenced testing does hold promise for the development of instructional strategies for learning-disabled and retarded students (Gillespie & Johnson, 1974; Proger & Mann, 1973). If adopted, this approach to reading assessment will necessitate a great deal of planning and preparation.

■ READING CHARACTERISTICS OF ADOLESCENTS ■ WITH LEARNING DISABILITIES

The literature is full of studies concerning the characteristics of children labeled poor readers. In the few studies conducted on children and adolescents labeled learning-disabled, children are generally labeled dyslexic rather than learning-disabled. Some of these studies are reviewed here.

JOHNSON AND MYKLEBUST

Johnson and Myklebust (1965) investigated the reading characteristics of sixty dyslexics, aged seven to eighteen, who were referred to the Institute for Language Disorders because of school difficulties. These researchers defined dyslexia as part of a basic language disability more than as a reading disorder. Students who exhibited primary aphasic symptoms or who were slow learners were not included in the study. Twenty-four of the sixty subjects were adolescents. No control group was used. The mean intelligence quotient on the WISC or the WAIS was 103.9, and the range was 89 to 129. When tests for oral reading, reading vocabulary, and comprehension were made, the grades showed that reading quotients were substantially below average compared to the intelligence quotients.

Other tests administered were the Detroit Test of Learning Aptitude, an informal measure of memory, left-right orientation, body image and body concept, spelling measures, laterality, the EEG, and neurological examination. As a group, the dyslexics showed memory impairments as defined by the digit span subtest of the WISC and WAIS, the memory subtests of the Detroit Test of Learning Aptitude, and such informal measures as repeating in sequence the months of the year and the alphabet. Mental age scores, determined by drawing a human figure on the Goodenough Draw-a-Man Test, were below the chronological and mental age levels. Problems appeared with numerical symbols and positive funding of neurological dysfunction (90 percent of the cases). Parenthetically, abnormal EEG reading of dyslexic readers has been found by Ayres and Tarres (1967), Liberson (1966), and Vogel and Broverman (1964); however, the evidence that learning-disability and dyslexic readers have abnormal EEGs is not conclusive (Hartlage & Green, 1973; Koppitz, 1971).

179

In the Johnson and Myklebust study, the nature of the reading difficulties was presented case by case. Johnson and Myklebust observed such problems as auditorizing while reading, inability to distinguish differences in letter sounds of syllables, and difficulties in sound blending. They categorize three types of dyslexic readers: (1) visual dyslexics who have problems in discrimination of words and retaining visual images; (2) auditory dyslexics who have adequate visual skills but have problems with auditory discrimination blending and auditory memory; and (3) those dyslexics who have difficulty integrating auditory and visual stimuli.

BODER

Boder (1970) uses three similar characterizations of reading disorders. In studying dyslexics aged eight to eighteen, she noted three types of reading problems:

1. *Dysphonetic,* with the primary deficit in letter-sound integration and the inability to develop phonetic skills. Spellings are nonphonetic and unintelligible. Substitutions in reading include use of *funny* for *laugh, airplane* for *train.*

2. *Dyseidetic,* with primary deficit in the ability to perceive whole words as gestalts. Reading is by phonetics rather than by sight.

3. Combination of dysphonetic and dyseidetic. Boder describes this category as the most serious reading disorder.

NAIDOO

Naidoo (1972) divided ninety-eight specific dyslexic boys aged eight to thirteen into reading-retarded and spelling-retarded groups. A control group consisted of ninety-eight boys matched for age, types of school, and class background. Naidoo defined dyslexia as "a condition causing difficulty in learning to read and spell in physically normal intelligent children in spite of continuous schooling and in the absence of severe emotional problems."

Naidoo found that the dyslexic students were reading at least two years below their chronological age, while the control group was reading at grade level or above. (This finding is not surprising, since

Naidoo's students at the Word Blind Center had already been identified as having severe reading problems.) Scores from standardized word recognition and reading comprehension tests were obtained. Significant differences were found in reading accuracy, rate, word recognition and reading comprehension as measured by these tests. Sound blending of the reading retardates, as measured by an informal test, was found significantly below that of the control group. The majority of the dyslexic boys could not blend sounds until age eleven, while most of the control group had done this at age eight.

MYKLEBUST

Myklebust (1973) studied a group of students who had been classified by the schools as reading-disabled and placed in remedial reading classes. A control group was selected from the same schools. Age ranges were divided into groups with two-year intervals: seven, nine, eleven, thirteen, and fifteen years. Students below age eight were not found in remedial reading classes, and the majority in these classes were between the ages of eleven and thirteen. The fifteen-year-olds were inferior to the control groups on cognitive ability, as measured by the Primary Mental Abilities Test and the Draw-a-Man Test.

Students who had reading difficulties scored lowest on the subtests requiring verbal ability, but scores were better, within normal limits, on several of the nonverbal tasks. As compared to the normal students, the reading-disabled students generally scored lower as they became older. Myklebust attributes this to the students' inability to achieve at the normal rate; he does not see it as a reflection of their reading potential. This lack of achievement is frequently reflected as a negative correlation between age and reading scores. Both groups showed a plateau at age thirteen on auditory receptive language. Poor readers achieved a level of function at thirteen years; normal readers, at nine years.

Test II matched auditory instruction to instructions on the printed page. Rate of gain on the test at the two-year interval exceeded that of controls, and, by age fifteen, rate corresponded to the normals. Fifteen-year-olds who were reading-disabled were like eleven-year-old normal readers in ability to comprehend instruction auditorially and to relate it to reading. The reading-disabled group was from three to four years below the average in auditory reception.

On auditory expression, the reading-disabled were three to four years below normal in their ability to give opposites. Fifteen-year-olds had obtained a level of auditory expressive language equivalent to that of a nine-year-old. They were also deficient in the definition of words and reached a plateau in this skill at age thirteen.

Eleven- and thirteen-year-olds scored half of the average on word recognition as measured by the Columbia Vocabulary Test; fifteen-year-olds were one-third the average. The reading-disabled did not make expected gains as they grew older. Myklebust drew these conclusions:

Their inferiority is revealed further in that at fifteen years of age their capability was at third-to-fourth grade level. Characteristic of children with reading disability, they did not make the expected gains as they became older. It is not uncommon to find poor readers who evidence greater retardation year by year. Nevertheless, this group showed advancement from eleven to thirteen, but at a rate below that of the control group. They made no gains from thirteen to fifteen years, whereas the normals advance rapidly during this age.

■ FOLLOW-UP STUDIES OF LEARNING-DISABLED ■ READERS

While Myklebust's findings on the reading gains of disabled readers have been observed by other special educators as well, the prognosis for learning-disabled readers is not clearly established.

HERJANIC AND PENICK

Herjanic and Penick (1972) reviewed the "history of childhood reading disorders" and noted that few studies have been conducted to determine the long-term effects of reading retardation. Further, they criticize the few available studies for their disregard of IQ, race, SES, and emotional problems. The authors concluded that the results vary to the extent that no definitive conclusions can be drawn as to the achievement patterns of adult dyslexics. (See Herjanic & Penick, 1972, for a thorough summary of the studies that include follow-up of students labeled dyslexic.)

182

KOPPITZ

Koppitz (1971) conducted a follow-up study of learning-disabled students ranging in age from eleven to eighteen. The youngsters had been enrolled in a public school learning-disabilities program. Although the follow-up did not continue into adult life, it is still valuable because of its implications for placement and programming for the learning-disabled. The students entered the program during a four-year span, and, when possible, they were studied for five years following admission. The entire study covers a period of eight years.

Koppitz defined learning-disabled students as those who (1) demonstrate an achievement more than one year below their mental age, and (2) though possessing normal intellectual potential and no gross motor impairment, cannot profit from attendance in a regular public school class. The term did not indicate any specific underlying etiology, but Koppitz concluded that observed learning problems were primarily the result of some degree of "brain dysfunction."

In summary, Koppitz stated that, before learning-disabled students age nine or older can succeed in a regular class, they should be able to read at least at the level of fourth or fifth grade. She stated:

The findings of the follow-up study convinced me that a child who is still reading at the preprimer or primer level at age ten or eleven will not become a fluent reader by the age sixteen. Chances are he will never progress far beyond the second or third grade reading level, if that far.

She found that learning-disabled pupils who were returned to regular classes were, from the beginning, better readers than were the long-term learning-disabled. In addition to their differing reading achievement, learning-disabled students exhibited varying degrees of learning and behavior disorders. Koppitz found that learning-disabled pupils were more often referred to the learning-disabilities program for behavior problems than for reading problems; that older learning-disabled children had reported soft neurological signs when they were younger but that these seemed to disappear as they got older; that, overall, student EEGs did not show abnormalities; and that those learning-disabled children who were able to profit from the regular class had parents who were "interested, cooperative, and supportive." Those who did not profit from learning-disabled classes or who were referred for residential treatment often came from unstable or deprived homes.

MUEHL AND FORELL

Muehl and Forell (1973) conducted a follow-up study of disabled readers who had been referred to a reading clinic five years before. Classifying the poor readers according to their performance on the EEG, they designate three groups: (1) normal EEGs; (2) abnormal EEGs with fourteen- and six-per-second positive spike pattern (PSP) (related to severe behavior disorders and lack of impulse control by some investigators, for example, Freeman, 1971); and (3) abnormal EEGs other than the fourteen and six PSP. After five years, no significant relationship was found between EEG findings and reading achievement, although the reading performance of the third group tended to be better than that of the other two groups.

The subjects took both the Iowa Tests of Educational Development (ITED) and reading tests dealing with materials in social studies, natural sciences, and literature. The results of the reading tests showed that only two of the subjects had reading scores above the fifteenth percentile; five students had dropped out of high school (four of these were described as having severe reading retardation); and twelve were in college. Muehl and Forell concluded that poor readers in elementary and junior high, as a group, continue to be poor readers in high school. The better group of readers in their study had higher IQs, were younger when first referred for remedial reading, had spent more time in clinical instruction, and had professional or white-collar parents who sought early help for their children.

Similarly, other follow-up studies of dyslexics have concluded that specific reading retardation tends to be a persistent handicap (Rutter & Yule, 1975).

■ INSTRUCTIONAL STRATEGIES IN READING ■
FOR THE LEARNING-DISABLED

Special educators have assumed that adolescents designated dyslexic, minimally brain-injured, or learning-disabled need differential programming to learn to read. Many remedial reading programs have been developed for such special populations. (See Bannatyne, 1968; Fernald, 1943; Fitzhugh & Fitzhugh, 1966; Gillingham & Stillman, 1965; Heckelman, 1969; Hegge, Kirk, & Kirk, 1955; Hillis, 1971.)

Other programs used with learning-disabled children are Distar (Engelmann & Bruner, 1969); Words in Color (Gattegno, 1962); programmed readers (Buchannon & Sullivan Associates, 1963); readers not employing traditional orthography, such as the Peabody Rebus Reading Program (Woodcock & Clark, 1969) and the initial Reading Alphabet (ITA) (Downing, 1967); and such special approaches as language experience (Lee & Allen, 1963) and organic reading (Fries, Fries, Wilson, & Rudolph, 1966). Howard (1969) characterized corrective reading programs used with young and adolescent dyslexics as those with large doses of isolated letter phonics and exercises in perceptual-motor development and tactile-kinesthetic exercises.

Some educators note that the methods used with learning-disabled students appear no different from those used with other students (Lerner, 1969). These authors observe that while instruction in reading for learning-disabled children and adolescents includes instruction in word recognition and comprehension, it differs from typical remedial reading practices. Remedial reading contains more instruction in the area of the reading correlates based upon the ITPA or Peabody Language Development Kits (Dunn & Smith, 1965, 1966, 1967; Dunn, Horton, & Smith, 1968), perceptual-motor skills based upon Kephart's program (1971), visual-perceptual training (as in the Frostig & Horne Program in Visual Perception, 1964), and auditory perception programs such as the Auditory Conceptualization Test (LAC Test; Lindamood & Lindamood, 1971). These programs, typically used with younger students, are also used in remedial programs for adolescents, especially the perceptual-motor training exercises (Howard, 1969). This training assumes that the relationships between these skills and reading are causal, and that enhancement in these areas will increase reading achievement; but the relationship between training and reading achievement is still not definite (Allen, Dickman, & Haught, 1966; Balow, 1971; Black, 1974; Buckland & Balow, 1973; Gillespie & Johnson, 1974; Hammill, Goodman, & Wiederholt, 1974; Hammill & Larson, 1974; Hammill & Wiederholt, 1973; Keough, 1974; Samuels, 1973; Sedlack & Weener, 1973).

Moreover, the assumption that special populations read differently or require reading instruction different from other readers has not been clearly established (Gillespie & Johnson, 1974). Orlando (1973) states that the research is inconclusive and negligible. Reed, Rabe, and Mankinen (1971), in reviewing the effectiveness of reading instruction for brain-injured children, conclude that there is little evidence to suggest that teaching procedures for these children should differ significantly from those for other children with reading problems. Further, the research literature offers little to support the superiority of one method of teaching reading over another (L. Blanton, Sitko, & Gillespie, in press; Bond & Dykstra, 1967; Cawley, Goodstein, & Burrow, 1972; Gillespie & Johnson, 1974).

Generally, gain-score studies have been used to determine the superiority of one method over another in teaching students with similar characteristics. Designs are used in which deficits are presumed for an entire group of students, and special and traditional programs are compared (Ysseldyke, 1973). According to Ysseldyke, this type of research has been criticized for various reasons: a failure to consider the Hawthorne effect, inadequate controls, regression effects, linearity across different levels, and lack of reliability among diagnostic devices. The homogeneity among populations that this research assumes has not been found among learning-disabled students. In addition, this approach does not necessarily provide information that will be beneficial to the teacher, since it is difficult to define just how one approach is different from another. Most methods contain such similar elements as the teaching of the alphabet, comprehension, structural analysis, or word recognition. Moreover, comparison studies do not reveal the strong or weak points of a particular program (Engelmann, 1967).

Some developers of instructional strategies for learning-disabled students emphasize teaching to the strengths (Johnson & Myklebust, 1967). Others stress teaching toward the weaknesses (Bannatyne, 1971). Multisensory training (Fernald, 1943; Gillingham & Stillman, 1965) is advocated by some clinicians, as is training toward intact modalities. Johnson and Myklebust, in particular, contend that some learning-disabled students can be overloaded with stimuli if multisensory techniques are used.

The efficacy of modality training with normal and poor readers (designating children as visual, auditory, or tactile-kinesthetic learners and then teaching toward the preferred modality) has been studied (W. Blanton, 1971; Waugh, 1973). The results show a lack of evidence for the effectiveness of modality preference training.

For a thorough discussion of reading approaches that have been used with learning-disabled students, including ones stressing modality preference, see Gearheart (1973) and Gillespie and Johnson (1974).

DIAGNOSTIC-PRESCRIPTIVE APPROACHES

Recognizing that individual students in special-education classes have different needs (Kirk & Kirk, 1971), some professionals are developing techniques based on the most effective strategies for "specific variables believed to be related to academic learning" (Ysseldyke & Salvia, 1974). However, in a review of diagnostic-prescriptive training programs (Ysseldyke, 1973), little empirical support was found for the diagnostic-prescriptive approach.

According to Ysseldyke, the use of correlational and gain-score results to determine differential instruction is an inadequate technique. He states that aptitude treatment research is appropriate in investigations of diagnostic-prescriptive programs, but he concludes "that very little research in special education has employed aptitude-treatment interaction designs." Those studies that have used the method have failed to demonstrate significant treatment interactions. Reasons for some of the failure to demonstrate significant treatment interactions between personological variables and instructional strategies include lack of valid, reliable, and educationally relevant instruments.

Ysseldyke and Salvia noted that effective diagnostic-prescriptive teaching depends on four critical assumptions:

1. Children enter a teaching situation with strengths and weaknesses.

2. These strengths and weaknesses can be reliably and validly assessed.

3. These strengths and weaknesses are causally related to the acquisition of skills.

4. There are well-identified links between the child's strengths and weaknesses and the relative effectiveness of the instruction.

Ysseldyke and Salvia question the empirical support for all four underlying assumptions in education of handicapped children. (These assumptions are discussed elsewhere in this chapter.) Such reading programs for the learning-disabled are based upon the skills measured in the ITPA and the DTVP.

TASK ANALYSIS

Ysseldyke and Salvia describe the task-analysis model of instruction as one which places emphasis

on observed inter- and intra-individual differences in skill development. Assessment of strengths and weaknesses within this model is restricted to evaluation of the child's position on skill continuance. Emphasis is placed on the child's current level of skill development, the next skill to be mastered, and the behavioral components of that next skill.

According to Lerner (1975), task analysis is used in the field of learning disabilities to determine the processing abilities required of the individual. On the other hand, she states that task analysis in reading involves analysis of the task itself. If this is the case, problems occur within both approaches. First, the underlying processes necessary for reading achievement have not been clearly established. For example, a learning-disabilities specialist may conduct a task analysis of visual-perceptual tasks to train areas that have not been established as ones that will directly enhance reading achievement. Second, a hierarchy of reading progression and subtasks needed for competence in reading remains to be clearly demonstrated. Many task analyses of reading skills tend to be in areas that reflect taxonomical models of reading instruction (word recognition, phonetic approach, and structural analysis skills). Such an approach may encourage training in isolated word-attack skills simply because they are the easiest to analyze according to subtasks with a certain amount of face validity, for example, word recognition and phonetic analyses.

Perhaps more extensive investigations of the reading process will enable educators to develop adequate task-analytic approaches that can transfer more readily into instructional strategies.

READING INSTRUCTION GEARED SPECIFICALLY TO LEARNING-DISABLED ADOLESCENTS

Most of the literature concerning learning disabilities emphasizes early identification and intervention, yet many students who receive early remedial instruction still have reading difficulties in secondary school. According to Wepman et al. (1975), intervention for learning-disabled students over age twelve should be compensatory rather than developmental. Learning-disabled adolescents should be taught to utilize their best skills to meet the academic requirements of the secondary school.

More attention is now focusing on programming basic skills for learning-disabled adolescents and adults (Bailey, 1975; Giles, 1975). Suggested methods of working with this population include the use of high interest–low vocabulary materials, development of study skills, and variety of presentation, such as films and cassettes on the secondary and college level.

As interest in developing reading strategies for learning-disabled adolescents increases, we fear the promulgation of materials and programs that have not been carefully validated for use with adolescents. The adoption or adaptation of assessment techniques and instructional strategies that have had questionable efficacy with younger learning-disabled students is no answer to meeting the needs of older students who have reading problems. More analysis—both of the reading characteristics of learning-disabled adolescents and of the requirements of secondary curricula—is needed before programming can be truly effective.

■ CONCLUSIONS ■

The conclusions of the preceding review of the research concerning the reading difficulties of learning-disabled adolescents are as follows:

Ascribing specific reading characteristics to adolescents classified as learning-disabled is difficult because of the many interpretations of learning disabilities, dyslexia, minimal brain damage, and the like. Definitional confusions and varying identification procedures are reflected in the heterogeneity that exists in groups designated as learning-disabled. Researchers in reading and other disciplines define the reading process in different ways, and research in learning disabilities reflects these various interpretations. Most past research depicted a simplistic view of the reading process, and many investigations dealt with reading correlates rather than with the reading process itself.

Assessment techniques in reading, for the most part, lack validity, reliability, and true diagnostic value. Quantitative rather than qualitative differences are most often measured by these tests.

Clinical and empirical data indicate that "learning-disabled adolescents" possess reading characteristics that are similar to younger students with learning disabilities. Difficulties in basic sight vocabulary, reading comprehension, rate of reading, auditory and visual discrimination difficulties, and sequencing of letters are examples of these difficulties.

Few follow-up studies have been conducted concerning the long-term effect of reading programming for learning-disabled elementary students or of the problems accrued by adolescents and adults with reading disorders. What studies exist indicate that reading problems tend to persist into adolescence and adult life. In addition, the younger the student at the time of intervention, the more successful the programming; and the less severe the reading problem(s), the more chance there is for success in the secondary special education program or regular class.

Reading programs are more fully developed on the elementary level, but attention is now focusing on the reading and learning problems of learning-disabled adolescents. Moreover, those special and regular educators who are developing effective instructional strategies on the secondary level are faced with the critical lack of carefully validated programming developed for younger learning-disabled.

Two critical issues should be addressed in programming for learning-disabled adolescents. First, more research should be focused on the current theories in the field of reading. The lack of specificity of the research describing the reading characteristics of normal and inadequate readers is apparent. Most often, because of the utilization of a taxonomic model of reading, investigators who have studied the characteristics of poor readers have reported only reading levels and a few clinical observations of oral reading errors. More studies dealing with involvement of linguistic and information processing skills in the reading process should be conducted.

Most promising is the research conducted by Levitt (1972), Blanton et al. (1974), and Bilsky and Evans (1970) with poor readers in exceptional populations. Research conducted by K. Goodman (1965, 1968, 1972), Venezky and Calfee (1970), Smith (1971), Elkind et al. (1965), and Gibson et al. (1970) seems to have promise in determining reading characteristics of learning-disabled adolescents.

If educators are to consider the individual reading needs of learning-disabled students, a reorientation in research methodology, programming, and teaching training must occur. Rather than attempting to isolate or ameliorate various deficits using generic intervention programs, it seems more feasible to conduct task analyses of students' behaviors in learning to read. Reading approaches used in classes for the learning-disabled often employ phonics or whole word approaches that consider the word as the basic unit of reading. These methods neither attend to the communicative nature of reading nor address themselves to the relevance of linguistic context—particularly to semantic and syntactic relationships in sentence structure in determining word perception and comprehension. Reading investigators must develop training techniques that enhance the ability of learning-disabled students to attend and utilize relevant linguistic strategies that take advantage of the basic structures of the materials themselves.

Second, students classified as learning-disabled tend to exhibit a wide range of abilities and disabilities. The heterogeneity of a supposedly homogeneous population has been cited countless times in the literature. Although researchers may be able to identify the learning-disabled with similar clusters of characteristics (McCarthy, 1975), the development of instructional programming necessitates focusing on the individual and situation-specific assessment rather than merely determining general clusters of behavior. Particular reading difficulties may be remediated by specific instructional strategies, but this may not be the case with every adolescent possessing that particular reading characteristic. Motivational factors, the influence of previous instruction, and the nature of the course content will influence the efficacy of the intervention.

Because of the many variables involved in establishing programs for learning-disabled adolescents, we have proposed a decision-making model for programming (Gillespie & Sitko, 1974). Major stages of the model are assessment, implementation, and evaluation. In assessment the teacher establishes the instructional needs of the students by gathering data from a variety of sources (pupil records, information from resource personnel, and classroom information). The classroom information should be used primarily for establishing instructional objectives. In planning a program for adolescents, the teacher must conduct a task analysis of the reading materials and strategies available and a learner analysis of the adolescent. There should be a match between the cognitive demands of the approach and the learning characteristics of the student. All programs established should consider as much data as possible, including the teacher's preferred teaching style and the characteristics of the influence of other pupils in the classroom. Instructional needs should be considered tentative by the teacher. Diagnostic teaching lessons should serve as trial lessons. Data gathering should continue during this process. All instruction should be part of assessment; hence, lessons are part of the continual and ongoing assessment of instructional needs. Evaluation should be in terms of effectiveness of the teacher and the gains of the pupil. The teacher needs to evaluate his or her effectiveness in implementing and monitoring instructional programs. Concise objectives for the students are equally important in evaluating their progress.

■ REFERENCES ■

Adams, R. B. Dyslexia: A discussion of its definition. *Journal of Learning Disabilities,* 1969, *2,* 616–633.

Allen, R. M., Dickman, I., & Haught, R. A pilot study of the immediate effectiveness of the Frostig-Horne training program with educable retardates. *Exceptional Children,* 1966, *31,* 41.

Ashton-Warner, S. *Teacher.* New York: Bantam Books, 1963.

Ayres, F. W., & Tarres, F. The incidence of EEG abnormality in a dyslexic and control group. *Journal of Clinical Psychology,* 1967, *23,* 334–336.

Bachmann, R. Uber Kongenitale Worblendhict (angeborene Lesichwache). *Neur. Psych. Grenzgeh.,* 1927, *40,* 1–72. As cited by D. M. Critchley, *Developmental dyslexia.* Springfield, Ill.: Charles C Thomas, 1964.

Bailey, E. J. *Academic activities for adolescents with learning disabilities.* Evergreen, Colo.: Learning Pathways, 1975.

Balow, B. Perceptual-motor activities in the treatment of severe reading disabilities. *The Reading Teacher,* 1971, *24,* 513–525; 542.

Bannatyne, A. *Psycholinguistic color system: A reading, writing, spelling, and language program.* Urbana, Ill.: Learning Systems Press, 1968.

Bannatyne, A. *Language, reading, and learning disabilities.* Springfield, Ill.: Charles C Thomas, 1971.

Bateman, B. Three approaches to diagnosis for children with learning disabilities. *Academic Therapy,* 1966–1967, *2,* 215–222.

Beery, Keith C. *Visual motor integration.* Chicago: Follett, 1967. (Monograph)

Bijou, S. W., et al. *The Edmark reading program*. Seattle: Edmark Associates, 1972.

Bilsky, L., & Evans, R. A. Use of associative clustering techniques in the study of reading disability: Effects of list organization. *American Journal of Mental Deficiency*, 1970, 74, 771–776.

Birch, H. G., & Belmont, L. Auditory-visual integration in normal and retarded readers. *American Journal of Orthopsychiatry*, 1964, 34, 852–861.

Black, F. W. Achievement test performance of high and low perceiving learning disabled children. *Journal of Learning Disabilities*, 1974, 7, 60–69.

Blanton, L. *The relationship of organizational abilities to the comprehension of connected discourse in educable mentally retarded and nonretarded children*. Unpublished doctoral dissertation, Indiana University, 1974.

Blanton, L., Sitko, M., & Gillespie, P. Reading and the mildly retarded: Review of research and implications. (In press.)

Blanton, W. Eric Crier: Review of modality research. *The Reading Teacher*, 1971, 25, 83–89.

Blanton, W. Guest editorial: Targeted Research and Developmental Program on Reading as an answer to problems of reading, behavior research, and a basis for future directions. *Reading Research Quarterly*, 1973, 8, 115–120.

Blanton, W. E., Farr, R. E., & Tuinman, J. J. (Eds.). *Measuring reading performance*. Newark, Del.: International Reading Association, 1974.

Bloom, R. D. Learning to read: An operant perspective. *Reading Research Quarterly*, 1973, 8, 147–166.

Boder, E. Developmental dyslexia. *Journal of School Health*, 1970, 40, 289–290.

Bond, G., & Dykstra, R. The cooperative research program in first-grade reading instruction. *Reading Research Quarterly*, 1967, 2, 125–126.

Bryant, N. D. Some principles of remedial instruction for dyslexia. In W. Otto & K. Koenke (Eds.), *Remedial teaching: Research and comment*. Boston: Houghton Mifflin, 1969.

Buchannon, C. D., & Sullivan Associates. *Sullivan programmed readers*. New York: McGraw-Hill, 1963.

Buckland, P., & Balow, B. The effect of visual perception training on reading achievement. *Exceptional Children*, 1973, 39, 299–304.

Burke, C. L., & Goodman, K. S. *Theoretically based studies of patterns of miscues in oral reading performance. Final report*. Detroit: Wayne State University, 1973. (ED 079 708)

Carner, R. L. The adult dyslexic—Dilemma and challenge. In G. Spache (Ed.), *Reading disability and perception.* Newark, Del.: International Reading Association, 1969.

Cawley, J., Goodstein, H. A., & Burrow, W. H. *The slow learner and the reading problem.* Springfield, Ill.: Charles C Thomas, 1972.

Clements, S. D., & Peters, J. E. Minimal brain dysfunction in the school-age child. *Archives of General Psychiatry,* 1962, *6,* 185–197.

Critchley, M. *Developmental Dyslexia.* Springfield, Ill.: Charles C Thomas, 1964.

Downing, J. A. ESA school teachers assess i.t.a. *Special Education,* 1967, *56,* 12–16.

Dunn, L. M., & Smith, J. (Eds.). *Peabody language development kit: Level number 1.* Circle Pines, Minn.: American Guidance Service, 1965.

Dunn, L. M., & Smith, J. (Eds.). *Peabody language development kit: Level number 2.* Circle Pines, Minn.: American Guidance Service, 1966.

Dunn, L. M., & Smith, J. (Eds.). *Peabody language development kit: Level number 3.* Circle Pines, Minn.: American Guidance Service, 1967.

Dunn, L. M., Horton, R. B., & Smith, J. O. *Peabody language development kit: Level P.* Circle Pines, Minn.: American Guidance Service, 1968.

Elkind, D. Piaget's theory of perceptual development: Its application to reading and special education. *Journal of Special Education,* 1967, *1,* 357–361.

Elkind, D., Horn, J., & Schneider, G. Modified word recognition, reading achievement, and perception de-centralization. *Journal of Genetic Psychology,* 1965, *107,* 235–251.

Ellehammer, M. Assessment progress in reading. In M. D. Jenkinson (Ed.), *Reading instruction: An interdisciplinary forum proceedings of international reading* (Vol. 1). Proceedings of International Reading Association World Conference on Reading, 1967.

Englemann, S. Teaching reading to children with low mental age. *Education and Training of the Mentally Retarded,* 1967, *2,* 193–201.

Englemann, S., & Bruner, E. C. *Distar reading: An instructional system.* Chicago: Science Research Associates, 1969.

Evans, R. A. Use of the associative clustering technique in the study of reading disability: Effects of presentation mode. *American Journal of Mental Deficiency,* 1970, *74,* 765–770.

Farr, R., & Tuinman, J. The dependent variable: Measurement issues in reading research. *Reading Research Quarterly,* 1972, *7,* 418–423.

Fernald, G. *Remedial techniques in basic school subjects.* New York: McGraw-Hill, 1943.

Fitzhugh, K., & Fitzhugh, L. *The Fitzhugh plus program.* Galen, Mich.: Allied Education Council, 1966.

Freeman, R. D. Special education and the electroencephalogram: Marriage of convenience. In D. Hammill & N. Bartel (Eds.), *Educational perspectives in learning disabilities.* New York: Wiley, 1971.

Fries, C. C., Fries, A. C., Wilson, R., & Rudolph, M. *Merrill linguistic readers.* Columbus, Ohio: Charles E. Merrill, 1966.

Froese, V. Word recognition tests: Are they useful beyond grade three? *The Reading Teacher,* 1971, *24,* 432–438.

Frostig, M., & Horne, D. *The Frostig program for the development of visual perception.* Chicago: Follett, 1964.

Fry, E. The orangutang score. *The Reading Teacher,* 1971, *24,* 360–361.

Gagné, R. M. *The conditions of learning* (2nd ed.). New York: Holt, Rinehart and Winston, 1970.

Gallagher, J. R. Specific language disability (dyslexia). In W. Otto & K. Koenke (Eds.), *Remedial teaching: Research and comment.* Boston: Houghton Mifflin, 1969.

Gattegno, C. *Words in color.* Chicago: Learning Materials, 1962.

Gearheart, B. R. *Learning disabilities: Educational strategies.* St. Louis: C. V. Mosby, 1973.

Gibson, E. J., Gibson, J. J., Pick, A. D., & Osser, H. A. A developmental study of the perception of letter-like forms. *Journal of Comparative and Physiological Psychology,* 1962, *55,* 897–906.

Gibson, E. J., Shurcliff, R., & Yonas, A. Utilization of spelling patterns by deaf and hearing subjects. In H. Levin & J. P. Williams (Eds.), *Basic studies on reading.* New York: Basic Books, 1970.

Giles, M. T. *Adolescent screening instrument.* Evergreen, Colo.: Learning Pathways, Inc., 1975.

Gillespie, P. H., & Johnson, L. *Teaching reading to the mildly retarded child.* Columbus, Ohio: Charles E. Merrill, 1974.

Gillespie, P. H., & Sitko, M. C. A decision-making model for training pre-service teachers in diagnostic-prescriptive teaching. Bloomington: Indiana University, Center for Innovation in Teaching the Handicapped, 1974.

Gillingham, A., & Stillman, B. *Remedial work for reading, spelling, and penmanship* (7th ed.). Cambridge, Mass.: Education Publishing Service, 1965.

Goodman, K. S. Reading: A linguistic study of cues and miscues in reading. *Elementary English Review*, 1965, *42*, 639–643.

Goodman, K. S. (Ed.). *The psycholinguistic notion of the reading process.* Detroit: Wayne State University Press, 1968.

Goodman, K. S. Reading: A psycholinguistic guessing game. In K. S. Goodman (Ed.), *Individualized instruction: A reader.* New York: Holt, Rinehart and Winston, 1972.

Goodman, Y. M., & Burke, C. L. *Reading miscue inventory.* New York: Macmillan, 1972.

Guralnick, M. Alphabet discrimination and distinction test: Research and educational implications. *Journal of Learning Disabilities,* 1972, *5*, 428–438.

Hammill, D., Goodman, L., & Wiederholt, J. L. Visual-motor process: Can we train them? *The Reading Teacher,* 1974, *27*, 469–481.

Hammill, D., & Larson, S. The effectiveness of psycholinguistic training. *Exceptional Children,* 1974, *41*, 5–14.

Hammill, D., & Wiederholt, J. L. Review of the Frostig visual perception test and the related training program. In L. Mann & D. A. Sabatino (Eds.), *The first review of special education.* Philadelphia: JSE Press, 1973.

Haring, N., & Hauch, M. A. Improving learning conditions in the establishment of reading skills with disabled readers. *Exceptional Children,* 1969, *35*, 341–352.

Hartlage, L. C., & Green, J. B. The EEG as a predictor of intellectual and academic performance. *Journal of Learning Disabilities,* 1973, *6*, 239–242.

Hearns, R. S. Dyslexia and handwriting. *Journal of Learning Disabilities,* 1969, *2*, 25–26.

Heckelman, R. G. The neurological impress methods of remedial reading instruction. *Academic Therapy,* 1969, *4*, 277–282.

Hegge, R. C., Kirk, S. A., & Kirk, W. P. *Remedial reading drills.* Ann Arbor, Mich.: George Wohr, 1955.

Herjanic, B. M., & Penick, E. Adult outcomes of disabled child readers. *Journal of Special Education,* 1972, *6*, 397–410.

Hewett, F. *The emotionally disturbed child in the classroom.* Boston: Allyn and Bacon, 1969.

Hillis, V. The multisensory linguistic approach: The key to language problems. *Reading Newsreport,* 1971, *6*, 18–26.

Howard, M. An interpretation of dyslexia: An educator's viewpoint. In G. Spache (Ed.), *Reading disability and perception.* Newark, Del.: International Reading Association, 1969.

Isom, J. B. An interpretation of dyslexia: A medical viewpoint. In G. Spache (Ed.), *Reading disability and perception*. Newark, Del.: International Reading Association, 1969.

Johnson, D. G., & Myklebust, H. R. Dyslexia in childhood. In J. Hellmuth (Ed.), *Learning disorders* (Vol. 1). Seattle: Special Child Publications, 1965.

Johnson, D. G., & Myklebust, H. R. *Learning disabilities: Educational principles and practices*. New York: Grune & Stratton, 1967.

Johnson, M. S., & Kress, R. A. Task analysis for criterion-referenced tests. *The Reading Teacher*, 1971, *24*, 355–359.

Kass, C. E. Psycholinguistic disabilities of children with reading problems. *Exceptional Children*, 1966, *32*, 533–539.

Keough, B. K. Optometric vision training programs for children with learning disabilities: Review of issues and research. *Journal of Learning Disabilities*, 1974, *7*, 219–229.

Kephart, N. C. *The slow learner in the classroom* (2nd ed.). Columbus, Ohio: Charles E. Merrill, 1971.

Kirk, S., & Kirk, W. *Psycholinguistic learning disabilities: Diagnosis and remediation*. Urbana: University of Illinois Press, 1971.

Koppitz, E. M. *Children with learning disabilities: A five year follow-up study*. New York: Grune & Stratton, 1971.

Lahaderne, H. M. Attitudinal and intellectual correlates of attention: A study of four sixth-grade classrooms. *Journal of Educational Psychology*, 1968, *59*, 320–324.

Lee, D., & Allen, R. V. *Learning to read through experience* (2nd ed.). New York: Appleton-Century-Crofts, 1963.

Lefcvre, C. A. *Linguistics and the teaching of reading*. New York: McGraw-Hill, 1964.

Lennon, R. T. What can be measured? In L. Hafner (Ed.), *Improving reading in secondary schools: Selected readings*. New York: Macmillan, 1967.

Lerner, J. W. Dyslexia or reading disability: A thorn by any name. In *Selected papers of learning disabilities: Progress in parent information, professional growth, and public policy*. Proceedings of Sixth Annual Conference, Association for Children with Learning Disabilities, Pittsburgh, Pennsylvania, 1969.

Lerner, J. W. Two perspectives: Reading and learning disabilities. In S. A. Kirk & J. M. McCarthy (Eds.), *Learning disabilities: Selected ACLD papers*. Boston: Houghton Mifflin, 1975.

Levitt, E. Higher-order and lower-order reading responses of mentally retarded and nonretarded children at the first grade level. *American Journal of Mental Deficiency*, 1972, 77, 13–20.

Liberson, W. T. EEG and intelligence. *Proceedings of the American Psychological Association*, 1966, 56, 514–543.

Lindamood, C., & Lindamood, P. *Lindamood auditory conceptualization test (LAC)*. Boston: Teaching Resources, 1971.

Lovell, K. *The growth of basic mathematical and scientific concepts in children*. London: University of London Press, 1966.

Maurogenes, N. A., Winkley, C., Hanson, E., & Vacca, R. I. Concise guide to standardized secondary and college reading tests. *Journal of Reading*, 1974, *18*, 12–22.

McCarthy, J. Report of Leadership Training Institute. Presented at ACLD, New York, February, 1975.

McLeod, J. Some perceptual factors related to childhood dyslexia. In M. D. Jenkinson (Ed.), *Reading instruction: An interdisciplinary forum*. Proceedings of International Reading Association World Conference on Reading (Vol. 1), 1967.

Money, J. Dyslexia: A post conference review. In J. Money (Ed.), *Reading disability: Progress and research needs in dyslexia*. Baltimore: Johns Hopkins Press, 1962.

Muehl, S., & Forell, E. R. A follow-up study of disabled readers: Variables related to high school reading performance. *Reading Research Quarterly*, 1973, 9, 110–122.

Myklebust, H. R. *Development and disorders of written language: Studies of normal and exceptional children*. New York: Grune & Stratton, 1973.

Naidoo, S. *Specific dyslexia*. London: Pitman Press, 1972.

Neisser, V. *Cognitive psychology*. New York: Appleton-Century-Crofts, 1967.

Orlando, C. P. Review of the reading research in special education. In L. Mann and D. A. Sabatino (Eds.), *The first review of special education*. Philadelphia: JSE Press, 1973.

Orton, S. T. *Reading, writing, and speech problems in children*. New York: Norton, 1937.

Popp, H. Visual discrimination of alphabet letters. *The Reading Teacher,* 1964, *18,* 221–226.

Prescott, G. A. Criterion referenced test interpretation in reading. *The Reading Teacher,* 1971, *24,* 347–354.

Proger, B., & Mann, L. Criterion-referenced measure: The world of gray vs. black. *Journal of Learning Disabilities,* 1973, *6,* 72–84.

Rabinovitch, R. D. Dyslexia: Psychiatric considerations. In J. Money (Ed.), *Reading disability: Progress and research needs in dyslexia,* Baltimore: Johns Hopkins Press, 1962.

Reed, J. C. The deficits of retarded readers—Fact or artifact? *The Reading Teacher,* 1970, *23,* 347–352.

Reed, J. C., Rabe, E. F., & Mankinen, M. Teaching reading to brain-damaged children: A review. In D. Hammill & N. Bartel (Eds.), *Educational perspectives in learning disabilities.* New York: Wiley, 1971.

Rutter, M. E., & Yule, W. The concept of specific reading retardation, *Journal of Child Psychiatry,* 1975, *16,* 181–197.

Ryan, E. B., & Semmel, M. I. Reading as a constructive language process. *Reading Research Quarterly,* 1969, *5,* 59–93.

Sabatino, D. A., & Hayden, D. L. Information processing behaviors related to learning disabilities and educable mental retardation. *Exceptional Children,* 1970, *37,* 21 30.

Samuels, S. J. Success and failure in learning to read: A critique of the research. *Reading Research Quarterly,* 1973, *8,* 200–239.

Satz, P., & Friel, U. Some predictive antecedents of specific reading disability. *Journal of Learning Disabilities,* 1974, *7,* 437–444.

Satz, P., & Sparrow, S. Specific developmental dyslexia. In D. J. Bakker and P. Satz (Eds.), *Specific reading disability: Advances in theory and method.* Rotterdam: University of Rotterdam Press, 1970.

Sedlack, R., & Weener, P. Review of the research on the Illinois test of psycholinguistic abilities. In L. Mann & D. A. Sabatino (Eds.), *The first review of special education.* Philadelphia: JSE Press, 1973.

Senf, G. M. Memory and attention factors in specific learning disabilities. *Journal of Learning Disabilities,* 1971, *4,* 94–106.

Shedd, C. L. Ptolemy rides again or dyslexia doesn't exist? *Alabama Journal of Medical Science,* 1968, *5,* 484–488.

Simmons, G. A., & Shapiro, P. J. Reading expectancy formulas: A warning note. *Journal of Reading,* 1968, *11,* 626–629.

Skinner, B. F. *Verbal behavior.* New York: Appleton-Century-Crofts, 1957.

Smith, F. *Understanding reading: A psycholinguistic analysis of reading and learning to read.* New York: Holt, Rinehart and Winston, 1971.

Staats, A. W., Staats, C. K., Schultz, R. E., & Wolf, M. M. The conditioning of reading response using "extrinsic" reinforcers. *Journal of Experimental Analysis of Behavior,* 1962, *5,* 33–40.

Sullivan, M. W. *Sullivan reading program.* Palo Alto, Calif.: Behavioral Research Laboratories, 1966.

Tarnopol, L. Delinquency and learning disabilities. In L. Tarnopol (Ed.), *Learning disabilities: Introduction to educational and medical management.* Springfield, Ill.: Charles C Thomas, 1970.

VandeVoort, L., & Senf, G. M. Audiovisual integration in retarded readers. *Journal of Learning Disabilities,* 1973, *6,* 170–179.

Van Meel, J. M., Vlek, C. A., & Bruijel, R. M. Some characteristics of visual information-processing in children with learning difficulties. In D. J. Gakker & P. Satz (Eds.), *Specific reading disability: Advances in theory and method.* Rotterdam: Rotterdam University Press, 1970.

Venezky, R. L., & Calfee, R. C. The reading competency model. In H. Singer & R. B. Ruddell (Eds.), *Theoretical models and processes of reading.* Newark, Del.: International Reading Association, 1970.

Vogel, W., & Broverman, D. M. Relationship between EEG and test intelligence: A critical review. *Psychological Bulletin,* 1964, *62,* 132–144.

Waugh, R. P. Relationship between modality preference and performance. *Exceptional Children,* 1973, *39,* 465–469.

Wepman, J. M., Cruickshank, W. M., Deutsch, C. P., Morency, A., & Strother, C. R. Learning disabilities. In N. Hobbs (Ed.), *Issues in the classification of children* (Vol. 1). San Francisco: Jossey-Bass, 1975.

Williams, J. P. Learning to read: A review of theories and models. *Reading Research Quarterly,* 1973, *8,* 121–146.

Woodcock, R., & Clark, C. L. *Rebus reading program.* Circle Pines, Minn.: American Guidance Service, 1969.

Woolman, M. *A progressive choice reading program.* Chicago: Science Research Associates, 1966.

Ysseldyke, J. E. Diagnostic-prescriptive teaching: The search for aptitude treatment interactions. In L. Mann & D. A. Sabatino (Eds.), *The first review of special education.* Philadelphia: JSE Press, 1973.

Ysseldyke, J. E., & Salvia, J. Diagnostic-prescriptive teaching: Two models. *Exceptional Children,* 1974, *40,* 181–186.

CHAPTER 9

AN INSTRUCTIONAL
DESIGN
IN MATHEMATICS

JOHN F. CAWLEY

The design of instructional programs in mathematics for learning-disabled students at the secondary school level must reflect many concerns. The first of these is the need to think of such programs in terms of both ideals and realities. The reality issues lead to rapid decision making about curricula and to preparation of instructional materials and instructional activities. These efforts often are conceived in haste, and they tend to represent fragmented attempts to solve problems that in themselves are not clearly understood. Necessarily limited in scope and effectiveness, these realities-based attempts underscore the imperative to program in terms of ideals. Programs based on ideals will be rooted in theory, will challenge current practices, and will lead to the meaningful integration of basic constructs such as maximum potential into the programmatic design.

A second concern that any instructional program must address involves the *source* of the serious deficiencies in mathematics that characterize many learning-disabled students at the secondary school level. These deficiencies may be rooted in mathematics per se, or they may grow out of disabilities in other academic skills that influence proficiency in mathematics. One student may fail in mathematics because of strictly mathematical disabilities. Another student, one whose basic mathematical abilities are relatively intact, may fail in math because of poor reading or language skills. A model program for instruction in math, therefore, must include both developmental and remedial components. A diagnostically based remedial component will serve the student who manifests clear and specific learning disabilities in mathematics. A developmental program that systematically corrects or partials out the effects of other learning disabilities on performance in mathematics will help to meet the needs of the student who is disabled in other areas.

The ideal in conjunction with the real, the developmental in conjunction with the remedial: such are the avenues along which instructional design in mathematics for the learning-disabled must proceed. At present, the state of our knowledge in this area is so limited that the

AUTHOR'S NOTE: In preparing this material, I was aided by a grant from the United States Office of Education, Bureau of Education for the Handicapped, No. OEG-070-2250 (607), Proj. No. 162008.

This chapter would have been impossible to complete without the assistance of Dr. Anne Marie Fitzmaurice, who provided the illustrations and considerable guidance. I am appreciative of the time and effort that she put into this endeavor.

best we can do is to offer alternatives, not solutions. The instructional design proposed in this chapter is simply that—an alternative.

■ REMEDIAL MATHEMATICS ■

Many learning-disabled students are capable of demonstrating mathematical proficiency—*regardless of the level of content*—if their specific learning disabilities can be partialed out of the task. The needs of some students with learning disabilities might be met in a college preparatory program, whereas the needs of others might be met through a course in functional mathematics. In either case, the student may require varying degrees of remedial assistance as preparation for a developmental program. We can vary method as well as content in order to meet these different needs.

Henderson (1970), noting that various methods can be used in the teaching of concepts, presents three examples of teaching the concept of a trapezoid. In one example the teacher draws several representations of a trapezoid while telling the students that a trapezoid is a quadrilateral having two sides parallel. In the second example the teacher tells the students two meanings for the word *trapezoid* while drawing two figures, one meeting the conditions of one meaning and the other meeting conditions of the other. The figures are then contrasted, and a definition is agreed upon. In the third example the teacher draws some geometric figures on the board, labeling some trapezoids and some not trapezoids. Reasons for the labels are developed in each example.

In Henderson's exposition, a basic attempt is made to mediate differing positions regarding a concept either as an abstraction where no name is involved or as a set of conditions for the use of a name. Henderson's position is that the formal education of the secondary school mathematician focuses on efficiency in the teaching of a concept by relying on other concepts already taught (and supposedly learned).

It is essential that mathematics programs for learning-disabled pupils insist upon mastery of each concept as a prerequisite for other concepts. Mathematics lends itself nicely to mastery through the teaching of concepts because, as Henderson points out, there are a number of ways to present a concept.

It is not enough, however, simply to master a concept. Concept attainment at the formal level of thinking must include the ability to identify new instances of the concept (Klausmeier, Ghatala, & Frayer, 1974). In formulating concepts, one must consider classifications that are supraordinate, subordinate, and coordinate to the concept at hand. Efforts should be made to formulate hierarchies, to establish cause-and-effect relations, and to help the pupil understand the interrelationships of attributes and rules. All of these can be presented to the learner or to the instructor through alternative modalities.

Furthermore, Klausmeier et al. (1974) point out that effective teaching involves more than the transmission of information and knowledge; it also makes efforts to facilitate learning behaviors. Restated for purposes of the present writing, the issues concerning Klausmeier et al. are as follows:

Teaching mathematics for the sake of mathematics is a limited proposition. Remediating learning disabilities for the sake of remediating learning disabilities is a limited proposition. Enhancing the status of the learner during instruction in mathematics serves the purpose of remediating specific problems and at the same time presents substance to the student.

The structure of mathematics is such that a comprehensive mathematics program can focus on perceptual and cognitive development, language improvement, problem-solving facilitation, reading and writing, and a host of other behaviors.

A good program will attend to the needs of the learner and the demands of the subject area simultaneously. Romberg (1970) cites the learner and the subject matter as the two necessary components of curriculum development in mathematics. These two crucial components must be interrelated in mathematics programs for the learning-disabled. Regarding principles of instructional design, Gagné and Briggs (1974) set out four assumptions:

1. Instructional planning *must* be for the individual.

2. Instructional design has phases that are both immediate and long range.

3. Systematically designed instruction can greatly affect human development, beyond the limits of the instruction itself.

4. Instructional design must be based on knowledge of how human beings learn.

Let us examine these assumptions in reverse as they relate to learners disabled in mathematics. There are, by agreement, pupils with disorders in learning. If we know how intact students learn (if we truly know!), we may then have a basis for directing the learning characteristics of nonintact students in appropriate learning sequences and styles. It is this redirection of learning behavior into new patterns that must be considered in teaching mathematics to the learning-disabled. The skills, principles, and attitudes necessary for effective performance in mathematics cannot otherwise be attained by the nonintact student.

The effect of mathematics on human development is unquestionably important. The highest incidence of failure in secondary schools is in mathematics, and the long-term effect of this failure is harmful to individuals, their self-concept, and their motivation. Appropriate instruction can mitigate such problems. Also, interpersonal relationships can be modified by way of the instructional design. For example, situations in which instructors and learners manipulate two-dimensional or three-dimensional objects or representations of objects during the instructional activity may have more favorable effects than those in which the instructor assigns a page in a text or workbook for the student to work at individually (and quietly). The mathematics instructor assisting secondary learning-disabled pupils must use systematic instructional designs to provide alternative strategies that positively affect interpersonal relations.

An understanding of the immediate and long-range phases of the instructional design is necessary when planning for the pupil with learning disabilities. The immediate phases should establish a diagnostically based plan, to be followed by remedially oriented instruction that—with full consideration for the incorporation of an appropriate rule or algorithm—integrates specific content through the modality hierarchy that is most effective for the learner. The long-range phase involves comprehensive curriculum planning for preschool through the secondary school level. The curriculum must provide for different stages of proficiency and competency in all students.

Instructional planning for the individual is, of course, where it all begins and ends. Such planning must include provisions for poor readers who are capable in mathematics to attain their maximum potential in mathematics *regardless of their inability to read*. It must include diagnostics, supplementary services, and modification of instructional strategies and styles. These are components of the principles of instructional design that connect the educational system to the individual.

Mathematics, I believe, ought to provide as much attention to facilitating learning behavior as it does to specifically developing the skills, principles, and attitudes of mathematics. Attention to the learner's behavior must, of course, be related to the complexities of the subject matter itself. To facilitate understanding of this point, let us pose a question: Does a rule that is well learned among younger students fail to transfer effectively at the upper grade levels because of quantitative complexity? Here we might look at Jensen's (1972) discussion of functions, where a function is a pairing of the elements of two sets of objects. In example A, the "add 1" function is applied to a set of ordered pairs called P.

Example A: $P = (0,1), (1,2), (2,3), (3,4), (4,5), (5,6)$

In example B a different illustration of function is presented; here the basic rule is "to square."

Example B: $P = (0,0), (1,1), (2,4), (3,9), (4,16), (5,25)$

A learning-disabled student who grasped the significance of functions might be unable to proceed from mastery of example A to mastery of example B because content (rule of square) was not effectively integrated into his program, which attended solely to his learning-disability traits.

The content and skill requirements of mathematics become more complex as learners move through the school system. Whereas most students learn most of the rules of their native language early in life and know how to read by the fifth or sixth grade, they have far to go in mathematics beyond these levels. By sixth or seventh grade, children are ordinarily able to perform the basic operations on whole numbers through long division. Somewhere in these grades they may begin to translate their skills in the operations to rational numbers. Students experience a subtle but formidable transfer of learning experiences as they progress in mathematics, as can be seen in the following mathematical progression:

A. Divide 6 by 2.

B. Divide 2 into 6.

C.   Divide 92 by 36.

D.   Divide $\frac{1}{2}$ by $\frac{1}{4}$.

E.   Divide $\frac{1}{2}$ into $\frac{1}{4}$.

F.   Divide .92 by .36.

If the above are approached symbolically, using rote rules, students will probably never understand the tasks, nor will they have acquired alternative means by which to demonstrate proficiency. Most of us in special education could take a set of blocks and demonstrate the differences between items A and B in the above list. How many of us can do the same for items D and E? (See Figure 9–3, pages 220–221.) Many times the issue boils down to how far the instructor can take the learner, and not just how far the learner can go.

■ UNDERACHIEVEMENT IN MATHEMATICS ■

The problem of pupil failure in secondary school mathematics is not a recent one, if there is any substance to an article written in 1925 by W. J. Osborn entitled *Ten Reasons Why Pupils Fail in Mathematics.* Osborn felt that the root of the problem rested "in the existence of individual differences in pupils to an extent hitherto undreamed of." The major problems, he said, were these: (1) problems relating to propositions that require the learner to see analogies, (2) problems requiring generalization and transfer, (3) tasks in which contradictory conditions exist (specifically, activities with negative numbers), and (4) problems requiring the pupil to select the correct information and to know how and where to use it.

The fascinating aspect of Osborn's article is that, some fifty years later, learners still perform poorly in these same areas. One explanation for the persistence of this problem is the fact that secondary mathematics educators have devoted most of their attention to college preparatory instruction. One recent book, *A History of Mathematics Education in the United States and Canada* (NCTM, 1970), reflects this focus. The book pays scant attention to the matter of failure; on the contrary, the central theme of the document relates to mathematics as an entity in and of itself, with particular reference to college-bound students. The University of Illinois' Committee on School

Mathematics has concentrated on the preparation of college-bound pupils, and the School Mathematics Study Group has also concentrated its efforts in this direction. Rudman (1934), Eisner (1939), Reeve (1944), Sobel (1959), and Elder (1967) are among the educators who have recounted the problems of and made recommendations on secondary school mathematics for underachieving pupils.

Mathematics educators understand that failure in arithmetic has many causes. There may be problems relating to cognitive complexity, method of instruction, and mastery of prerequisite learnings. The math may be too abstract for the pupil, or the instruction may be initiated before the pupil is ready to deal with the concepts. The pupil may not have had the prerequisite skills for going on to a new skill. Some educators have suggested that poor teaching is sometimes responsible for student failure (Schonell & Schonell, 1957; Reisman, 1972).

Difficulties with mathematics are frequently viewed by experts as problems of the "system," including both curriculum and method. Reeve's 1923 statement exemplifies this concern: "I think it [poor performance] is largely due to the stupid way in which mathematics is too often presented to the pupil" (NCTM, 1970). Whitcraft (1930) presented a somewhat more balanced set of concerns. He felt that failure could be traced to (1) the materials of mathematics (textbook, practice exercises, and special devices), (2) the teacher's method of instruction and manner of presentation, or (3) the pupil's processes and methods.

■ LEARNING DISABILITIES IN MATHEMATICS ■

In a recent summary of literature about overachievement and under-achievement in mathematics, Asbury (1974) cited a number of variables that contribute to underachievement. An examination of these variables shows that many of them are similar to those that special educators ascribe to the learning-disabled. Besides general and specific cognitive factors, they include noncognitive factors such as emotional problems.

Despite the apparent similarities among these variables, regular and special educators approach mathematics differently (Schonell &

Schonell, 1957; Reisman, 1972; Johnson & Myklebust, 1967; Lerner, 1971).

Unlike mathematics educators, special educators tend to look for problems within the pupil as explanations of the disability. Johnson and Myklebust, for example, have indicated that dyscalculics (1) are deficient in visual spatial organization and nonverbal integration, (2) have superior auditory abilities, (3) may excel in reading vocabulary and skills, (4) may have disturbances of body image, (5) have possible disorientation problems, (6) show poor social perception, and (7) have higher verbal than nonverbal functions.

Lerner (1971) speaks in much the same tone as Johnson and Myklebust (1967) relative to arithmetical disturbances. Her list of characteristics does not extend the development of a theoretical approach to identification or remediation. She suggests that materials for teaching arithmetic should be considered as tools that are useful when they fit the pupil, the disability, the diagnosis, and the teaching plan. Lerner recommends materials (such as Cuisenaire rods), but she does not elaborate on the implications for selecting these materials. (For example, Cuisenaire rods suggest a measurement approach to numbers, whereas our own work in Project MATH is a set approach.)

Cohn's (1971) longitudinal study of thirty-one pupils stands alone as a contribution to our knowledge in the area of arithmetical disabilities among handicapped students. Eighty percent of these students were observed four or five times, and in only a few instances were the pupils unable to develop reasonable arithmetical ability. Overall improvement in arithmetical operations occurred in direct relation with improvement in general neurological status and in the language functions.

Cohn described a number of instructive cases in detail. One boy who, at eight years, three months of age, wrote numerals as $\int \mathcal{B} \mathcal{I} \mathcal{Q}$ was able, ten years later, to complete $3x + 9y = 7$ and $6x + 9y = 8$ correctly. In cases such as this, Cohn emphasizes the symbolic nature of mathematics and its interrelationships with verbal and nonverbal logical processes. His extensive work in the psychoneurological correlates of arithmetic disabilities has led him to conclude that arithmetic disabilities constitute a subset of language disabilities that should be superordinated into a classification properly designated as a disorganization syndrome.

Patterson (1974) suggests that attempts to deal with the language and reading elements in mathematics problems should attend to two factors: language patterns and language units. *Language patterns* are of two types, explanations and problems. (Explanations consist of extensive presentations or word problems or concept-testing tasks.) *Language units* consist of sentences, paragraphs, and chapters. The use of written material in sentences, paragraphs, and chapters can be effectively enhanced by appropriate attention to vocabulary. Our work in Project MATH has demonstrated the value of controlling language factors in mathematics instruction (Bessant, 1972).

According to Hammill and Bartel (1974), students with problems in arithmetic are as handicapped as students who cannot read. They will have difficulty in making purchases, balancing checkbooks, filling out tax returns, and so forth.

Myers and Hammill (1969) have reviewed various theoretical and programmatic considerations relative to methods for learning disorders. The various authorities whose work came under consideration (Friedus, Lehtinen, Cruickshank, Myklebust) showed only scant attention to arithmetical disabilities and their remediation. Mathematics disabilities at the upper grade levels were almost completely ignored.

Spencer and Smith (1969) demonstrated how little attention has been given to the problem of mathematical disabilities. In a relatively brief chapter, they devote two full pages to data from a study on types of arithmetic habits observed in elementary pupils; however, the source of their data is a 1925 study. Even the 1972 Yearbook of The National Council of Teachers of Mathematics, *The Slow Learner in Mathematics,* does not provide significant insights into mathematics disabilities at the secondary school level.

■ **INDIVIDUALIZATION OF INSTRUCTION** ■

Fitzmaurice and I (Cawley & Fitzmaurice, 1972) developed a set of principles that we believe establish minimal guidelines for mathematical instruction of learning-disabled pupils in mathematics at the secondary school level.

Principle I   Mathematics programs for learning-disabled pupils must include instructional procedures and alternatives that reduce the

210

influence of age-in-grade relationships on curriculum and material development.

This principle recognizes that pupils with learning disabilities demonstrate variable developmental patterns. Some read fairly well but are impaired mathematically, others are inordinately impaired in both reading and math, and others are adequate in math but deficient in reading.

A mathematics program that fails to recognize variability in students' developmental patterns usually increases the difficulty of all parameters of mathematical learning simultaneously. Thus there may be a simultaneous increase in mathematical difficulty, reading vocabulary level, semantic complexity, and cognitive sophistication. As one component of the program becomes more difficult, so do all the others. The problem this poses should be clear. Learning-disabled pupils are basically students whose performance in one or more areas of development is deficient. Instructional programs for learning-disabled pupils must be capable of systematically partialing out the effects of any single variable (or combination of variables) interfering with success. For example, reading skills should not be necessary for achievement in mathematics. The effects of age-in-grade should be reduced through multimedia instruction and through the use of instructional practices that independently vary reading, language complexity, and the like.

Principle II   Individualized mathematics programs must be based on the principle that successful performance facilitates learning.

Success is an essential element in learning. In the context we are considering, success refers to satisfactory performance on a given mathematical task. Success is such that mastery of one task provides the prerequisite behavior for subsequent ones. A learner who finishes a marking period in school with an average grade of 20 percent has a greater problem than the F that is likely to be recorded will suggest. The student has been reinforcing incorrect responses about 80 percent of the time. At this rate, it is unlikely that he or she will ever demonstrate proficiency. Our second principle, therefore, obligates the instructor to assign tasks that the learner can successfully perform.

Principle III   Mathematics programs for learning-disabled pupils must produce alternatives to the fixed-frequency system.

211

Basic mathematics texts and their accompanying workbooks are fixed-frequency systems. Each problem or task in the book has a specific frequency of occurrence which, one must assume, represents a data base beyond the fact that the student is presented with mathematics for approximately 40 minutes per day, 180 days per year.

What performance traits of the learner determine the number of book pages devoted to a given topic? Why are certain problems or practice tasks presented a specific number of times on a given page? Is the frequency of presentation sufficient to enable the least proficient child to attain mastery? These are questions that must be answered.

Principle IV   Mathematics programs for learning-disabled pupils must be capable of providing the teacher with qualitative options.

The instructor working with learning-disabled pupils may find that the material is not sufficient to insure original learning or original mastery. If this is the case, the student will have little opportunity for overlearning, retention or recall will be negatively affected, and transfer of learning is likely to be reduced. It is necessary, therefore, that the instructor supplement the basic mathematics test and workbooks with other materials in order to facilitate a pupil's mastery of the material.

Instructional practice with learning-disabled pupils must include qualitative options such as recommendations for divergent instructional practices and supplementary activities for the teacher. Such qualitative options emphasize the development of concepts, principles, and understanding rather than rote computational skills.

Principle V   Mathematics programs for learning-disabled pupils must be capable of providing instant diagnostic feedback to the instructor.

This principle stresses that continuous diagnosis is an integral component of the instructional design. Diagnostic feedback is essentially a process that is undertaken during instruction. Fremont (1975) recommends that diagnostics be action-based and conducted as the learner is engaged in problem-solving experiences requiring mathematical skills. The learner's specific problems then become the diagnostic referent. Fremont points out, however, that it is difficult to construct valid and reliable diagnostic techniques, and that an overdependence on testing as a means of diagnosis may well be creating failure experiences that further discourage an already discouraged pupil.

Schmidt (1975) recommends a simple reorganization of standard practices to expand the diagnostic base from which a child can be viewed. An example of this would be the use of a standard geoboard (5 rows × 5 columns) and a nonstandard geoboard (5 rows × 5 columns, with one square removed or punched out). He notes that a comparison between the learner's performance on the standard and the nonstandard geoboards may serve as a diagnostic technique because of the perceptual problems that may be encountered with the nonstandard board.

Principle VI   Mathematics programs for learning-disabled pupils must be efficient in terms of instructor/learner time and effort.

This principle focuses on the teacher and learner as cooperating agents in the instructional design. Neither instructor nor learner should have to spend excessive time and effort in homework. Activities that use multimedia materials should be prepared cooperatively, with the learner assisting the instructor. In this way students become directly involved in the lesson, their motivation is facilitated, and they may obtain additional insight into the lesson. Further, instructors should develop a partnership with learners and help them to conceptualize each of the steps leading to proficiency.

■ AN INSTRUCTIONAL PROGRAM ■

Figure 9-1 presents a model for an instructional program for secondary school students with learning disabilities in mathematics. The rationale for this program has its roots in Project MATH, which was funded by the Bureau of Education for the Handicapped, U.S. Office of Education, and carried out by Anne Marie Fitzmaurice and me. The design can best be understood by following the paths of a group of learners entering the system.

All learners who have been referred because they seem to be experiencing difficulty in math are screened on the Mathematics Concept Inventory (MCI). An evaluation of each student's mathematical

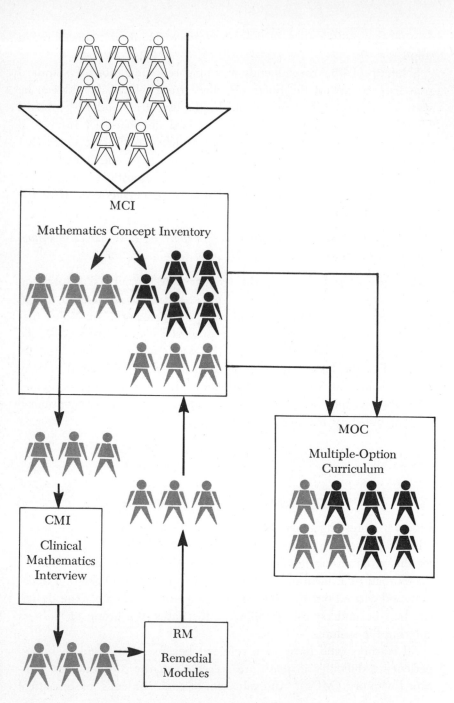

Figure 9-1   Components of the instructional design

status is made on the basis of MCI performance. Students who demonstrate abilities in the basic operations of mathematics are referred to the Multiple-Option Curriculum (MOC) for instruction. Students who show marked deficiencies in mathematics are referred to a Clinical Mathematics Interview (CMI) for an intensive diagnostic appraisal. After the appraisal, these students are instructed in the Remedial Modules (RM), have another go at the MCI, and then, their deficiencies remediated, move to the MOC.

THE MATHEMATICS CONCEPT INVENTORY

The Mathematics Concept Inventory is presented as a domain-referenced instrument that assesses learner proficiency in a sample of selected mathematics concepts. It has two roles. The first is to serve as a general screening device to arrive at a determination of general and specific areas of strengths and weaknesses. Second, it serves as a decision referent for pupils who manifest disabilities appropriate for attention within the learning-disabilities concept.

A student's performance on the MCI will suggest one of two courses. One of these courses is to use the results of the Mathematics Concept Inventory in conjunction with other psychoeducational information as placement data to enter the pupil into the Multiple-Option Curriculum. The Mathematics Concept Inventory is composed of a set of items devised directly from the concepts presented in the Multiple-Option Curriculum. Its item pool contains at least one item for each concept developed in the curriculum. The other course is to refer the pupil for intensive evaluation via the Clinical Mathematics Interview. This option is recommended only when the student shows extensive disability on items requiring the use of the basic operations of addition, subtraction, multiplication, or division with whole numbers, fractions, percentages, or decimals.

THE DEVELOPMENTAL COMPONENT OF THE PROGRAM

CURRICULUM DESIGN   Curriculum design is usually introduced in a conceptual framework referred to as a model. The model presented here is a modification of the approach taken to develop Project MATH. Project MATH's model has been included as an exemplar for curriculum development in special education (Mayer, 1975), and it is gaining popularity in the professional literature (Hammill & Bartel, 1974; Smith, 1974). The organizer of this model is the Interactive Unit. This unit has been modified since its inception (Cawley & Vitello, 1972) so as to provide greater specificity and variability for curriculum development. The original Interactive Unit used nine combinations of input (instructor) and output (learner). In its current form, there are sixteen combinations of instructor-learner interaction, each of which is defined and briefly illustrated in Figure 9-2. The Interactive Unit constitutes the basis for cognitive and affective signals and the alternatives of the Multiple-Option Curriculum.

DIMENSIONS OF THE INTERACTIVE UNIT   A curriculum in special education must, at minimum, possess these four fundamental qualities:

1. The curriculum must be capable of partialing out or circumventing the effects of a disability upon other areas of development. In this instance, for a student who cannot read, mathematics must be presented in such a way that the effects of reading disabilities are circumvented.

2. The curriculum must be capable of interrelating with divergent management strategies and teaching styles in order to facilitate appropriate effect. Let us take two of the sixteen combinations assembled in Figure 9-2 and describe these in terms of affective potential. One combination is construct-construct (C-C); the other is graphically symbolize–graphically symbolize (GS-GS). It is the latter (students working with workbooks, ditto sheets, or textbooks) that tends to be the dominant classroom practice. Students work quietly and independently, with little or no interaction with others. In preparing for the graphically symbolize–graphically symbolize combination, the instructor anticipates the type of affect in this situation and also considers the accompanying management components (for example, what to do when students talk with one another; how to traverse the room in order to relate to different learners). The construct-construct combination signals a different set of conditions to the instructor. It is an ideal combination for having learners within close proximity to one another and to the instructor; it is an effective means of organizing instruction in order to have one pupil—say, one who tends to isolate herself—operate amid a group. It is a difficult combination if students

tend to push, shove, or harass one another, because it only increases the opportunity for such behaviors to occur. (The graphically symbolize–graphically symbolize combination might be better used in this latter instance.)

3. The curriculum must be capable of transmitting knowledge and information to the learner. In this situation, we are referring to knowledge and information about the concepts and skills of mathematics.

4. The curriculum must be capable of providing continuous diagnostic information to the instructor.

THE MULTIPLE-OPTION CHARACTER OF THE INSTRUCTIONAL PROGRAM   The multiple-option character of the design described herein is provided through the Instructional Guide. Guides may be developed so as to represent a complete scope and sequence for a curriculum, or they may be developed to represent particular topics.

The guide signals three elements of content: strand, area, and concept (see Figure 9-3, pages 220–221). The *strand* is the highest level of categorization employed. Within each strand there are a number of *areas*. Each area specifies a broad range of mathematical topics. These areas recur throughout the curriculum. Each area contains a number of *concepts*. The concept is the most specific signal for a mathematical topic within the Multiple-Option Curriculum. Within the present frame of reference, the term *concept* includes both skills and principles. It is essential that students with learning disabilities be taught and helped to discover the principles (rules, ideas, algorithms, and the like) of mathematics in order to increase their own capacity to "learn to learn" and to transfer and generalize.

Each individual guide signals an input (instructor) and output (learner) interaction. The guide also includes a behavioral objective that is stated in terms of both instructor and learner behavior. Note in Figure 9-3 the variation in the style of the behavioral objective from that typically used in the literature. It has been my experience that behavioral objectives written in the traditional format inhibit the instructional and developmental components of curriculum. Each guide should contain a set of instructional activities written in such a way that they can be used repeatedly. The evaluative criteria provide the basis for continuous diagnostic feedback.

Assume that a teacher had administered the Mathematics Concept

Figure 9-2   The Interactive Unit of the instructional design: components, definitions, and examples

Input (from instructor)	C,	P,	S,	or	GS
Output (from learner)	C,	I,	S,	or	GS

Construct   Instructor manipulates the learning environment, and learner makes constructive or manipulative responses.

Present   Instructor presents learner with fixed nonsymbolic visual displays (arrangements of materials, pictures, or pictorial worksheets).

State   Instructor and learner rely on oral discourse.

Graphically   Instructor and learner work with written or drawn
symbolize   symbolic stimulus materials.

Identify   Learner responds in a multiple-choice framework.

Concept: Division of a whole number by a proper fraction

Instructor	*Learner*
Constructs by separating a number of wholes into halves, fourths, etc.	*Constructs* by separating a number of wholes into halves, fourths, etc.
Constructs by separating a number of wholes into halves, fourths, etc.	*Identifies* a fixed representation of the same number of wholes divided into the same parts.
Constructs by separating a number of wholes into halves, fourths, etc.	*States* a description of what the instructor has done and names the number of pieces resulting.
Constructs by separating a number of wholes into halves, fourths, etc.	*Graphically symbolizes* by writing the numeral naming the number of pieces resulting.
Presents fixed representations of a number of wholes divided into halves, fourths, etc.	*Constructs* by separating the same number of wholes into the same number of parts.

218

Presents fixed representations of a number of wholes divided into halves, fourths, etc.	*Identifies* a fixed representation of the same number of wholes divided into the same parts.
Presents fixed representations of a number of wholes divided into halves, fourths, etc.	*States* a description of what the instructor has shown and names the number of pieces.
Presents fixed representations of a number of wholes divided into halves, fourths, etc.	*Graphically symbolizes* by writing the numeral naming the number of pieces shown in each representation.
States what division by a proper fraction means and gives directions for showing this.	*Constructs* representations of division by a proper fraction according to the instructor's directions.
States what division by a proper fraction means and gives directions for showing this.	*Identifies* a representation of division by a proper fraction.
States what division by a proper fraction means and gives directions for showing this.	*States* what division by a proper fraction means.
States what division by a proper fraction means and gives directions for showing this.	*Graphically symbolizes* by drawing a picture to represent division by a proper fraction.
Graphically symbolizes by drawing a picture representing division by a proper fraction and writing the number expression represented.	*Constructs* a representation of what the instructor has drawn and written.
Graphically symbolizes by drawing a picture representing division by a proper fraction and writing the number expression represented.	*Identifies* a fixed representation of what the instructor has drawn and written.
Graphically symbolizes by drawing a picture representing division by a proper fraction and writing the number expression represented.	*States* the meaning of the number expression by describing the picture and names the number of parts resulting.
Graphically symbolizes by drawing a picture representing division by a proper fraction and writing the number expression represented.	*Graphically symbolizes* by copying the instructor's picture, writing the number expression, and writing the numeral to name the resulting number of parts.

Figure 9-3   A sample Instructional Guide from within the Multiple-Option Curriculum. This one provides direction for teaching division of a whole number by a proper fraction.

Strand	Fractions
Area	Operations
Concept	Division of a whole number by a proper fraction
Input	Construct
Output	Graphically symbolize

Behavioral objective

Instructor	*Learner*
Constructs by separating a number of wholes into halves, fourths, etc.	*Graphically symbolizes* by writing the appropriate division expression and the numeral naming the number of pieces resulting.

Illustrative materials

Geometric regions, scissors, paper, pencil, chalkboard, chalk

Activities

Review the meaning of division and a division expression. Write the expression $10 \div 2$ on the chalkboard. Remind the learners that the expression represents the number of groups of 2 that are in 10. Then write $10 \div 1/3$

Inventory to a group of ten students who were referred for screening and that there was reasonable variation in the performance of these pupils. The decision was made to place seven of these youngsters in the Multiple-Option Curriculum. The teacher now has, among others, the following options:

1. Different students could be assigned to different strands.

2. All seven could be assigned to the same strand, but to different areas.

3. All seven could be assigned to the same strand and the same area, but to different concepts.

4. All seven could be in the same strand, same area, and same concept, but in different interactive combinations.

Figure **9-3** (cont.)

on the board. Ask the learners what this expression should mean. Elicit the response, "The expression represents the number of 1/3 pieces in 10."

1. *How Many Parts Have Been Cut from the Wholes?* Give each learner paper and pencil. Use a set of geometric regions cut from paper. Tell the learners that you are going to cut a number of wholes into parts. They are to write the division expression that tells what you have done. Begin by holding up two circular regions. Tell the learners that you will be starting with two wholes. They are to write down the numeral 2. Since you will be dividing the wholes, they are to write the division sign ÷ after the 2. Cut the two circular regions into thirds. Ask the learners to write the fraction 1/3 after the division sign. Ask one learner to tell how many pieces resulted from the division. Tell the learners to write the equal sign = after the 1/3, and then to write the total number of pieces, six. The complete number sentence should read $2 \div 1/3 = 6$.

Repeat the procedure, using three square regions and cutting the regions into fourths. Guide the learners step by step in writing the number sentence $3 \div 1/4 = 12$. Repeat the activity several times using different regions and dividing them into different parts.

2. *How Many Folded Parts Are There?* Follow the procedure outlined in activity 1, but fold the regions into parts instead of cutting. In each case, ask the learners to write the division sentence that tells what you have done.

Evaluative criteria

Give each learner paper and pencil. Cut three straws in half. Ask the learners to write the division sentence that tells what you have done. They should write $3 \div 1/2 = 6$.

---

5. All seven could be in the same strand, same area, same concept, and same interactive combination but be presented with different materials (in most instances).

The Multiple-Option Curriculum design for mathematics is a diverse and comprehensive approach to the individualization of instruction for students with learning disabilities.

THE DIAGNOSTIC COMPONENT OF THE PROGRAM

According to Reisman (1972), diagnostic teaching approaches the hierarchy of the learning processes and the level of the student's functioning. Through diagnostic teaching, the teacher identifies strengths and weaknesses, formulates strategies for ameliorating problems, and applies remedial techniques. Compensatory strategies utilizing the pupil's strengths can also be applied.

Glennon and Wilson (1972) have elaborated on the diagnostic-prescriptive model. They see it as interrelated with two essential variables: the curriculum variable and the method variable. The curriculum variable focuses on the mathematics that are of most worth, whereas the method variable focuses on the question of what method is of most worth in the diagnosis of and prescriptions for learning disabilities. Of the two, Glennon and Wilson say that the latter is "far more complex." These authors suggest the need to consider a triad consisting of content, behavior, and psychological learning products. In this taxonomy, content relates to the curriculum of elementary school mathematics; behavior relates to components of the cognitive domain, after Bloom; and learning products are modeled after Gagné's eight types of learning.

It is ironic that the instructional elements of mathematics have persistently highlighted the use of manipulatives or pictorial representations and other processes in instruction, but that our diagnostics have failed to differentiate themselves accordingly. It is even more interesting to note that the variety of algorithms that students may choose to employ in their performance is consistently neglected in diagnostics. In effect, what we have diagnostically are content instruments that require learners to perform selected tasks in mathematics without attention either to their most efficient and least efficient modes of performance or to the appropriateness or efficiency of the algorithm they employ. This is especially evident at the secondary school level, where most testing is done with graphic-symbolic modes such as reading and writing. It is equally interesting to note that instruction and learning at the secondary school level also make extensive use of the graphic-symbolic mode. Let us look at diagnostic procedures. Key Math (Connolly, Nachtman, & Pritchett, 1971) is one of the few commercial tests that claims to be diagnostic. It actually lends itself more to grade placement than to diagnosis. This is because failure on an item on the test does not give the teacher a clear view of where or how remediation should take place, for the process that the student used to solve the problem is not apparent. Key Math computational subtests do not cover the subskills involved in computational accuracy well enough to insure that remediation will take place at the proper subskill (Goodstein, Kahn, & Cawley, 1976).

For example, Key Math presents two fraction items. The first shows the pupil a picture of four rabbits and asks, "If half of these rabbits ran away, how many would be left?" A second item, nearly six grade-equivalents higher, shows the child a picture of eight ducks and asks, "Three-fourths of this group of ducks is how many?" A student who applied the same algorithm to both tasks (for example, $\frac{1}{2} \times 4$ and $\frac{3}{4} \times 8$) would have demonstrated a different level and character of performance than did a student who used different algorithms to solve each (for example, half of 4 is 2, $4 - 2 = 2$ for the first problem; $\frac{3}{4} \times 8 = (3 \times 8)/4 = 6$ for the second), particularly if one response was correct and the other incorrect. Buswell and John's Diagnostic Chart for Individual Difficulties: Fundamental Process in Arithmetic provides for individual analysis of a pupil's difficulties in the four basic operations with whole numbers. The problems are arranged according to the difficulty of each operation. Teachers use a checklist of errors as the pupils orally explain their methods of solving the problem. The test is not excessively long and is relatively easy to analyze for sequence of processes. However, the Buswell-John is primarily a graphic-symbolic instrument in which the modes of performance are reading and writing. Through these channels the learner performs nearly 180 items relative to basic concepts in mathematics.

One aspect of the diagnostic component of the Buswell-John that has been shown to be effective is an oral interview with the pupil (Cox, 1973; Langford, 1974; Lepore, 1974; Schonell & Schonell, 1957). The pupil is asked to do problems "out loud," verbalizing each step. Through the use of the oral interview, the student's strategies can be studied and improper algorithms can be discovered. The pupil may be using rules that vary greatly from the norm, or the rules may be only a slight departure from the conventional algorithm. The pupil may recognize the pattern and structure for completing the computation but may be using the wrong procedure. A teacher needs to be familiar with the pupil's set of rules in order to remediate effectively.

Defective algorithms have been found to be the major cause of computational inaccuracy (Ashlock, 1972). Lepore found that learning-disabled students and educable mentally retarded students, when compared by mental age, made the same types of errors in the four basic operations of whole numbers, with defective algorithms the most prominent error type. Cox also found that normal and handicapped pupils made similar systematic errors in addition, subtraction, multiplication, and division of whole numbers.

THE CLINICAL MATHEMATICS INTERVIEW   The Clinical Mathematics Interview is an intensive diagnostic procedure that integrates content, mode, and algorithm (or rule). *Content* is the mathematical skills and knowledge that are focused on; *modes* are interactive combinations of the Interactive Unit; *algorithms* (rules) are the mathematical or cognitive strategies that the individual uses during performance.

Think back to the group of pupils who were referred for screening via the Mathematics Concept Inventory. Some of these students were recommended for placement in the Multiple-Option Curriculum, while others were referred for intensive diagnosis. Basically, the students who were referred for diagnosis were deficient in one or more of the four basic operations in numbers and operations, fractions, and decimals and/or percentages.

Figure 9-4 illustrates the model for the Clinical Mathematics Interview. The first step is to have the learner complete the given computation tasks in the graphic symbolic–graphic symbolic mode. After the test is scored, the student is asked to verbalize the procedure that he or she used to do both the correct and the incorrect problems. The student then works with the examiner to complete representative problems in each of the other modality combinations.

Making the content $\times$ mode $\times$ algorithm inquiry to each learning-disabled student is essential if we are to plan an educational problem adequately. This is illustrated in the following response of a student to the problem "$64 - 35 = ?$":

$$
\begin{array}{r}
5^{1} \\
\not{6}4 \\
-35 \\
\hline
39
\end{array}
$$

The response is incorrect. Is it because the student erred in subtraction? No! *The student inappropriately used a nonconventional algorithm.* This learner subtracted from left to right. The student subtracted 3 (30) from 6 (60) and then subtracted 5 from 4 by renaming,

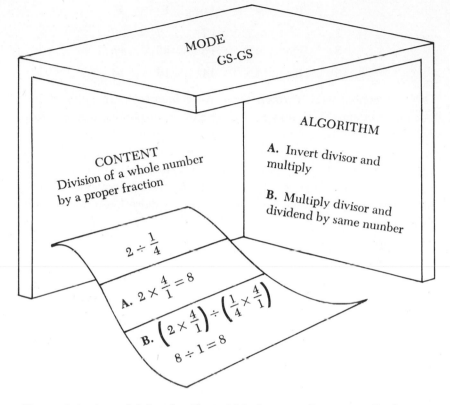

Figure 9-4 A model for the Clinical Mathematics Interview. In this part of the interview, an instructor and learner will work in the graphic symbolic–graphic symbolic mode on division of whole numbers by proper fractions.

which was done correctly. The error exists in the source of the student's retrieval of the "10" that was borrowed. Lepore's work uncovered numerous similar instances of algorithm deficits. The instructional question is one of deciding whether to correct the left-to-right algorithm (ordinarily this is easily done) or to convert the student to the standard right-to-left algorithm. In the present case, the instructor might have perceived the student's problem as a content one (not knowing $5 - 3$).

Nor is the algorithm relevant only when the response is incorrect. Take the task "$7 + 8 = ?$" as given to six learners who responded as follows:

A	B	C	D	E	F
7	7	7	7	7	7
+8	+8	+8	+8	+8	+8
15	15	15	14	16	14

Three responses were correct; three were incorrect. In spite of the fact that students D, E, and F made incorrect responses, it is possible that the algorithms they used were more sophisticated than those used by students A, B, and C. Suppose A, B, and C simply responded from rote memory but, when requested to prove their answers in an alternate mode, were unable to do so. Assuming D, E, and F *were* able to work out proofs in an alternate mode, who, then, is more likely to respond correctly to

$$\begin{array}{ccc} 796 & & 709 \\ 834 & \text{or} & \times 807 \\ 756 & & \overline{} \\ \overline{} & & \end{array}$$

when "memory" is partialed out?

Another example of the need to control specific variables and to integrate these with the content × mode × algorithm is illustrated in the work of Sherman (1972). The student is asked to complete the following:

$$(a + b)^2 = a^2 + b^2 + 2ab, \qquad \text{where } a = 3 \text{ and } b = 5$$

When this task is represented symbolically as shown above, the symbolically deficient student may be unable to perform the computation or to analyze the concept. When presented in a less symbolic manner as

$$(3 + 5)^2 = 3^2 + 5^2 + 2(3 \times 5)$$

the task can be completed with pictorial or manipulative materials like the following:

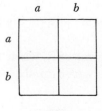

226

The learner is aided in the discovery of the mathematical principle in this task by the use of alternative modes. This provides the basis for an integration of symbolic concepts with operational ones as indicated in

$$(5a^2 + 6b^2 - 3ab)(4a - 2b)$$

These illustrations are used to show a particular instance, rather than to suggest that all learning-disabled students ought to attain similar standards.

THE REMEDIAL MODULES   Work in the Remedial Modules is based on an extensive task analysis of the content, mode, and algorithm (or rule) that constitute a module. A given curriculum plan may call for the use of many modules. The remedial effort undertaken with a module or modules is designed to prepare the learner for placement in the Multiple-Option Curriculum after retaking of the Mathematics Concept Inventory.

As can be seen in Figure 9-5, the design for the Remedial Modules provides for a comprehensive attack on a specific disability. It is my general feeling that error behaviors should be attacked one at a time. For example, if a pupil uses bizarre rules, errs in computation, and is unable to vary modality, the modality sequence should be utilized first. This tends to establish correct patterns of behavior. If, on the other hand, a student uses a nonconventional algorithm correctly but errs on computation, it seems wise to continue the use of the nonconventional algorithm and to work solely on the learner's computation deficiencies. Mastery is essential in the Remedial Modules. It is here that the most intensive instructor-learner interactions will be undertaken, and it is here that the learner must have successful experiences.

While the overall instructional design presented in the preceding pages may appear complex, it is, in reality, quite simple. There are only five administrative steps involved.

1. Administer the Mathematics Concept Inventory.

2. Place the student in the Multiple-Option Curriculum or refer him or her for further diagnosis with the Clinical Mathematics Interview.

3. Follow the Clinical Mathematics Interview with work in the Remedial Modules.

CONTENT

ADDITION OF
SINGLE-DIGIT NUMBERS

NAME_____ DATE_____
SCHOOL_____ GRADE_____

$\begin{array}{r}1\\+2\\\hline\end{array}$	$\begin{array}{r}2\\+3\\\hline\end{array}$	$\begin{array}{r}4\\+3\\\hline\end{array}$
$\begin{array}{r}2\\+0\\\hline\end{array}$	$\begin{array}{r}0\\+5\\\hline\end{array}$	$\begin{array}{r}5\\+4\\\hline\end{array}$
$\begin{array}{r}8\\+3\\\hline\end{array}$	$\begin{array}{r}7\\+6\\\hline\end{array}$	$\begin{array}{r}7\\+7\\\hline\end{array}$
$\begin{array}{r}9\\+8\\\hline\end{array}$	$\begin{array}{r}7\\+8\\\hline\end{array}$	$\begin{array}{r}9\\+9\\\hline\end{array}$

ALGORITHM

RULES

COUNTS TO SUM USING SOME CONCRETE OBJECTS

COUNTS TO SUM WITHOUT AID OF CONCRETE OBJECTS

OPERATES FROM KNOWLEDGE OF FACTS

FOR SUMS GREATER THAN 10, GROUPS FIRST 10 AND THEN FINDS REMAINDER

MODALITIES

MODE		MODALITIES					
INSTRUCTOR	LEARNER	INSTRUCTOR	LEARNER	INSTRUCTOR	LEARNER	INSTRUCTOR	LEARNER
CONSTRUCTS SUBSETS REPRESENTING ADDENDS	CONSTRUCTS SET REPRESENTING SUM	PRESENTS PICTURES OF TWO SUBSETS REPRESENTING ADDENDS	CONSTRUCTS SET REPRESENTING SUM	STATES TWO ADDENDS	CONSTRUCTS SET REPRESENTING SUM	GRAPHICALLY SYMBOLIZES TWO ADDENDS	CONSTRUCTS SET REPRESENTING SUM
CONSTRUCTS SUBSETS REPRESENTING ADDENDS	IDENTIFIES PICTURE OF SET REPRESENTING SUM	PRESENTS PICTURES OF TWO SUBSETS REPRESENTING ADDENDS	IDENTIFIES PICTURE OF SET REPRESENTING SUM	STATES TWO ADDENDS	IDENTIFIES PICTURE OF SET REPRESENTING SUM	GRAPHICALLY SYMBOLIZES TWO ADDENDS	IDENTIFIES PICTURE OF SET REPRESENTING SUM
CONSTRUCTS SUBSETS REPRESENTING ADDENDS	STATES SUM	PRESENTS PICTURES OF TWO SUBSETS REPRESENTING ADDENDS	STATES SUM	STATES TWO ADDENDS	STATES SUM	GRAPHICALLY SYMBOLIZES TWO ADDENDS	STATES SUM
CONSTRUCTS SUBSETS REPRESENTING ADDENDS	GRAPHICALLY SYMBOLIZES SUM	PRESENTS PICTURES OF TWO SUBSETS REPRESENTING ADDENDS	GRAPHICALLY SYMBOLIZES SUM	STATES TWO ADDENDS	GRAPHICALLY SYMBOLIZES SUM	GRAPHICALLY SYMBOLIZES TWO ADDENDS	GRAPHICALLY SYMBOLIZES SUM

Figure 9-5   A sample Remedial Module consisting of algorithm, content, and mode sequences that allow error behaviors to be attacked one by one.

4. Transfer the student from the Remedial Modules, via readministration of the Mathematics Concept Inventory, to the Multiple-Option Curriculum.

5. Provide developmental mathematics via the Multiple-Option Curriculum or place the student in a regular program.

THE ADMINISTRATIVE COMPONENT

The resource center is the primary administrative unit used to serve learning-disabled students. (I feel that there is still room for self-contained units for some pupils but that the resource center is a valid approach.) The relationships between mathematics educators and special educators can be best fostered through the resource center. The flexible scheduling used by secondary schools provides numerous opportunities for mathematics teachers to work intensively in the resource center while the special education teacher covers one or more regular classes.

The Multiple-Option Curriculum will include much the same content as the general mathematics program. There is, therefore, a logical basis for a partnership approach to learning disabilities in mathematics. The teachers could develop instructional guides that cover the same content in different modalities. Proficiency can be developed while the student is attending the resource center. The regular class teacher could parallel the content of the resource center by selecting guides in the same concept but in different modalities.

The resource center relationship can be maintained with special subject areas such as a career education and work-study, which includes mathematics. The guides can be exchanged among instructors, and selected instructional activities on each guide can be made directly applicable to the specific subject area. By transmitting information on strand, area, concept, and interactive combinations, different teachers can work independently to meet specific learner needs.

In another effort (Cawley, Calder, Mann, McClung, Ramanauskas, & Suiter, 1973; Cawley, 1977), my coworkers and I demonstrated that it is possible to take almost any psychoeducational assessment data on a pupil and relate these to any subject matter of the school (for example, we can prepare a biology program that is based on tactics such as the ITPA). We did this in order to meet the needs of students with learning disabilities and/or behavioral disorders on an all-day basis.

Integrating mathematics within this system meets more fully the goal of educational services to the handicapped student.

Administrative provisions for curriculum development and in-service training are a final component of the instructional design.

Special education has not devoted many resources to secondary education. Teachers of the learning-disabled tend to have a remedial orientation, which generally focuses on the elementary level. As we are well aware, however, the concept of learning disabilities has not been fully remedial; our efforts must now include curricula. The initial step in the development of an effective training program should be to acquire a body of knowledge on which to build the program. As that is unlikely to happen, I suggest that we select educators who have a background in mathematics and that we train them in the cognitive-linguistic area, in psychodiagnostic procedures, and in modification and development of curricula and instruction. I believe that the dynamics of the secondary school are such that while non-subject-matter specialists might plod through the school's remedial program, they will not have sufficient influence on curricula or pupil scheduling to set up effective remedial programs.

Our work in Project MATH suggests that it is possible to design a multimedia self-instructional [or group-instructional) in-service training program for working with learning-disabled pupils at the secondary level. Such a program should represent the concerns both of the mathematics educator and of the special educator.

■ REFERENCES ■

Asbury, C. A. Selected factors influencing over- and underachievement in young school-age children. *Review of Educational Research*, 1974, *44*, 409–428.

Ashlock, R. B. *Error patterns in computations: A semi-programmed approach.* Columbus, Ohio: Charles E. Merrill, 1972.

Bessant, H. P. *The effects of semantic familiarity and information load on the arithmetical verbal problem solving performance of children in special classes for the educable mentally retarded.* Doctoral dissertation, University of Connecticut, 1972.

Buswell, G. T., & John, L. *Diagnostic chart for individual difficulties: Fundamental processes in arithmetic.* Indianapolis: Bobbs-Merrill.

Cawley, J. F. Curriculum: One perspective for special education. In R. D. Kneedler & S. G. Tarver (Eds.), *Personal perspectives in special education.* Columbus, Ohio: Charles E. Merrill (in press).

Cawley, J. F., Calder, C. R., Mann, P. H., McClung, R., Ramanauskas, S., & Suiter, P. *Behavior resource guide.* Wallingford, Conn.: Educational Sciences, 1973.

Cawley, J. F., & Fitzmaurice, A. M. *The individualization of instruction: Illustrations from arithmetical programming for handicapped children.* Unpublished manuscript, University of Connecticut, 1972.

Cawley, J. F., Fitzmaurice, A. M., Goodstein, H. A., Lepore, A. V., Sedlak, R., & Althaus, V. *Project MATH, Level 1.* Tulsa, Okla.: Educational Progress, a division of Educational Development Corporation, 1976.

Cawley, J. F., & Vitello, S. J. Model for arithmetical programming for handicapped children. *Exceptional Children,* 1972, *39,* 101–110.

Cohn, R. Arithmetic and learning disabilities. In H. Myklebust (Ed.), *Progress in learning disabilities* (Vol. 2). New York: Grune & Stratton, 1971.

Connolly, A. J., Nachtman, W., & Pritchett, E. M. *Key math.* Circle Pines, Minn.: American Guidance Service, 1971.

Cox, L. S. *Systematic errors in the addition algorithm in normal and handicapped populations.* Unpublished manuscript, University of Kansas, 1973.

Eisner, H. The challenge of the slow pupil. *The Mathematics Teacher,* 1939, *32,* 9–15.

Elder, F. Mathematics for the below-average achiever in high school. *The Mathematics Teacher,* 1967, *60,* 235–239.

Fremont, H. Diagnosis: An active approach. *The Mathematics Teacher,* 1975, *68,* 323–326.

Gagné, R. M., & Briggs, L. J. *Principles of instructional design.* New York: Holt, Rinehart and Winston, 1974.

Glennon, V. J., & Wilson, J. W. Diagnostic-prescriptive teaching. In *The slow learner in mathematics* (35th Yearbook, NCTM). Washington, D.C.: National Council of Teachers of Mathematics, 1972.

Goodstein, H. A., Kahn, H., & Cawley, J. F. The achievement of educable mentally retarded children on the Key Math Diagnostic Arithmetic Test. *Journal of Special Education,* 1976, *10,* 61–70.

Hammill, D. D., & Bartel, N. *Teaching children with learning and behavior problems.* Boston: Allyn and Bacon, 1974.

Henderson, K. B. Concepts. In *The teaching of secondary school mathematics* (33rd Yearbook, NCTM). Washington, D.C.: National Council of Teachers of Mathematics, 1970.

Jensen, R. Chapter 4, pp. 73–116. In P. H. Martorella (Ed.), *Concept learning: Design for instruction.* Scranton, Pa.: Intext Educational Publishers, 1972.

Johnson, D., & Myklebust, H. R. *Learning disabilities: Educational principles and practices.* New York: Grune & Stratton, 1967.

Klausmeier, H. J., Ghatala, E., & Frayer, D. *Conceptual learning and development: A cognitive view.* New York: Academic Press, 1974.

Langford, F. S. What can a teacher learn about a pupil's thinking through oral interviews? *Arithmetic Teacher,* 1974, *21,* 26–32.

Lepore, A. *A comparison of computational errors between educable mentally handicapped and learning disability children.* Unpublished manuscript, University of Connecticut, 1974.

Lerner, J. *Children with learning disabilities.* Boston: Houghton Mifflin, 1971.

Mayer, W. *Planning curriculum development.* Boulder, Colo.: Biological Sciences Curriculum Study, 1975.

Myers, P. I., & Hammill, D. D. *Methods for learning disorders.* New York: Wiley, 1969.

National Council of Teachers of Mathematics. *A history of mathematics education in the United States and Canada* (32nd Yearbook). Washington, D.C.: NCTM, 1970.

National Council of Teachers of Mathematics. *The slow learner in mathematics* (35th Yearbook). Washington, D.C.: NCTM, 1972.

Osborn, W. J. Ten reasons why pupils fail in mathematics. *The Mathematics Teacher,* 1925, *18,* 234–238.

Patterson, J. H. Techniques for improving comprehension in mathematics. In *Reading in the middle school.* Newark, Del.: International Reading Association, 1974.

Reeve, W. D. In defense of Donald Dull (by M. A. Potter). *The Mathematics Teacher,* 1944, 37, 195–201.

Reisman, F. K. *A guide to the diagnostic teaching of arithmetic.* Columbus, Ohio: Charles E. Merrill, 1972.

Romberg, T. A. Curriculum, development, and research. In *The teaching of secondary school mathematics* (33rd Yearbook, NCTM). Washington, D.C.: National Council of Teachers of Mathematics, 1970.

Rudman, B. Causes for failure in senior high school mathematics and suggested remedial treatment. *The Mathematics Teacher,* 1934, *27,* 409–411.

Schmidt, P. A. A non-simply connected geoboard based on the "what if not" idea. *The Mathematics Teacher,* 1975, *68,* 384–389.

Schonell, F. J., & Schonell, F. E. *Diagnosis and remedial teaching in arithmetic.* London: Oliver & Boyd, 1957.

Sherman, H. *Common elements in new mathematics programs: origins and evolutions.* New York: Teachers College Press, 1972.

Smith, R. *Clinical teaching.* New York: McGraw-Hill, 1974.

Sobel, M. A. Providing for the slow learner in the junior high school. *The Mathematics Teacher,* 1959, *52,* 347–353.

Spencer, E. F., & Smith, R. Arithmetic skills. In R. Smith (Ed.), *Teacher diagnosis of educational difficulties.* Columbus, Ohio: Charles E. Merrill, 1969.

Whitcraft, L. H. Remedial work in high school mathematics. *The Mathematics Teacher,* 1930, *23,* 36–51.

CHAPTER 10

EDUCATIONAL PROGRAMMING: A SURVEY OF CURRENT PRACTICE

LIBBY GOODMAN

Despite the impressive accomplishment of the past few years, the learning-disabilities field has, with very few exceptions, been preoccupied with the learning problems of younger pupils while ignoring the older learning-disabled student. The disparity between the many programs and services for the primary pupil and the few that are available for the secondary school student is evidence of the pronounced elementary bias that has characterized the learning-disabilities field—a characteristic that applies to much of special education.

Our minimal efforts on behalf of junior and senior high learning-disabled students have precipitated the criticisms of learning-disabilities professionals which have appeared in the literature (Kline, 1972; Hammill, 1975). While there are no acceptable excuses for the blatant neglect of the older student, there are any number of explanations which could be offered (Goodman & Mann, 1976). Perhaps the simplest is the most revealing. Too many professionals and parents believed that learning disabilities could be "cured" if identified and remediated at a very early age. Indeed, primary programs were supposed to negate the need for services in our secondary schools. After many years of programming for learning-disabled children, we know now that many learning disabilities are not cured. Some learning problems persist despite our best educational efforts. Some of the learning-disabled pupils who participated in good, sound remedial programs at the elementary level still need academic support and assistance through their secondary school programs. Widespread recognition of this fact is long overdue.

On the positive side, after years of neglect many efforts in program development at the secondary level are now emerging. Although a formidable distance exists between the current level of services and the unmet need for services, the mounting interest in, commitment to, and efforts on behalf of, the secondary learning-disabled student indicate that we stand on the threshold of far-reaching program development at the secondary school level.

The special educator attempting to initiate a program for secondary learning-disabled students will find, as we did in Montgomery County (Pennsylvania), that there are few information sources available. The purpose of this chapter is, therefore, to review and discuss model learning-disabilities programs for secondary students. I hope to familiarize the reader with a sampling of current programs and to highlight current programming trends. Key issues that affect program development are discussed, and some tentative guidelines are offered.

As a prelude to my survey of specific programs, I should specify the population to which the term *secondary-level learning-disabled* is to be applied. Who shall be served by the new secondary-level programs? Indeed, where were the learning-disabled pupils before the new programs were created? Many of the learning-disabled pupils coming into secondary schools were in remedial programs in elementary school but have a continuing need for academic assistance. Perhaps more than any others, these students exemplify the need for a *continuum* of services from the elementary through the secondary school. The other candidates for secondary learning-disabilities programs are underachieving students who did not have the benefit of special elementary programs (and whose problems are just now being identified as being due to learning disabilities). It may be that many of these students were over-age for the elementary programs that were being started; misdiagnosed; or mislabeled (the labels *emotionally disturbed, delinquent,* and *retarded* have obscured many cases of learning disability). We know, too, that many learning-disabled students attending private educational facilities could be educated in their home schools if the appropriate programs and services were available. In sum, the secondary learning-disabled population attending public schools for the next few years will be made up of "graduates" from elementary school learning-disabilities programs who have a continuing need for special services; students with long-standing histories of academic difficulty who have yet to receive the educational assistance that they need; academically marginal students who squeaked through the elementary grades only to find themselves unable to cope with the added requirements and stresses of secondary schools; and students transferring from private school facilities.

I am well aware that the enumeration of different sources for secondary learning-disabled students skirts the issue of definition. The avoidance is deliberate at this point. The problems that beset the definition question at the elementary level are compounded when the special educator tries to define—in operational terms—the learning-disabled student at the secondary level. Despite the difficulties, however, an operational definition is essential, even critical, when one recognizes that the number of school failures increases in the move from elementary to secondary school. And we simply do not have (nor can we anticipate) sufficient funding to extend special-education services to all underachievers in our secondary schools. If learning disabilities are to be a workable category of special education, we must be able to distinguish the truly learning-disabled from the larger number of underachieving secondary students. The questions of definition and specific identifying criteria are a primary concern in any appraisal of programs for secondary-level learning-disabled students. We shall return to this issue later in the chapter.

The specific programs reviewed in this chapter do not represent an exhaustive or all-inclusive cataloging of secondary programs now in operation. Instead, the discussion is limited to Title III and Title VI-G projects. Focus on Title III and Title VI-G does not suggest that these are the only sources of funding for learning-disabilities programs. Title IV and Title VI-B funds have also supported learning-disabilities projects, and many locally funded efforts are also under way; but some arbitrary restrictions were necessary in order to keep this presentation within manageable proportions.

Since the express intent of federal assistance programs is to stimulate innovative and pioneering practices, I feel that federally funded projects are most likely to represent the best examples of current programming attempts. While not all Title III or Title VI projects are discussed, the selected projects do, I believe, offer sufficient depth and variety to illustrate current programming trends. They also allow for some generalizations about the intent, purposes, and direction of secondary learning-disabilities programming.

This overview of selected programs does not include a discussion of residential or private daycare facilities that offer programs for learning-disabled adolescents. By omitting them, I do not intend to slight their value or to deny their role in the education of handicapped students. Private residential and daycare schools that work with older learning-disabled students are generally better equipped than are the public schools to handle cases of very severe disabilities that are often compounded by emotional disturbance or maladjustment. Despite the current and relentless trend toward mainstreaming, private schools do offer a much needed service. Students who cannot cope in the normal school setting—even within a more sheltered environment of the special class—are likely candidates for private school placement.

■ PROGRAMS FUNDED UNDER TITLE VI, PART G ■

As of this writing, twenty-nine Title VI-G model demonstration centers in learning disabilities are in operation. Of the twenty-nine Child Service Demonstration Centers (CSDCs), eighteen, or 60 percent, include secondary-age students in their target population. While all the projects share a concern for the learning-disabled pupil, particularly the secondary student, they vary greatly in their objectives, range of services offered, techniques, and so on. Five CSDC projects in progress or concluded will be described in greater detail in this section. Table 10-1 contains information on CSDCs in operation during the 1976–1977 school year. (The number and location of the centers varies from one year to the next as some projects are concluded and new ones are begun.) The location, age, and type of student served and the contact person for each of the twenty-three CSDC programs that were serving secondary students in 1976–1977 are provided in the table.

WEST VIRGINIA CHILD SERVICE DEMONSTRATION CENTER

The West Virginia Child Service Demonstration Center is concerned primarily with teacher training and staff development activities, with only an indirect service delivery system for learning-disabled students. The project is an extension of a pre- and in-service training center previously established by the Kanawha County Schools, by means of Title I and Title III funding and local school system support. The Kanawha County pre- and in-service training center had developed a clinical service model for learning-disabled pupils. The West Virginia CSDC seeks to replicate and propagate the clinical model within Kanawha County and to the remaining fifty-four counties of the state.

The clinical model involved a "four part series of interrelated diagnostic, prescription, intervention, and consultation [D-PIC] skills." In order to foster the adoption of the model by other school systems, the West Virginia CSDC offers an internship training experience at the center and/or field visits by project personnel to cooperating districts. As a result of participation in the internship training program, teachers should gain proficiency in the various components of the D-PIC clinical model. They will become more confident about the diagnostic-prescriptive process as they acquire the skills and knowledge to recognize

Table 10–1 Child Service Demonstration Centers serving secondary learning-disabled students, 1976–1977

LOCATION	TITLE	POPULATION SERVED	CONTACT PERSON
Alabama	Alabama A & M University Interdisciplinary Child Service Demonstration Center	Junior high, urban, suburban	Dr. Donna Griggs, Department of Special Education, Alabama A & M University, Normal, Alabama 35762 (205) 859–7367
Alabama	Project MELD: Molding Education for Learning Disabled Students at the Junior High School Level	Junior high, urban, suburban	Mrs. Ida Johnson, Tuscaloosa County County Board of Education, P.O. Box 2568, Tuscaloosa, Alabama 35401 (205) 758–0411
Arkansas	Child Service Demonstration Center for Children with Learning Disabilities	Secondary, small city	Mrs. JoAnne Brown, El Dorado School District 15, 700 Columbia St., El Dorado, Arkansas 71730 (501) 863–3541
California*	California Child Service Demonstration Center System	Secondary, urban, suburban, rural	Dr. Charles W. Keaster, California State Department of Education, 721 Capitol Mall, Sacramento, California 95814 (916) 445–9420
Georgia	Project ACTION: A Model Child Service Demonstration Center Emphasizing the Adjustment of the Child's Teaching Based on an Interdisciplinary Orientation to Needs	Secondary, urban	Dr. Mary Ben McDorman, The Howard School, Inc., 1815 Ponce de Leon Avenue, N.E., Atlanta, Georgia 30307 (404) 337–7436

240

Illinois	Northeastern Illinois University Child Service Demonstration Center	Secondary, urban	Dr. Janet Lerner, Northeast Illinois University, Department of Special Education, Bryn Mawr at St. Louis Avenue, Chicago, Illinois 60625 (312) 583–4050
Indiana	Ball State University Child Service Demonstration Center for Children and Young Adults with Specific Learning Disabilities	Postsecondary, urban	Dr. James A. Poteet, Ball State University Teachers College, Department of Special Education, 2000 University Avenue, Muncie, Indiana 47306
Iowa	Project Clue: Career Laboratories Utilizing Experience	Secondary, urban	Ms. Diane Finley, Director, Des Moines Independent Community School District, 1800 Grand Avenue, Des Moines, Iowa 50309
Kentucky	Kentucky Child Service Demonstration Center	Junior high, suburban, rural	Mr. Fred West, Director, Kentucky CSDC, Bureau for Exceptional Children, Capitol Plaza Tower, Frankfort, Kentucky 40601 (502) 564–2067
Louisiana	Project HOLD: Helping Operation in Learning Disabilities	Secondary, urban, rural	Dr. Levelle Haynes, Director, Northeast Louisiana University, Strauss Hall, Room 112, Monroe, Louisiana 71201 (318) 342–3189
Massachusetts	Project OPEN: Optimal Procedures for Educational Needs	Junior high, urban	Ms. Paula T. Downs, East Junior High School, 464 Central Street, Brockton, Massachusetts 02402 (617) 588–7800

* California CSDC is actually a network of affiliates that span the entire state; there are a number of CSDC centers in various locations.

(cont.)

Table 10–1   Child Service Demonstration Centers serving secondary learning-disabled students, 1976–1977 (cont.)

LOCATION	TITLE	POPULATION SERVED	CONTACT PERSON
Minnesota	Step Up with SIMS (Systematic Instructional Management Systems)	Secondary, urban, suburban	Ms. Marie Blackburn, Armatage Learning Center, 2501 West 56th St., Minneapolis, Minnesota 55410 (612) 926–1693
Minnesota	Minnesota Learning Disabilities Consortium	Junior high, rural, suburban, institutional	Ms. Von Valletta, Minnesota State Department of Education, 550 Cedar St., St. Paul, Minnesota 55101 (612) 296–2774
Nebraska	Child Service Demonstration Center for Children with Learning Disabilities	Secondary, rural	Ms. Polly Feis, Educational Service Unit #9, P.O. Box 2047, Hastings, Nebraska 68901 (402) 463–5611
New York	Project CHILD: Model Programs for Children Having Individual Learning Disabilities	Secondary, urban, suburban	Dr. Robert T. Smith, East Ramapo School District, 50A South Main Street, Spring Valley, N.Y. 10977 (914) 356–4100
North Carolina	Child Service Demonstration Center for Replication of Mainstream Environments for Children with Specific Learning Disabilities	Junior high, small city	Mr. Robert Carmichael, Salisbury City Schools, 314 North Ellis Street, Salisbury, North Carolina 28144 (704) 636–7500
Oklahoma	Oklahoma Child Service Demonstration Center for Secondary Students	Secondary, rural	Ms. Deborah Murphy, Hillside School, Route 3, Cushing, Oklahoma 74023 (918) 225–1882

242

Ohio	Project Expand: A Child Service Demonstration Center to Provide Services for Learning Disabled Children in the State of Ohio	Secondary, urban, suburban, rural	Ms. Shirley Moorehead, Ohio Division of Special Education 933 High Street, Worthington, Ohio 43085 (614) 466–2652
Oregon	Oregon Child Service Demonstration Center Project	Secondary, urban, suburban, rural	Dr. Thomas D. Rowland, Oregon College of Education, Monmouth, Oregon 97361 (503) 838–1220
Pennsylvania	Child Service Demonstration Center for Urban Secondary Students with Learning Disabilities	Secondary, urban, suburban	Dr. Naomi Zigmond, School of Education, Division of Specialized Professional Development, University of Pittsburgh, 4616 Henry Street, Pittsburgh, Pennsylvania 15260 (412) 624–5197
Vermont	Chittenden South Supervisory School District Consulting Teacher Program	Junior high, rural, suburban	Mr. Joseph P. Loretan, Chittenden South Supervisory District, P.O. Box 127, Shelburne, Vermont 05482 (802) 985–3356
Virginia	Virginia Child Service Demonstration Learning Disabilities Center	Secondary, suburban	Ms. Irene Nassor, Director, Springfield Estates Elementary School, 6421 Meriwether Lane, Springfield, Virginia 22150 (703) 971–4302
Wyoming	Child Service Demonstration Center in Learning Disabilities—Regional and Statewide Technical Assistance	Secondary, rural	Dr. Joseph Reed, Region V Board of Cooperative Educational Services, P.O. Box 112, Kemmerer, Wyoming 93101 (307) 877–3991

SOURCE: Compiled from data presented in the 1976–1977 Special Issue (Directory) of "Centerfold," published by NaLDAP, the National Learning Disabilities Assistance Project.

children whose disabilities are so severe that their needs cannot be adequately met within the regular school program.

During its first three years of operation, the West Virginia CSDC Project provided some degree of training to every elementary teacher in Kanawha County. Many of the other counties in the state have also sent intern teams to the Kanawha Center. Ideally, this visiting team consists of an administrator, a teacher, a teacher's aide, and a parent. In reality, few administrators have had the time to participate in the program, and few teaching aides have been involved, since teacher's aides per se are a rarity in West Virginia. The intern team receives three five-day training sessions, and a project staff member later visits each team in their home school district. It is hoped that, in addition to acquiring confidence in diagnostic-prescriptive skills, each team that is trained will become the catalyst for a training program within its own school district.

Teachers who opt for more intensive training in preparation for the role of resource room specialists may pursue a more intensive training program at the center. The project will ultimately gauge the success of its efforts in terms of quality and extent of replication of the D-PIC Model throughout the state. More immediately, project personnel are involved in an evaluation to determine the quality of the teacher training and internship training program and in upgrading the skills of participating teachers.

TEXAS CHILD SERVICE DEMONSTRATION CENTER

The Texas Child Service Demonstration Center, termed Project ECHO, services secondary students with language and/or learning disabilities. Project ECHO is the successor of an earlier CSDC project that was located in Corsicana, Texas. The Corsicana Project was responsible for the development of a model of service for fifteen- and sixteen-year-old students who are learning-disabled. The major components of the service model were in-depth diagnosis of students, the development of exportable instructional materials (mini modules) in three subject areas (math, science, and language), and the development of a management system capable of bringing the services and resources to the classroom. Project ECHO is charged with reproduction of the Corsicana Model in five additional school sites within various areas of the state and with the evaluation of the mini modules and classroom management system.

Participation in Project ECHO is limited to fifteen-year-old students who must (1) be of average intellectual ability (intellectual quotient not falling more than two standard deviations below the norms of the general school population); (2) be three or more years deficient in one or more of the basic auditory, visual, or haptic processes, intersensory integration, or concept formation; (3) demonstrate a difference of two or more years between achievement in math or reading skills and expected grade level performance based upon mental age; (4) demonstrate a four-year discrepancy from the national or local norms of academic achievement for their age group; and (5) have no apparent psychological deficiencies. Students screened for the program undergo extensive preplacement evaluation. Those students who are selected to participate are placed at the recommendation of the Admissions, Review, and Dismissal (ARD) Committee at each project school—the only body that can legally place students in special-education programs within the state of Texas.

At each designated school site, the staff consists of a site coordinator, three teachers in language-learning disabilities (one each for science, math, and language arts), two teacher aides, and a secretary. Since Project ECHO is dedicated to mainstreaming, student participants remain in their regular school program while receiving supportive services from the language-learning disability teachers. An individual educational plan is prepared for each student cooperatively by the language-learning disability teacher and the site coordinator. Resource room assistance is available for those students who may need it.

The language-learning disability teachers utilize the mini modules as well as commercial materials to assist in the teaching of handicapped students. At present ten modules for academic and vocational education have been developed for each of the three primary subject areas. Each module includes pre, post, and mastery tests to assist in pacing students through the instructional material. Mini modules may require anywhere from a few days to a few weeks of instruction for completion, and the materials may be used in both the resource room and the regular classroom. The mini modules are not, however, complete curricula in and of themselves. Rather, they were designed to be supplements to a regular instructional program. In addition to the curricular modules, Project ECHO has produced two orientation training modules for use in teacher and staff development programs.

The short-range goals of Project ECHO focus on student achievement gains, improved attendance with a corresponding decrease in the dropout rate, greater parental involvement, and greater cooperation by the business community in the project's efforts. The long-range objective is to foster the adoption and implementation of the project model in other school locations.

OKLAHOMA CHILD SERVICE DEMONSTRATION CENTER

The Oklahoma Child Service Demonstration Center for Secondary Students is attempting to bring educational services to junior and senior high school students handicapped by learning disabilities in six rural and semirural districts of the state. To date 150 students have been served. To participate in the program, students must (1) demonstrate normal intellectual abilities; (2) evidence signs of central nervous system involvement; (3) have learning disabilities that disrupt perceptual, conceptual, or integrated functions; (4) not be handicapped by severe emotional disturbance, sensory deficits, mental retardation, or severe organic insult to the central nervous system; and (5) be lagging four or more years below grade placement in the areas of reading, spelling, arithmetic, or social studies.

The intervention model embodies the diagnostic-prescriptive teaching approach with the diagnostic assessment of the student being carried out by an itinerant team comprised of the school psychologist and two learning-disabilities teachers. The team develops an individualized prescriptive learning program for each student reflecting the results of the in-depth diagnostic testing. Attention is paid not only to students' academic needs but also to the social and emotional pressures that weigh heavily on secondary students. The overall goal of the project is to foster normal academic and social growth for each adolescent.

The project staff attempts to provide the needed instructional intervention with the least disruption to the student's regular school program. When they program and schedule, therefore, they first try modifying a regular classroom program rather than relocating the student to a special class. If placement in a special class is indicated, it will be a resource room rather than a self-contained program. The extent and duration of the youngster's participation in the program is determined by the degree of the pupil's disability and the rate of amelioration; special services are continued until the student can succeed in a regular program without academic assistance. Students may come to the resource room for instruction instead of attending classes in which they are failing. Conversely, at no time and for no reason are students removed from classes in which they are succeeding.

The Oklahoma CSDC Project is striving to produce products and techniques that can be diffused throughout the state. One of the tangible outcomes of the project thus far is a multimedia materials catalog of curricular materials suitable for use with secondary-level learning-disabled students. It has an extensive listing of materials for reading, language arts, math, social studies, science, and vocational education, as well as periodicals, games, equipment, professional materials, and tests. Copies of the catalog are available from the project.

MISSISSIPPI CHILD SERVICE DEMONSTRATION CENTER

Mississippi's Child Service Demonstration Center is one of the few Title VI-G projects that has a primary commitment to teacher training. Headquartered at Mississippi State University in Starkville, the project trains graduate and undergraduate students to work with the learning-disabled. Approximately one hundred students per year are involved in this training effort. The project's graduates are meeting the state-wide need for personnel qualified to teach the learning-disabled.

The services of the Mississippi CSDC are many. It created a multi-disciplinary team for disagnostic-prescriptive and remedial servicing of children with specific learning disabilities, and it provides in-service training and supervision of teacher trainers. The CSDC works with parents, teachers, and administrators; recommends successful educational techniques to professionals and parents; evaluates the center's program effectiveness; and puts out a technical manual to facilitate replication of the center's program regionally and nationally.

The center's services are available to pupils between the ages of five and eighteen. Eligibility for services is restricted to those whose intellectual functioning places them within the average or above-average category but whose academic performance falls significantly below their ability. Pupils referred to the center receive extensive diagnosis by teacher trainees under direction of a doctoral student.

The trainees' teaching of the youngsters at the center serves as a practicum experience and their diagnostic and prescriptive work is closely supervised. An individualized prescription is developed for each youngster; and a case coordinator, who functions as a liaison between the CSDC Project and the home school, interprets the diagnostic summary and makes recommendations to parents and school personnel.

The effectiveness of the Mississippi CSDC Project rests upon the academic growth of the student trainees and the demonstrable benefits for the handicapped youngsters (that is, effectiveness of the diagnostic-prescriptive program implemented in the home school). Project personnel believe that the center's models provide the basis for a viable teacher training program, and that the center's design also lends itself to application with a wide range of educational professionals (guidance counselors; reading, speech, and hearing specialists; and psychologists) as well as teachers. They hope that the model will be replicated in whole or in part in other locations.

PITTSBURGH CHILD SERVICE DEMONSTRATION CENTER

The Pittsburgh Child Service Demonstration Center offers a resource room program for learning-disabled inner-city youths in grades six through twelve. The intentions of the project are to design a model of comprehensive educational service, to replicate the model in both urban and suburban school sites, and to extend services to regular classroom teachers and to the parents of the learning-disabled students.

The resource rooms ("learning labs") are housed in a middle school and a high school. Each learning lab can serve up to twenty students; the lab is staffed by a lab teacher and consultant teacher. The resource room program offers both direct and indirect services. Direct service is the remedial programming for students, which emphasizes basic academic and school survival skills, social interaction, values clarification, and career exploration. Indirect services include consultation to regular classroom teachers and a parent education program.

To be eligible for services a student must have a full-scale IQ of 80, have a discrepancy of two or more years between achievement and potential for achievement (three or more years discrepancy for high school students) in reading or math, and be free of emotional problems.

The program begins with referral, followed by assessment and intervention. Features worthy of note are self-referrals, student participation in weekly group meetings to acquire school survival skills, and participation in the career education program that is provided to all students in the Pittsburgh School System for students beginning in grade six. Parent involvement is encouraged.

The success of the program will be gauged by its impact on students' achievement and self-concept; the project's impact on teachers will be evaluated by examination of rate and kind of referrals, attitude changes regarding learning disabilities, knowledge acquired, and degree of modification in classrooms to accommodate the needs of the learning-disabled.

■ PROGRAMS FUNDED UNDER TITLE III ■

Many innovative projects have been sponsored under Title III funding. Five Title III secondary projects are described in the following sections.

ALTERNATIVES TO FAILURE

A learning-disabilities program for junior and senior high students within the Des Moines (Iowa) public school system is called Alternatives to Failure.* The program is part of a comprehensive continuum of school programming (kindergarten through grade twelve) for learning-disabled students in the Des Moines schools. The program for secondary students can, without exaggeration, be termed a community-based program, as the involvement of pupil, peers, staff, parents, and community is an integral component of the total project structure.

The classroom model is one that has become familiar to us by now—the resource room. The instructional orientation is decidedly remedial and utilizes the diagnostic-prescriptive approach. Assessment of each student's areas of weakness is followed by individualized programming to "help the child with his problem areas in learning." The basic

---

* The description of the Alternatives to Failure program in this section is based on personal communication from J. Richardson, Project Manager (1974).

instructional strategy "remediation of deficits" is apparently adhered to at all levels, with the teachers substituting tests and materials appropriate to the student's age.

In each school the program is backed up by a team comprised of the learning-disabilities specialist, the resource teacher, four regular teachers (one from each content area), the principal or his representative and, when requested, the nurse, psychologist, speech therapist, or social worker. The content area teachers will attend Drake University for graduate work in learning disabilities, and one will go on to complete twenty-one college hours in an approved training program in order to become a resource teacher. The involvement of teachers with both special education and regular education backgrounds greatly facilitates the acceptance of the program and the adapting of curriculum in content subjects to meet the needs of learning-disabled students.

CROSSOVER ASSISTANT TO CHILDREN WITH HANDICAPS

Project COACH (Crossover Assistant to Children with Handicaps) is a Pennsylvania Title III project currently operating in the Central Dauphin School District.* The program is designed to provide assistance to seventh and eighth graders who are unable to cope with the scholastic demands of junior high school. The students included in the program are those identified as low achievers and/or learning-disabled. A low achiever is defined as a student whose academic performance is one or more years below his actual grade placement. The learning-disabled are identified by their classroom teachers and receive help from a learning therapist assigned to their school.

The experimental program focuses on math and social studies and is based on a multimedia instructional approach and a philosophy of continuous progress from the student's own baseline of achievement (the unrealistic and often harmful standard of on-grade level performance was avoided). In comparison to their peers, underachieving adolescents are constantly losing academic ground, falling

* The description of the COACH program in this section is based on personal communication from J. Hines, Administrative Assistant for Curricular Development (1974).

farther and farther behind. Through Project COACH, the school personnel hope to reverse the trend toward academic deterioration among these students. Just "holding the line" in math or social studies would represent progress; gains would be doubly rewarding to both the students and the project staff.

As a result of the project, significant changes have occurred in regular classroom procedures. One of these changes was a shift from traditional lecture and textbook approaches to small-group instruction utilizing a variety of approaches (audio-visuals, manipulatives, simulations, and so on). Other noted effects included a marked decrease in discipline problems and improvement in student attitudes toward school reported by teachers and parents. Many of the students made impressive academic gains. During the project's second year (1973–1974), the number of seventh graders who gained academically in math and social studies was 73 percent and 83 percent respectively. Among eighth graders, 86 percent and 65 percent demonstrated improvement in math and social studies. In math 27 percent of the seventh graders and 11 percent of the eighth graders made no gains or lost ground; in social studies, the percentage of students who regressed was 17 percent at the seventh-grade level and 35 percent at the eighth-grade level. Though the project did have a designated control group, statistical comparisons between experimental and control subjects were not available.

LANDIS CURRICULAR MODIFICATION PROJECT

This secondary-level program is intended to meet both the "subject matter needs and remedial needs of the learning-disabled student" by extensive curricular modifications of the existing reading program. (See Landis, Jones, & Kennedy, 1973.) Teachers of English I, Mathematics I, and Science I were urged to substitute a multisensory learning approach for traditional textbook-oriented instruction. The teachers also had to structure course content in terms of behavioral objectives and to prepare appropriate auditory, visual, and kinesthetic learning aids and materials to facilitate the student's acquisition of skill and knowledge in the content areas.

A basic remedial program parallels the new, modified instructional program. Here students, removed from the demands and pressures of the content reading situation, are able to profit from reading instruction in both word recognition and comprehension of content. Study skills are stressed in the remedial instructional program.

As a result of the program, learning-disabled students are passing their academic courses. (And Landis insists that the courses are not "watered down"—that they differ in method of presentation, not content.) There has also been marked improvement in attitudes and behavior. Apparently, success in content subjects and the self-respect it engendered were the impetus for improvement in both remedial and general reading.

The three projects described above have at least one important element in common: the involvement of secondary content-area teachers. By this means each project was able to stimulate alterations and modifications of methods and materials in a regular class to bring academic instruction more in line with the needs of learning-disabled adolescents. Experimental programs designed to achieve this kind of effect are particularly promising. Secondary students have two needs: remedial or compensatory aid and "school survival therapy" (Ansara, 1972). We have to help adolescents to achieve not only in separate special programs but in regular courses, the mainstream, with their nonhandicapped peers. Unfortunately, this task is not going to be an easy one. Too few secondary teachers outside the realm of special education view themselves as responsible to teach basic skills, particularly reading skills, along with the subject matter of their discipline (Early, 1973).

THE AREA LEARNING CENTER

The Area Learning Center program (Huizinga & Smalligan, 1968) involves the establishment of a regional diagnostic learning center offering comprehensive social, medical, and educational services. This project features a multidisciplinary team service for students with classroom learning problems. The center staff includes reading, psychological, psychiatric, pediatric, and academic professionals. After a student is referred from a local school system, a center consultant will observe the student in his own classroom and complete some preliminary testing. Thereafter two courses of action are possible: an educational plan may be developed by the consultant working cooperatively with the teacher and school principal; or the student

252

may receive further diagnostic testing, in which case an evaluation is scheduled for the Area Learning Center. The assessment probes intellectual, perceptual, academic, and personality factors. Following the evaluation, a conference is held with the center and school personnel, and an educational plan is formulated. The plan is then implemented in the school with back-up support provided by the center's consultant.

By the end of the center's first year in operation, some secondary benefits of the center concept came to light. In the course of evaluation for learning disabilities, numerous health problems were detected and appropriate medical treatment was given. The interdisciplinary team approach made it possible to coordinate the services of many organizations avoiding wasteful duplication of services. Finally, the project staff found that the center concept was very well accepted by parents and school personnel.

MONTGOMERY COUNTY LEARNING-DISABILITIES PROGRAM

A secondary learning-disabilities project, titled Curricular Development for Secondary Level Learning Disabilities, was sponsored by the Montgomery County (Pennsylvania) Intermediate Unit. I was project director from July 1974 through June 1976. The express purpose of the project was to develop an intensive remedial academic program for severely educationally deficient (and learning-disabled) junior and senior high school students. The program's instructional objective was to upgrade the students' competencies in basic math and language skills to the level needed for successful reintegration into the regular secondary program, that is, full sixth-grade competency.

At the outset of the project, we, like other educators, faced the definitional dilemma. It was necessary for us to evolve specific criteria (based on our state definition of learning disabilities) that would differentiate the truly learning-disabled from the larger population of slow-learning or underachieving students. Selection criteria were established and subsequently applied to admissions for the secondary learning-disabilities program. To be eligible for participation in our program, a student must (1) demonstrate a full-scale intellectual quotient of 90 or better on an individually administered intelligence test; (2) lag two or more years below grade placement and also be functioning below the seventh-grade level in basic math and language skills; (3) be free of severe emotional and behavioral disorders; (4) demonstrate severe and specific process or cognitive disorders; and (5) willingly participate in the program. These criteria restrict the learning-disabilities program at the secondary level to students who, because they still have not mastered the elementary school curriculum, are high-risk candidates for failure at the secondary level if support is not provided to them. The intellectual criterion effectively screens out most slow learners; this was our intent. We believe that the slow learner is part of the normal, nonhandicapped school population and that responsibility for programming for such students rests with the regular educator. The various criteria further insure that students who participate in the program have good potential and motivation for learning despite severe academic disabilities and long histories of school failure. The requirement that testing reveal evidence of severe processing or cognitive deficits in effect seeks corroboration of the diagnosis of learning disability. The process/cognitive disorder criterion is useful for identification purposes but offers little useful information for instructional purposes.

The Montgomery County project has developed a basic education model for use in secondary learning-disabilities classrooms. The basic educational model is defined and delineated in terms of curricular content and grade level. We hold that the appropriate instructional concerns of the secondary learning-disabilities program are the basic math and language skills normally taught in grades one through six. We advise against both extending the instructional program to encompass the content areas of the secondary school and implementing a tutorial model for instruction in the various secondary content areas. Instruction in content areas is best left to professionals trained specifically for this purpose. Special educators should focus their attention on those areas to which their training and background apply—fundamental skills.

The selection and use of core curricular programs is an important component of the basic educational approach. Our project staff has not been concerned with the development of new materials but rather have selected appropriate and adaptable materials from among the array of commercial products already on the market. Contrary to what most teachers believe, many materials suitable for use with secondary-level learning-disabled students are currently available; the problem is that teachers are not aware of what is actually already available to them.

The manner in which materials are utilized is critical. We firmly believe in the structured management of curricular materials if students are to make optimal academic progress. Our management approach is founded on the concept of mastery learning that has been popularized in the writings of Carroll (1963), Block (1971), and Bloom (1973). Criterion-referenced and norm-referenced testing, pre- and post-assessment, placement and diagnostic testing, segmentation of curricular content into manageable instructional units, and intensive instruction are important components of our management strategy.

Individualization of instruction is achieved by varying the amount of instruction and the rate at which the youngster progresses through the standard curricular program rather than utilization of individualized programs. The amount of instruction students may receive varies according to their needs; individual schedules may vary from a self-contained program to a partial remedial program in a resource room in place of some regular class periods. Both types of programs are directed from the same classroom base and by the same staff. We feel that the critical consideration is not the label or model attached to the program; rather, it is the provision of enough remedial instruction to students to ameliorate their learning difficulties.

During the 1975–1976 school year, our seven operational classes served eighty-two students. Student achievement was assessed by means of both normative and criterion-referenced measures; norm-referenced measures were used to determine the students' achievement relative to their nonhandicapped peers while criterion-referenced measurements were used to determine the extent and rate of mastery of the curriculum material. Results on the criterion tests, which parallel the core curricular programs utilized in our program, documented an accelerated rate of progress for the majority of students in the program as compared to their learning rate prior to participation in the special program. In addition, Stanford Achievement Tests were administered on a pre- and post- basis to all students. Gain scores computed for reading comprehension indicate that 64 percent ($N = 54$) of the students who were instructed in reading made at least one year of progress in this particular reading skill; 35 percent of the students made gains of two or more years. For math concepts, 52 percent ($N = 54$) gained at least one year, while 26 percent demonstrated gains of two or more years in math concepts. Improvement in math computational skills were almost identical to those for math concepts; 54 percent ($N = 54$) gained one year, and 27 percent of the students gained two or more years in computational skills.

Additional activities of the project were a two-phase needs assessment survey to determine the size of the potential secondary-level learning-disabilities population within Montgomery County; a three-day symposium on learning disabilities in the secondary school; a materials search of curriculum materials for use in secondary learning-disabilities classrooms; and a literature search of current information pertaining to learning disabilities in the secondary student. Each of these activities resulted in the preparation of a printed document; collectively the four documents represent the most extensive data base on the topic of secondary learning disabilities currently available. Copies of the documents may be secured from the ERIC information-retrieval system.

■ SUMMARY ■

In the near future we shall surely witness rapid growth of classroom programs and services for learning-disabled students in our junior and senior high schools. Developmental efforts are already under way, though many more will be needed to fill the void in service that exists at the secondary level.

Through its monetary assistance programs, the federal government has encouraged research and development projects for secondary learning-disabled students. Federal seed monies are generally directed toward innovative and exemplary programs. As a consequence, federally funded projects tend to be at the forefront of program development and to establish directions for the field at large. Major programming trends are apparent in the programs examined in this chapter.

Mainstreaming is a central theme in most of the projects that were reviewed. The mainstreaming concept, which stresses the desirability of the least restrictive educational placements for handicapped students, is exerting a strong influence on the relative appeal of different program models. Programs that involve minimal disruption and alteration of the student's regular school placement and schedule are generally preferred to programs that involve the isolation or segregation of students into special class situations. In other words, a modified regular program is much preferred to a resource room program or self-contained classroom. Of the two special programs, the resource room rather than the self-contained program is favored by far.

Another program trend that appeared in some form in almost every project discussed is diagnostic-prescriptive teaching. The emphasis on diagnostic-prescriptive teaching is very compatible with mainstreaming in that both conceptualizations focus upon individual learners and the adjustment of program to meet individual needs.

Individualization of the instructional process ideally results in the optimal matching of learner, methods, and materials to enhance student learning and achievement. In-service training, development of resource and information centers, and development of customized learning materials (prominent in many of the current projects) are offshoots of these major trends. All these resources are supportive services intended to help both special and regular teachers to meet the needs of learning-disabled students.

If one were to attempt—on the basis of the federal projects reviewed thus far—to project the ideal secondary-level learning-disabilities program, it would be one that could meet the needs of the individual student within a regular classroom setting. The blueprint of instruction would be an individualized educational plan resulting from an in-depth diagnostic evaluation of the student. The plan would, at the very least, detail the objectives, materials, and methods to be utilized. There would be a variety of supportive services that the teacher could call upon (consultation, evaluation, information resources, and the like), but it would be the teacher who would bear responsibility for dealing with the student's problems.

The acceptance of mainstreaming and diagnostic-prescriptive teaching is so strong at the present time that anyone who disagrees is likely to be in the minority. The learning-disabilities program of the Montgomery County Intermediate Unit, however, takes exception to both mainstreaming and the diagnostic-prescriptive teaching model.

We have found that severe learning problems require intensive remedial efforts and that the intensive instructional program required by some learning-disabled students cannot be provided in the regular classroom setting, where the handicapped student may have as many

257

as thirty classmates. For these severely disabled students, we provided a self-contained academic program removed from the regular classroom. The demonstrable academic growth of the students who are participating in the program reaffirms our belief that the self-contained classroom is a viable program option that may be the most beneficial educational service model for some handicapped students. Other special educators have come to the same conclusion. Project CLUE (Iowa's CSDC operating in the Des Moines Public School System) has identified 40 of 375 junior and senior high school students who "required more intensive assistance than the resource room/mainstreaming approach allowed" (NaLDAP, 1976). Project CLUE staff have developed three career laboratories in three school sites that focus on basic reading and math skill development and career education for these severely learning-disabled students in place of resource rooms/mainstream programs.

Despite the blanket acceptance of the diagnostic-prescriptive teaching model, this approach is not our method of choice for instructional planning. The diagnostic-prescriptive instructional model is essentially the translation of the goal of individualized instruction into practice. Many professionals believe that individualization of instruction is a unique and important contribution of special education to the education of handicapped learners. Unfortunately, the empirical evidence (Bracht, 1970; Ysseldyke, 1973) reveals that truly individualized instructional programming—that is, the ideal match between learner and method—is still an elusive goal for many handicapped children. In Montgomery County we have opted for the mastery learning approach, which we have found to be compatible with the curricular emphasis of our basic educational model. The success of this approach for nonhandicapped students is well documented. The academic success of our learning-disabled students, both at the elementary and secondary level, has demonstrated the utility of this model of instructional programming for handicapped learners as well.

We need to remember, too, that both mainstreaming and diagnostic-prescriptive teaching are concepts that require validation, particularly for learning-disabled adolescents. The popularity of mainstreaming and diagnostic-prescriptive teaching is not limited to learning disabilities or to adolescent pupils; rather these trends preceded the current interest in learning disabilities at the secondary level. How can we be so sure that this is the right and only educational model for these handicapped students? Our own experience points up at least one viable alternative. Are there no others?

In light of the heterogeneity that exists among the learning-disabled, it is very unlikely that one program—be it the resource room or an alternative—will be best for all pupils. We have yet to find the program panacea for elementary learning-disabled students. Are we going to repeat the same fruitless search at the secondary level? Our objective should be not to identify *the* right program or teaching approach, but rather to envision a range of services equal to the heterogeneity of the population to be served. It may well be that the range of services will vary along a continuum ranging from program segregation to total integration, depending upon the severity of the student's disabilities. Minskoff's (1971) suggested differentiation of curriculum for learning-disabled secondary students that extends from sheltered workshops for the most severely handicapped to college-preparatory programs for the more capable learning-disabled student is, I believe, a more realistic and promising approach to secondary programming than the pursuit of the ideal service model. Minskoff's curriculum differentiation embodies a realistic appraisal of the range of abilities and disabilities that characterize learning-disabled teenagers. We must be prepared to serve the broad range of needs that these students manifest with an equally broad range of program and curricular alternatives.

Another concern relative to secondary learning-disabilities programs is the issue of definition. Many of the project reports are not at all clear as to exactly which students these projects are serving. There is an urgent need to more clearly define the secondary learning-disabled population. As long as the issue of definition and the closely related issues of criteria and incidence remain unresolved, the limits, characteristics, and numbers of secondary learning-disabled students will vary from one locale to another as a function of the operational criteria being used. We must recognize, too, that the multiplicity of working definitions for identification of the learning disabled interferes with the provision of services, communication among professionals and between ourselves and parents. Until we can determine who the learning disabled are, the likelihood of developing an instructional technology to meet their needs is remote. And all the while, the lack of resolution to these basic questions jeopardizes the credibility of the whole field of learning disabilities.

A critical component of any project is its evaluation strategy. In general, this part of many projects tends to be weak or, in some instances, totally absent. I can appreciate the pressure for immediate program development, but this doesn't negate our responsibility to evaluate our programs, methods, and materials. (We need to remember, too, that the evaluation must encompass both the model of service and student performance outcomes.) From the last decade and a half of elementary learning-disabilities programming we should be well aware of the amount of time, money, and effort that was wasted on questionable and unproductive materials, curricula, and approaches. As we embark on large-scale programming at the secondary level, we need to look at educational innovations more critically and skeptically in order to avoid repeating past mistakes. By demanding evidence of a program's effectiveness, we can avoid wasted effort and resources.

And finally, access to information is one of our most invaluable resources. Particularly in a new area of inquiry such as secondary-level learning disabilities, it is a critical need. A federal clearing house for information on funded projects, their activities, and accomplishments would help the professional community immeasurably.

National Learning Disabilities Assistance Program, the technical assistance organization for Title VI-G projects, is an invaluable resource for information on Title VI-G projects for other professionals who are aware of the organization's existence. We hope to see similar efforts for other federal assistance programs.

■ **REFERENCES** ■

Ansara, A. Language therapy to salvage the college potential of dyslexic adolescents. *Bulletin of the Orton Society,* 1972, *22,* 123–139.

Block, J. H. (Ed.). *Mastery learning.* New York: Holt, Rinehart and Winston, 1971.

Bloom, B. S. Recent developments in mastery learning. *Educational Psychologist,* 1973, *10,* 53–57.

Bracht, G. H. Experimental factors related to aptitude-treatment interactions. *Review of Educational Research,* 1970, *40,* 627–645.

Carroll, J. A model of school learning. *Teachers College Record,* 1963, *64,* 723–733.

Early, M. Taking stock: Secondary school reading in the 70's. *Journal of Reading*, 1973, *16*, 364–373.

Goodman, L., & Mann, L. *Learning disabilities in the secondary school: Issues and practices.* New York: Grune & Stratton, 1976.

Hammill, D. D. Adolescents with learning disability. In *Learning disabilities in the secondary school.* Norristown, Pa.: Montgomery County Intermediate Unit, 1975.

Huizinga, R. J., & Smalligan, D. H. The area learning center—A regional program for school children with learning disabilities. *Journal of Learning Disabilities*, 1968, *1*, 502–506.

Kline, C. L. Adolescents with learning problems: How long must they wait? *Journal of Learning Disabilities*, 1972, *5*, 262–271.

Landis, J., Jones, R. W., & Kennedy, L. D. Learning disabled curricular modification for secondary school reading. *Journal of Reading*, 1973, *16*, 374–378.

Minskoff, J. G. Learning disabled children at the secondary level: Educational programming in perspective. In J. Arena (Ed.), *The child with learning disabilities: His right to learn.* Proceedings of the Eighth Annual International Conference of the ACLD, Chicago, March 1971.

National Learning Disabilities Assistance Project. *Catalogue of child service demonstration centers. 1975–76.* Merrimac, Mass. 1976.

Wiederholt, J. L. *A report on secondary school programs for the learning disabled.* Tucson: University of Arizona, Department of Special Education, 1975.

Ysseldyke, J. E. Diagnostic-prescriptive teaching: The search for aptitude-treatment interactions. In L. Mann & D. A. Sabatino (Eds.), *The first review of special education* (Vol. 1). Philadelphia: JSE Press, 1973.

CHAPTER 11

OCCUPATIONAL EDUCATION

PAUL IRVINE
LIBBY GOODMAN
LESTER MANN

The preparation of students for future careers is a major responsibility of our educational system. The public generally assumes that, as a result of their educational experience, students will learn the attitudes, values, and skills that will make them productive members in our society.

Career education—important for all students—may be more imperative for handicapped students' success than for their nonhandicapped schoolmates'. Nonhandicapped persons who have not had adequate vocational education may easily learn later from on-the-job training. Without prior school occupational training, handicapped persons' prospects for work success are, by contrast, poor.

Simches (1975), analyzing the poor prospects that certain economic situations hold for the handicapped, points out that, in time of high unemployment, workers without appropriate training are particularly vulnerable to unemployment and layoffs, and that the handicapped face more than usual difficulties in competing for limited jobs.

Despite their critical needs for career education, the handicapped were in the past frequently cut off from occupational training opportunities. General and vocational educators were often insensitive to their instructional needs, and society's attitudes did not support the participation of the handicapped in regular educational and training programs.

Fortunately, the outlook for the handicapped in the working world is improving. This changing outlook has been spurred on by several legislative mandates. The first was the Vocational Education Act of 1963, which urged that vocational education be more responsive to the needs of persons whose special problems make success in traditional vocational education programs more difficult. When the 1963 Act was amended in 1968 to require that 10 percent of federal funds for vocational education be earmarked specifically for use with the handicapped, the outlook became even brighter.

While the Vocational Education Act gained access to vocational training for some handicapped persons in principle, however, in reality only a small minority of special education students have profited from quality vocational programs (Matters, 1974). Vocational schools have tended to select only the handicapped students that they felt comfortable with, and sometimes they have relegated the handicapped to job training that offers little preparation for realistic postgraduate employment. Training in grounds keeping, for example, has been too popular a choice. Fortunately, there is evidence of other, more positive change.

The Vocational Rehabilitation Act of 1973 speaks to the issue of employment as well as training opportunities, in that it provides for equal employment opportunity for handicapped persons where federal contracts and grants are concerned. This act insists that employers take affirmative action toward the employment and advancement of qualified handicapped persons within their organizations, as they have been required to do with female and minority groups.

The Education of All Handicapped Children Act (1975), which stipulates that public school services be provided to all handicapped students between the ages of three and twenty-one, adds strength to legislation on vocational training for the older learning-disabled pupil. Since the importance of occupational preparation increases with the age of the pupils involved, this act, which extends educational opportunities until students are twenty-one (twenty-five in some states, such as Michigan), is most significant. Some states (for example, Washington) are even considering extension of educational services throughout the life of a handicapped person. As such developments give vocational education high priority in secondary and postsecondary education, we can expect new responsibilities for both special educators and vocational educators in preparing the handicapped for careers.

■ THE SPECIAL VOCATIONAL-EDUCATION NEEDS ■ OF THE LEARNING-DISABLED

Interest in occupational and vocational training programs for the learning-disabled is a consequence of the growth of programs for persons with all levels of handicaps. Programs for secondary level learning-disabled students are necessarily incomplete if they do not provide for *both* the continuing academic education *and* vocational training needs of the student. Educational programs for the secondary learning-disabled student fail if they do not provide comprehensive preparation for the world of work.

Unfortunately, directions for good occupational training programs for the learning-disabled are not clearly defined. Programs designed for students with handicaps other than learning disabilities (mental retardation, physical disabilities, and the like) do not address the special needs of this unique group. The consequences of a learning disability do not cause the limitations noted in other handicapped groups. Nor do the learning-disabled usually have the distinctive physical or intellectual deficits that often characterize other handicapped persons. Thus while the need for programs that are altered in content and format may be clearly perceived for physically or mentally disabled pupils, the need for special programming for the learning-disabled may be neglected. The learning-disabled may be caught between existing vocational programs for the handicapped—which may be too restrictive for their capabilities—and vocational programs for the nonhandicapped (among whom they often fit socially) in which the standards for performance, such as literacy skills, are unrealistic.

Learning-disabled adolescents urgently need programs in vocational education. This chapter will explore some of the issues that bear on special educators' work in this area.

■ ACADEMIC VERSUS VOCATIONAL PRIORITIES ■

As vocational programs for learning-disabled pupils become more prominent, educators will be faced with decisions about the best utilization of time for their secondary pupils. Given that there is a finite amount of utilizable time during the school day and year (never enough in any case for the handicapped individual), how shall the student's day be put to best use? In relation to the issues of concern in this chapter, shall the continuation of academic instruction in basic literacy training have priority over vocational instruction? There is no simple answer to these questions. Very likely, high school learning-disabled students have already been exposed to a prolonged, specialized, and intensive academic program meant to bridge the achievement gaps between them and their nonhandicapped peers. The relevance of intensive academic programming needs to be reassessed in light of each student's current educational status, past history, and future goals. For example, there will be different decisions required for students who have long histories of special programming and those who have only recently been identified as learning-disabled.

The decisions, too, will be very different for junior and senior high students. One would probably be reluctant to relegate academics to a secondary status for junior high students. Such training, however, should probably receive less emphasis for older high school students. Junior high students are in the midst, not at the end, of their academic careers. Educators should not, therefore, discount the possibility of significant academic progress for them, particularly if they are in their first special education program. Indeed, some research indicates that learning-disabled students may experience sudden and dramatic learning accelerations during their adolescent years (Williamson, 1974–75). However, while high school learning-disabled pupils may also be capable of learning much academically, their academic time clocks are running out. Priorities require an emphasis upon vocational rather than academic training.

In dealing with *both* high school and junior high school learning-disabled pupils, educators must recognize that *academic* training will most likely continue to be the most important focus for parents. Many of them fear that career education will represent a disruption of their children's academic experiences (Williamson, 1974–75). Thus new educational priorities that are set for the secondary-level learning-disabled student should be based on a consensus of student, parents, and teacher.

THE RANGE OF OCCUPATIONAL ROLES

A second dimension of vocational programming of particular importance for the learning-disabled is the range of occupational options. Students should be presented with a wide range of alternatives. The term *learning-disabled,* after all, applies to students of varying ability, accomplishments, and aspirations. We must avoid stereotyping their career options because of misconceptions of their potentials for future occupations.

Thus, for those learning-disabled students who have the general ability, and desire, college training should not be regarded as an unrealistic or unattainable goal despite specific learning disabilities (Ansara, 1972; Minskoff, 1971). However, there are only a handful of junior and four-year colleges which currently offer degree programs for learning-disabled students (Goodman & Mann, 1976).* Many more such programs are needed in the future.

An issue closely related to options is the employability of the learning-disabled. Vocational or college training that prepares a student for one specific working role and no other is certainly outmoded in our complex society, where jobs are created and eliminated at an alarming rate. Career planning for a learning-disabled student soon to be looking for a job should concern itself with marketable skills that apply to many occupations. The employability of learning-disabled pupils may be enhanced by defining their *occupational* strengths and matching these to specific job requirements (Wiig, 1972; Brutten, 1966).

Furthermore, of major importance to the exercise of occupational capabilities in learning-disabled pupils are the social skills that they have acquired. The emotional and social difficulties of learning-disabled pupils that interfere with job performance and employment acceptability must be dealt with, as well as their specific occupational concerns (Williamson, 1974–75).

FOCAL POINTS OF CAREER EDUCATION FOR THE LEARNING-DISABLED

The bulk of the literature on learning disabilities has dealt with pre-academic and academic preparation rather than with occupational role assignments; consequently, little interest has been generated in the goals of career education for the learning-disabled. Two educators in particular justify our attention among the few who have addressed themselves to these issues.

Washburn (1975) has specifically addressed herself to the vocational-educational preparation of secondary learning-disabled pupils. She recommends for this purpose a model of Vocational Entry-Skills for Secondary Students. This emphasizes the following:

1. *Vocational academics.* This includes survival reading, writing, spelling, and math, as they are relevant to vocational learning and everyday

---

* The Educational Testing Service now accommodates high school students who are learning-disabled by allowing untimed and orally administered tests. College level programs that do accept learning-disabled students tend to be both selective and costly (Goodman & Mann, 1976). Yet it is gratifying to know that for those who are able, the opportunity does exist.

living requirements (using the phone book, following written instructions, understanding advertising, and so on).

2. *Vocational physical education.* This is to further develop deficient visual-motor and coordination skills in learning-disabled youths.

3. *Vocational resources.* This is directed to training students to search out information they will require after their school years, that is, "school community, family and local businesses as resource helpers."

4. *Vocational know-how.* Here pupils receive training in the skills required to get and keep a desirable job. Students are provided experiences in interviewing, conversation, résumés, uses of money, transportation, and driver education. They are also assisted in developing personality and solving personal problems.

5. *Basic vocational entry skills.* Here the program develops all those basic work skills required for job success by hands-on experiences. Training aims at developing generalized work skills and appropriate attitudes toward work.

6. *Vocational placement.* All other efforts are fruitless unless learning-disabled pupils are actually able to come to grips with jobs themselves, as jobs. Vocational placement should be accomplished through volunteer work, work experience, and, finally, job placement (and replacement).

Williamson (1974–75) takes a broader view of occupational preparation for learning-disabled pupils. She talks about career education rather than vocational preparation and emphasizes offering choices to the pupil, rather than specific goal direction. She insists, for instance, that schools cannot decide for pupils whether or not they should go to college. Instead, she says, they can only present all of the alternatives to the students. The teacher of secondary-level learning-disabled pupils must be an effective counselor as well as a teacher to assist in this respect.

Williamson also notes that curriculum emphasis at the secondary level should move from remediating deficits to capitalizing on areas of strengths, and that these strengths should be matched with jobs or professional requirements.

Williamson insists that colleges should be willing to adapt curricula to meet the problems created by learning-disabled pupils' deficits or to exempt them from areas that they cannot manage. Employers, too, need to be educated in the problems of prospective learning-disabled employees so that they make allowances for reduced rates of performance (particularly in areas requiring perceptual and motor skills) if the learning-disabled employee is otherwise capable of producing acceptable results.

Williamson recommends that human service vocations may be particularly promising for employment of the learning-disabled. "Service careers tend to require a minimal degree of proficiency in high-level perceptual and motor skills in which many learning disabled pupils are deficient." While we are not in agreement that perceptual and motor dysfunctions are necessarily the critical ones in learning disabilities, we do agree with Williamson's statement that adults who have been learning-disabled pupils may feel, as she notes, "a strong identification for people in need, and have developed a compassion for people which enables them to find personal reward in the areas of social work, health careers, or other public service careers."

■ CAREER TRAINING PROGRAMS: WHERE ARE WE? ■

Most of the existing literature that does delve into vocational education for the handicapped relates to handicaps other than learning disabilities—most frequently, mental retardation, orthopedic handicaps, and visual and auditory impairments. The literature relative to career preparation for the learning-disabled is minute (Brutten, 1966; Kameny, 1967; Lurie, 1967; Martin, 1967; Schweich, 1975; Sunberg, 1970; Weening, 1969; Williamson, 1974–75; Washburn, 1975; Irvine, 1975; Colella, 1973).

Bergstein et al. (1973) offer a compilation of case studies for six career education programs for the handicapped. Of the programs reviewed, five serve pupils who might be considered learning-disabled and thus merit consideration from our readers: Career Development Center, Syosset, New York; Mobile Unit for Vocational Evaluation, Towson, Maryland; Project SERVE, St. Paul, Minnesota; Project Worker, Fullerton, California; Vocational Village, Portland, Oregon. Each case study includes a lengthy description of the program in terms of program operations, notable features, program personnel, program evaluation (internal program evaluation design), and recommendations regarding replication of the program for other locations.

Career preparation is also discussed by Koppitz (1971), who, in a five-year follow-up study of children with learning disabilities, outlined a comprehensive special education program after grade eight in which learning-disabled pupils have four major options: an academically oriented high school program; a general high school program; a self-contained, academically oriented special class; or a vocational program. Koppitz recommends that the vocational program include one or two years of prevocational training and the study of basic skills, followed by one or two years of skills training in a work-study program.

Finally, we might note a New Jersey Department of Education publication (Buontempo, McNulty, & Ringelheim, 1974) proposing "an educational strategy for employability" that may apply to learning-disabled pupils. It consists of five major phases: vocational evaluation, self and career awareness, skill training, getting started in a real job, and follow-up. The "self and career awareness" phase, in the middle school years or soon thereafter, offers students an opportunity to become acquainted with a variety of occupations and to become aware of their own abilities and interests in relation to the world of work, the end result being the establishment of realistic career goals. The "self and career awareness" phase as described by these authors resembles programs elsewhere referred to as "exploratory occupational education."

■ A MODEL PROGRAM FOR CAREER PREPARATION ■
FOR LEARNING-DISABLED ADOLESCENTS

The relationship of the major elements in a comprehensive model program of occupational preparation for learning-disabled youths is shown in Figure 11-1.* From a prevocational level, most often provided as a part of a special class or resource room program, a student moves into the exploratory level, most of them into the exploratory occupational education program, but with an alternative: an in-house, sheltered work experience program that may be more appropriate for those

* This model is one espoused specifically by the senior author of this chapter.

271

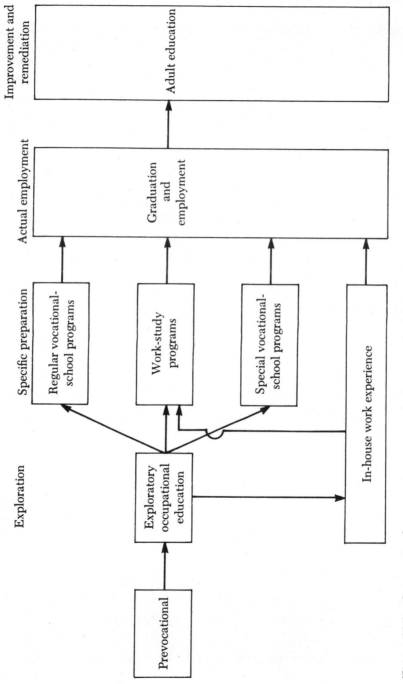

Figure 11-1 Occupational preparation patterns for learning-disabled youth

students with the most severe learning problems. From the exploratory level, the student moves into one of the four major alternatives for specific occupational preparation: regular vocational school programs, work-study programs, special vocational school programs, or the occupational preparation phase of the program that provides in-house work experience.

From specific occupational preparation, the student then moves into actual employment. Postgraduate (adult) education may then be required at times for improvement of specific skills or to prepare learning-disabled graduates for employment in a different field.

The model provides, however, for whatever movement is appropriate for a student, at whatever time it is needed.

An example of this model is the Exploratory Occupation Education (EOE) Program developed by the Board of Cooperative Educational Services (BOCES) of Putnam and Northern Westchester Counties, New York, a regional public school agency serving twenty-one public school districts.

The EOE program at BOCES serves approximately 320 pupils each year. About one-half of these pupils attend special classes operated either by BOCES or their home school districts. The other half are enrolled in regular school programs in the participating school districts.

Each pupil's application (upon referral by the home school or by the BOCES special education staff) for admission to the EOE program is considered in a conference attended by one or more representatives of the staff presently working with the pupil and a team of EOE staff members representing teaching, guidance, and administration.

The EOE program is designed to serve learning-disabled pupils along with pupils with other types of handicaps. Admission is based upon the pupil's need and readiness. The records of the pupils in the EOE program reveal a variety of diagnoses, but the program has essentially "delabeled" the students. In the EOE population, intelligence typically ranges from moderate mental retardation to bright-normal, and academic achievement in tool subjects from the level of first or second grade to that of the senior high school level. Class size is kept small, generally limited to ten, to allow for the individualization necessary in the rather heterogeneous groups.

While the qualifications and needs of each referred pupil are considered individually, the team making decisions regarding admission to EOE does have two guidelines:

1. Pupils will usually be admitted at age fifteen or sixteen.

2. To be admitted, pupils must have demonstrated a level of maturity that suggests they are ready to begin the process of occupational preparation. In assessing maturity and readiness, the team takes into consideration such factors as ability to accept direction, ability to work independently, attendance record, and safe work habits. Rigid admission requirements are, however, regarded as undesirable. The factors that enter into the assessment of readiness for the program should be applied with great sensitivity and insight, because pupil characteristics often change dramatically for the better when a pupil begins the EOE program.

Pupils attend the EOE program for half of each school day, either morning or afternoon, being transported to the regional campus from their home schools. The half-day at EOE is divided about equally between occupational instruction by a vocational teacher in a shop setting and related academic instruction provided by a teacher from special education. While an occupation is being explored in the shop, the related academic instruction focuses on the vocabulary of the occupation, the mathematics and reading skills needed, and a study of the occupation itself—working conditions, duties, required knowledge and skills, and so on. The shop and classroom areas are adjacent, fostering communication between the two teachers, who must function as a team to assure a high degree of relatedness between shop activities and academic instruction. There are eight such shops-classroom areas.

Listed below are the occupational areas that are available for exploration in the BOCES EOE program, with the specific occupations that are explored in each area.

1. *Metal Trades* Draftsman, drill press operator, appliance repairman, general machine operator, ironworker, lathe operator, machinist, sheet metal worker, welder

2. *Automotive trades* Auto body repairman, auto mechanic, oxyacetylene welder, service station attendant (lubrication specialist, pneumatic tire specialist), small engine repairman

3. *Building Trades I* Bricklayer, carpenter, concrete finisher, resilient tile mechanic, roofer

4. *Building Trades II* Dry wall applicator, electrician, insulation mechanic, maintenance man-custodian-cleaner, painter, plumber, taper

5. *Office Occupations / Distributive Education*   Bookkeeper, clerk, file clerk, messenger, receptionist, secretary, typist, cashier, receiving clerk–stock clerk, salesperson, shipping clerk, window trimmer, wrapper

6. *Food Trades*   Baker, beverage maker, cafeteria worker–steamtable, cashier, cook, counter person, dishwasher, salad maker, sandwich maker, short order cook, waiter-waitress

7. *Cosmetology / Health*   Beautician, day care center aide, home attendant, hospital housekeeper, hospital orderly, hospital tray person, hospital ward clerk, licensed practical nurse, nurse's aide

8. *Agriculture Occupations*   Florist, gardener, greenhouse worker, greenskeeper, groundskeeper, landscaper, nurseryman

Though pupils usually explore one occupational area per semester, they may change from one area to another at any time. Most pupils remain in the EOE program for two years, but arrangements can be made for them to advance to the next phase of occupational preparation whenever they are ready. The major alternatives for final occupational preparation are vocational school, a cooperative work-study program, and special vocational courses developed by the special education department to serve these pupils.

The success of the EOE program can be attributed to a number of factors:

1. Occupational education teachers are teaching the occupational aspects, and special education teachers are teaching the academic aspects of the program.

2. The occupational teacher and the special education teacher who form each team are working in adjacent spaces; they provide a unified program of occupational and academic instruction.

3. The program is adapted to each pupil's needs. Pupils are not expected to fit the program other than in terms of behavior that is acceptable and does not interfere with the learning of others.

4. Special attention is given to each student's disabilities so as to make instruction appropriate for him or her.

5. Attention is given to the development of realistic vocational and personal goals. The staff does not tell students that they lack the ability to perform a particular kind of work. Instead, they are given experience to help them reach their own conclusions.

6. Well-spelled-out short-term goals help to foster control.

7. There is an emphasis on a positive attitude toward work—the dignity of work—a concept that too often gets lost in occupational programs.

8. The Exploratory Occupational Education program demonstrates to students that they may enter and eventually master an occupation in spite of the learning problems that often made their school experiences demoralizing.

9. There is no failure.

Five years of experience with EOE in its present form have convinced us that learning-disabled students feel better about school and themselves, and achieve better in the final phases of their occupational preparation, in the EOE program than they do in traditional programs. The only real limitation of the program is the lack of college options.

■ **REFERENCES** ■

Ansara, A. Language therapy to salvage the college potential of dyslexic adolescents. *Bulletin of the Orton Society*, 1972, 22, 123–139.

Bamford, D., et al. *Curriculum guide for exploratory occupational education*. Yorktown Heights, N.Y.: Board of Cooperative Educational Services (in preparation).

Bergstein, P., and others. *Exemplary programs for the handicapped* (Vol. 2, Career education, case studies). Cambridge, Mass.: Abt Associates, 1973.

Brutten, M. Vocational education for the brain injured adolescent and young adult at the Vanguard School. In *International approach to learning disabilities of children and youth*. Proceedings of the Third Annual Conference of the ACLD, Tulsa, 1966.

Buontempo, G., McNulty, T., & Ringelheim, D. *Vocational education for the handicapped*. Trenton: State of New Jersey, Department of Education, 1974.

Colella, H. V. Career development center: A modified high school for the handicapped. *Teaching Exceptional Children*, 1973, 5, 110–118.

Goodman, L., & Mann, L. *Learning disabilities in the secondary school.* New York: Grune & Stratton, 1976.

Irvine, P. *Exploratory occupational education for learning disabled adolescents.* Paper presented at Learning Disabilities in the Secondary School, a symposium sponsored by the Montgomery County Intermediate Unit, Norristown, Pa., March 1975.

Irvine, P., & Plumpton, R. A. *A program for the vocational rehabilitation of emotionally disturbed and brain-injured adolescents in a public school setting.* Yorktown Heights, N.Y.: Board of Cooperative Educational Services, 1970.

Kameny, A. Prevocational retraining: A behavioral task-centered approach. In *Management of the child with learning disabilities.* Proceedings of the Fourth Annual Conference of the ACLD, New York, 1967.

Koppitz, E. M. *Children with learning disabilities: A five year follow-up study.* New York: Grune & Stratton, 1971.

Lurie, S. Experience and potentialities in vocational rehabilitation services. In *Management of the child with learning disabilities.* Proceedings of the Fourth Annual Conference of the ACLD, New York, 1967.

Martin, C. T. Prevocational services for secondary school children with learning disabilities. In *Management of the child with learning disabilities.* Proceedings of the Fourth Annual Conference of the ACLD, New York, 1967.

Matters, C. H. Serving the handicapped and disadvantaged in special programs. *American Vocational Journal*, 1974, 49, 34–35.

Minskoff, J. G. Learning disabled children at the secondary level: Educational programming in perspective. In J. Arena (Ed.), *The child with learning disabilities: His right to learn.* Proceedings of the Eighth Annual Conference of the ACLD, Chicago, March 1971.

Schweich, P. D. The development of choices—an educational approach to employment. *Academic Therapy*, 1975, 10, 277–283.

Simches, R. Economic inflation: Hazard for the handicapped. *Exceptional Children*, 1975, 41, 229–242.

Sunberg, N. Vocational rehabilitation cooperation in school. In L. Anderson (Ed.), *Helping the adolescent with the hidden handicap.* Los Angeles: California Association for Neurologically Handicapped Children, 1970.

Washburn, W. Y. Where to go in voc-ed for secondary LD students. *Academic Therapy*, 1975, 11, 31–35.

Weening, C. A. Program development for the learning disabled. In *Progress in parent information, professional growth, and public policy.* Proceedings of the Sixth Annual Conference of the ACLD, Fort Worth, 1969.

Wiig, E. The emerging LD crisis. *Journal of Rehabilitation,* 1972, *38,* 15–17.

Williamson, A. P. Career education: Implications for secondary LD students. *Academic Therapy, 10* (Winter 1974–75), 193–200.

Young, E. B., et al. *Vocational education for handicapped persons: Handbook for program implementation.* Washington, D.C.: U.S. Office of Education, 1971.

CHAPTER 12

COMPETENCIES
FOR TEACHERS

NAOMI ZIGMOND
RITA SILVERMAN
THERESA LAURIE

In the past few years educators have been interested in establishing special programs for secondary students with learning disabilities. Learning-disabled youngsters outgrow elementary programs, and many need supportive services as they enter middle and high schools. While we know that the programs are needed, we know little about the competencies required of teachers in these new programs. This chapter will examine that vital area.

Planners of teacher preparation programs are slowly responding to appeals (from state departments of education, from special education directors and supervisors, from parents, from teacher educators, and from teachers themselves) to develop training programs directed specifically at the secondary level. These new training programs reflect the continuing debate in the learning-disabilities field on definition, assessment, and instructional strategies: There is little agreement among teacher educators on the role of the secondary teacher and on the specific competencies needed to fill this role. Some programs emphasize teaching skills; others emphasize consultation skills. Some programs stress career and vocational preparation, while others stress academic learning.

This lack of standardization of teacher preparation programs is not simply a matter of academic freedom; it suggests that educators in the learning-disabilities field do not have a clear idea of what they are preparing teachers to do (or with whom they are to do it) and what they must know to do it well. At present we have no reason to believe that our graduates are, or will be, successful; follow-up data on teacher effectiveness are sorely lacking.

We cannot flounder this way forever. If we are committed to quality education for all learning-disabled students, we must begin to establish and maintain professional standards for personnel who educate our children. The dozens of articles listed in *Education Index* under "accountability in education" reflect the current interest in this topic. Moreover, in the decades ahead, teachers will be increasingly accountable for their behavior, and teacher educators must accept responsibility for defining and validating skills for the teacher of students with learning disabilities. The trend towards competency-based teacher education is a step in that direction.

In its simplest form, a competency-based teacher education program may be defined as one that specifies objectives for the training of teachers and holds prospective teachers accountable for meeting those objectives (Anderson et al., 1973). This approach allows clear specification of training outcomes for prospective teachers, thus facilitating the development of required teaching competencies. To design and implement such a training program, we must first be prepared to specify what knowledge we will expect of the teacher, and what skills are to be demonstrated upon completion of the program. This chapter proposes minimal competencies for teachers of secondary-aged learning-disabled students.

■ A MODEL FOR COMPREHENSIVE SERVICES ■

As part of a model for comprehensive services currently being implemented and validated in a Child Service Demonstration Center (Title VI-G) in Pittsburgh, Pennsylvania, these authors have established some tentative competencies for the participating teachers. In constructing the model, we made the assumption that the secondary student with learning disabilities should be provided with a special program in the least restrictive way possible, i.e., that special schools and self-contained classes are not appropriate, but that supportive services for mainstreamed students are. (See Commonwealth of Pennsylvania, Public School Code, 1971; Birch, 1973.)

The model for comprehensive services calls for two distinct roles for the secondary-level learning-disabilities teachers, since they must be able to work effectively with both students and other teachers.

The first role is that of the traditional learning-disabilities specialist or resource room teacher who is prepared to deal with the academic and social problems of students who are removed from their regular classes for part of the school day. For adolescents with significant deficiencies in basic skills, the need for effective, direct service is acute. And time is running out! Someone must help these students in a final attempt to reach literacy before school years run out. Since there is no time or place in a secondary curriculum, as it is presently constituted, for learning *how* to read or *how* to do elementary mathematics, one of the direct services that the learning-disabilities teacher must provide is intensive response-contingent instruction in basic skill areas.

However, identifying secondary students with learning disabilities and placing them in a program of direct intervention is insufficient.

281

The mainstream secondary curriculum requires reading, writing, comprehension, and computation skills without regard to individual learning problems. If the student is to survive the secondary curriculum, there must be a second role for the learning-disabilities teacher, that of teacher consultant (Reger et al., 1968; McKenzie et al., 1970; Shaw & Shaw, 1972; Newcomer, in press). As teacher consultant, a teacher has no direct classroom responsibilities and she or he does not work directly with a handicapped learner. Rather the teacher consultant is prepared to offer support to regular educators so that a secondary student can succeed in the mainstream. Without the indirect services of a teacher consultant, the direct remedial efforts of the learning-disabilities teacher may be without significance.

The special educators who work with regular educators must have all the skills of teachers who offer direct services to students with learning disabilities; in addition, the teacher consultant must be familiar with instructional programs in content areas and must be able to demonstrate to mainstream teachers the tactics and strategies of adaptive teaching within the regular class.

Teacher consultants must have the interpersonal skills to enable them to be supportive rather than critical. These teachers must be able to recognize and evaluate the constraints under which regular educators work (predetermined curricula, large class size, short class periods, limited materials) and to make suggestions that are reasonable for the situation.

INTERVENTION STRATEGIES

In our model the needs of secondary students with learning disabilities are seen as twofold: remediation of their basic learning disabilities and daily maintenance in the mainstream of school and society. To meet these needs, direct and indirect teacher intervention strategies are provided. Direct services include diagnostic-prescriptive teaching of basic skills, group meetings with learning-disabled students, and career exploration activities. Indirect services include one-to-one consultations with content-area teachers about necessary changes in teaching strategies for mainstreamed learning-disabled students, and parent education programs. Each phase of the model (outlined in Figure 12-1) is described in the sections that follow.

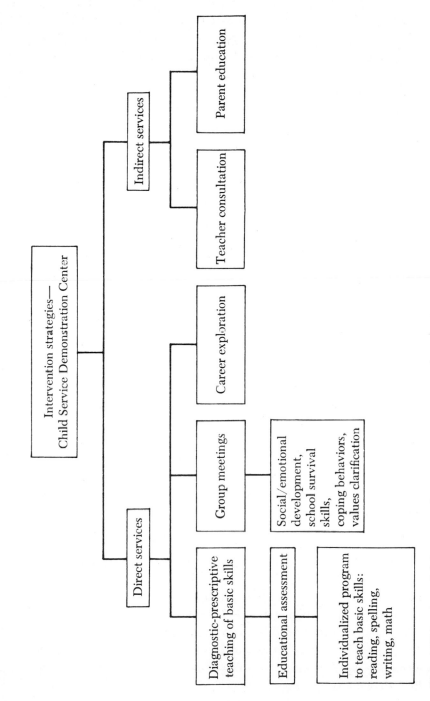

Figure 12-1 A model for comprehensive services to secondary students with learning disabilities

DIRECT SERVICES TO LEARNING-DISABLED STUDENTS

DIAGNOSTIC-PRESCRIPTIVE TEACHING   The primary objectives of this aspect of the direct services is the improvement of basic skills in reading, spelling, written language, and math. To accomplish this at the secondary level, students first undergo an educational assessment to determine error patterns in reading and math. The assessment consists primarily, though not entirely, of criterion-referenced measurements. In reading, skills in structural and phonetic analysis, sight vocabulary and comprehension are examined. In math, the teacher seeks to establish levels of entering behavior in computation and problem solving. Similar assessments are accomplished for spoken language, spelling, and writing.

Besides knowing how to assess basic skills, the teacher is expected to evaluate each student's interest areas and levels of motivation. This information, derived from structured interviews and ongoing observation, is used to select materials for instruction and to establish a behavior management strategy for the individualized teaching sessions.

Once the assessment has been completed, the teacher writes an instructional objective for each student. Sequences of tasks are generated according to individual needs and interests. Mnemonic devices, games, gimmicks, and gadgets are utilized, if necessary, to teach these hard-to-teach youngsters. Considerable use is made of commercially available material. Since most such materials are designed for younger students, however, an instructor may employ sources not usually considered to be instructional materials, but which are of immediate relevance to the world of the secondary pupil. These include drivers' manuals, comics, magazines, card or dice games, or other teacher-made materials, any of which can be used to help the teacher teach the task or skills in the instructional objective.

GROUP MEETINGS   Weekly meetings of small groups of students provide an opportunity for teaching "school survival tactics." This aspect of the direct services focuses on the academic, social, and emotional demands placed on the secondary student in the mainstream. The group meetings are an attempt to help learning-disabled adolescents deal more effectively with problems in these areas.

The emphasis is on exploring and developing coping skills. Since the secondary school faculty is typically large and diverse, learning-disabled students must acquire patterns that are appropriate to many kinds of adults. Typically, students learn the positive value of "teacher pleasing behaviors" (Brown, 1975) without specific instruction; many learning-disabled youngsters do not, and for these students instruction may be essential to survival. (See Chapter 4 of this book.) Group meetings emphasize the importance of getting to class on time, having a pencil and the right books, sitting straight and looking attentive, making eye contact with the teacher, responding to questions, and so on.

Sessions also deal with problems of how to study and how to prepare independently for various kinds of oral and written tests. The sessions are used for values clarification activities and for group discussions of career and vocational goals.

CAREER EXPLORATION Any program for adolescent students with learning disabilities would be incomplete if it did not provide both academic and vocational preparation. Learning-disabled teenagers require guidance and preparatory training if they are to find worthwhile and satisfactory careers. Most learning-disabled adolescents will not pursue academic training beyond high school. It is extremely important that these students use the remaining years of high school in a practical and realistic way as well as trying to achieve the highest possible level of academic success. The career exploration program attempts to meet this need.

INDIRECT SERVICES FOR LEARNING-DISABLED STUDENTS

CONSULTATION SERVICES TO MAINSTREAM EDUCATORS The plight of the student with a learning disability is accentuated at the secondary level because curriculum in the secondary school is developed, interpreted, and presented by specialists in subject matter. These teachers often lack the psychoeducational orientation useful in designing alternative teaching and assessment strategies. There is a need for an interpreter— a liaison between the student and the content-area teacher—to help this student "make it" in the mainstream. The learning-disabilities teacher in a teacher-consultant role works primarily on a one-to-one basis with content-area teachers who have learning-disabled students in their classes. The teacher-consultant helps the mainstream teacher to define instructional objectives and to develop alternative ways of presenting content information and of assessing knowledge. Courses are not watered down but are altered in terms of methods of presentation or methods of evaluation. For example, since curriculum at the secondary level is not ordinarily presented via multimedia or multi-sensory approaches, the teacher-consultant may recommend the use of supplementary materials such as filmstrips or tapes to a content-area teacher.

PARENT EDUCATION The parent education program in this model has two purposes. First, it provides parents with information about their children's learning problems, about the educational practices of their children's teachers, and about why certain methods are selected over others. Second, it attempts to teach parents new ways of dealing with learning problems that extend into the home, particularly problems of management and control.

Behavior management principles and practical solutions to problems are taught through modeling, role playing, and discussion. In addition, parents are helped toward a realistic appraisal of the student's strengths and weaknesses, and assisted in developing realistic short-term and long-term goals and career objectives for their child.

■ MINIMAL COMPETENCIES ■

Teacher educators must prepare personnel who can handle both the direct and indirect services described in the preceding section. The list of competencies in the next section is offered as a first step in specifying the critical skills needed by the secondary-level learning-disabilities teacher. This list is intended to serve as a general guide-line only. The organization of these competencies into sequential courses and experiences is considered the responsibility of individual teacher preparation programs. In order to be useful for specific application with teachers in a pre-service teacher-training program or an in-service teacher workshop, the competencies must be translated into the specific criteria required for demonstration of mastery. Of course, as Hammill and Newcomer (mimeo.) point out, there is no single correct criterion for mastery of any of the competencies. The biases, abilities, and preferences of those responsible for making these competencies functional will determine to a large extent the methods and means for attaining mastery. For example, one teacher trainer might be convinced that a broad competency such as the ability to teach reading might be accomplished by demonstrating effective use of a basal reading series; another might be equally positive that a language-experience reading program is appropriate. Certainly a thoroughly developed training program would provide several alternative approaches that pertain to each broad competency.

In proposing this list of competencies we have not attempted to be all-encompassing. We have focused almost exclusively on those skills needed for the day-to-day delivery of services to learning-disabled students and that can be demonstrated by the teacher on the job. No attempt has been made to specify personality or attitude variables that contribute to effective teaching of all secondary students. These might include the abilities to establish rapport with adolescents, to be flexible and adaptable, to recognize the need for continuous self-evaluation, and to communicate effectively with students, teachers, counselors, administrators, and parents. Certainly a strong desire to work with this age level would be essential. We hope that those who train teachers and those who employ them recognize the relationship between teachers' personalities and motivations and their successful teaching.

Also, we have not discussed those topics important to the general knowledge base of teachers about the field of learning disabilities. Such topics include causes of learning problems, theories of human learning and child development, history of the field of learning disabilities, and philosophical issues in the field, among others. We agree with those who say that no teacher should receive a degree or certificate in learning disabilities without consideration being given to each of these critical areas.

COMPETENCIES FOR PROVIDING DIRECT SERVICES

In the role of providing direct services to students, the learning-disabilities teacher must be able to do each of the following:

1. Interpret a psychological report and identify the educational relevance of findings in the report.

2. Assess the secondary-level learning-disabled student with appropriate informal, criterion-referenced, or competency-based tests as well as formal, standardized, norm-referenced assessments.

3. Conduct and interpret interviews with students and observations of them in and out of class, to learn about their particular interests and motivations.

4. Develop individualized instructional programs, utilizing the assessment information. This includes adjusting the difficulty level of a particular task and incorporating information regarding the child's attitude, interests, and values into the instructional plans.

5. Teach in the basic skill areas of reading, written language, and math.

6. Select commercially available instructional programs appropriate for the educational objectives as well as for the age and interests of adolescents with learning disabilities.

7. Create age-appropriate, high-interest instructional materials that may not be available commercially.

8. Use classroom management techniques with individuals and groups of students that motivate optimal efforts for achievement, reduce interfering maladaptive behaviors, encourage internal monitoring of behaviors, and enhance the students' self-concepts and peer interactions.

9. Engage groups of adolescents in discussion or activities that explore school survival skills, values clarification, attitudes, self-concept, and the like.

10. Provide learning-disabled students with an occupational exploration/preparation program which includes "hands on" experiences in one or more occupational fields.

COMPETENCIES FOR PROVIDING INDIRECT SERVICES

In the role of providing indirect services to students, teachers must be able to do each of the following:

1. Assess the receptivity of mainstream teachers for change.

2. Communicate effectively with other teachers—that is, transmit information at the readiness level of the listener.

3. Analyze the "system" operating within the secondary school and recognize the constraints under which the mainstream educator must function, including prescribed curricula, class size, time limitations, and requirements for or limitations on materials.

4. Analyze the teaching style of the mainstream educator, including the management strategies being employed, the manner (modalities) in which information is being conveyed to students, and the way in which student knowledge is being assessed.

5. Understand the content of a secondary curriculum well enough to be able to make suggestions for changes in methods of presentation of information and evaluation of knowledge.

6. Analyze mainstream curriculum materials, including testing readability levels of textbooks, so that they may direct the mainstream teacher toward selection of alternative or supplementary materials for learning-disabled students.

7. Suggest and model modifications of management strategies for individuals and groups of students, and modifications in teaching approaches (information delivery and knowledge assessment) to accommodate students with different learning styles and skill levels.

8. Apply learning principles to the teaching of teachers, including assessment of motivational levels, use of shaping, modeling and fading techniques, and reinforcement strategies.

9. Assume the role of child advocate and interact effectively on behalf of learning-disabled adolescents with all other members of the school staff.

10. Communicate with parents of the secondary learning-disabilities students, to help them to understand the implications of the students' learning styles in school, home, and community.

11. Help parents to find effective strategies for dealing with their learning-disabled adolescents in conflict situations.

12. Assist parents in developing realistic expectations in academic and occupational areas.

13. Direct parents and school staff to community and governmental agencies, volunteer and nonprofit groups and parent organizations that provide supportive services to learning-disabled students.

■ LIMITATIONS OF MINIMAL COMPETENCIES ■

The basic assumption behind the development of specific competencies for teachers of secondary-level learning-disabled students is that this population of students learn differently from other students (Anderson, 1970; Strother et al., 1971; Johnson, 1968; Johnson & Myklebust, 1967). A real problem with this assumption is that few research efforts have been directed towards secondary students with learning disabilities and even fewer toward the competencies their teachers should possess. The list of competencies which we have proposed is based entirely on the "expert opinion" of teacher educators, state education department leaders, and teachers in the field. Expert opinion is certainly an appropriate place to begin a definition of teaching competencies for secondary level teachers of learning-disabled students, but opinion alone does not constitute sufficient evidence that the abilities are critical to successful teaching (Shores et al., 1973). To validate competency statements one must demonstrate that successful teachers actually engage in those behaviors and that performance of the competencies discriminates between successful and unsuccessful teachers, when success is being defined as the production of desired effects in the learners' performance.

Thus, it is necessary to design research in which the curriculum, the teachers' behavior, and the learners' performance are dynamically related, and in which there is a systematic manipulation of teacher knowledge and skills with observation and measurement of the effect on the learners' performance (Rosenshine & Furst, 1971). In addition to serving as the basis for redefining competencies, such research would address the basic assumption that these competencies are unique. This would permit several important questions to be answered: Are the special learning needs of learning-disabled adolescents any different from those of their counterparts in the elementary school? Are the teacher behaviors that satisfactorily meet these needs different? Are the skills unique to the teacher of the learning-disabled youngster, or are they the competencies needed by any special educator or even by any mainstream teacher?

It is certainly possible that the answer to some of these questions is no. In fact, evidence is accumulating that learning-disabled children do not have learning characteristics different from those of mentally retarded or socially and emotionally maladjusted children, and that the same principles of learning and behavior change apply to all mildly handicapped students (Hammill & Bartel, 1975; Reger et al., 1968; Telford & Sawrey, 1968; Senf & Freundl, 1971; Haring, 1974).

It is clear that there is very little empirical data on which to base teacher preparation programs in secondary learning disabilities, a shortcoming that currently pervades the entire field of teacher education. Much research is needed. At the same time, we cannot abandon our efforts at preparing secondary personnel, nor curtail attempts to make programs competency-based until this research is available. On the contrary, we believe that the trend toward competency-based instruction has been responsible for significant advances in preparing teachers for special education, particularly in terms of setting specific program objectives, developing innovative teaching strategies, and evaluating both teachers and programs in relation to objective criteria (Shores et al., 1973). Still, we must accelerate research efforts aimed at validation of teacher competencies. Until we can answer some of the questions raised here with empirical data rather than with expert opinion, speculation, or passion, any programs that we design will be based on supposition.

■ REFERENCES ■

Anderson, D. W., Cooper, J. M., DeVault, M. V., Dickson, G. D., Johnson, C. D., & Weber, W. A. *Competency based teacher education.* Berkeley, Calif.: McCutchan Publishing Co., 1973.

Anderson, L. E. (Ed.). *Helping the adolescent with the hidden handicap.* Belmont, Calif.: Fearon Publishers, 1970.

Birch, J. W. *Retarded Pupils in Mainstream.* Prepublication manuscript, University of Minnesota, Leadership Training Institute of the Department of Special Education, 1973.

Brown, V. *Modifications in the Secondary Curriculum for the L. D. Student.* Paper presented at the Pennsylvania CEC Conference, November 1975.

Commonwealth of Pennsylvania, Public School Code, 24 Purd. Stat. Section 13-1372, 1971.

Hammill, D. D., & Bartel, N. R. *Teaching children with learning and behavior problems.* Boston: Allyn and Bacon, 1975.

Hammill, D. D., & Newcomer, P. *Minimum competencies for teachers of children with L.D.* A report based on the proceedings of the Professional Task Force sponsored by the Department of Educational and Cultural Services of the State of Maine. (Mimeograph)

Haring, D. G. *Behavior of exceptional children: An introduction to special education.* Columbus, Ohio: Charles E. Merrill, 1974.

Johnson, D. J. Educational principles for children with disabilities. *Rehabilitation Literature,* 1968, *28,* 317–322.

Johnson, D. J., & Myklebust, H. R. *Learning disabilities.* New York: Grune & Stratton, 1967.

McKenzie, H. S., Egner, A., Knight, M., Perelman, P., Schneider, B., & Garvin, J. Training consulting teachers to assist elementary teachers in the management and education of handicapped children. *Exceptional Children,* 1970, *37,* 137–145.

Newcomer, P. Special education services for the mildly handicapped. *Journal of Learning Disabilities,* in press.

Reger, R., Schroeder, W., & Uschold, K. *Special education,* New York: Oxford University Press, 1968.

Rosenshine, B., & Furst, N. Research on teacher performance criteria. In O. B. Smith (Ed.), *Research in teacher education—A symposium.* Englewood Cliffs, N.J.: Prentice-Hall, 1971.

Senf, G., & Freundl, P. Memory and attention factors in specific learning disabilities, *Journal of Learning Disabilities,* 1971, *4,* 94–106.

Shaw, S. F., & Shaw, W. K. The in-service experience plan, or changing the bath without losing the baby. *Journal of Special Education,* 1972, *6,* 94–126.

Shores, R. E., Cegelka, P. T., & Nelson, C. M. Competency based special education teacher training. *Exceptional Children,* 1973, *40,* 192–197.

Strother, C., Hagin, R., Giffin, M., & Lehtinen-Rogan, L. *The educator's enigma: The adolescent with learning disabilities.* San Rafael, Calif.: Academic Therapy Publications, 1971.

Telford, C., & Sawrey, J. *Educational psychology: Psychological foundations of education.* Boston: Allyn and Bacon, 1968.

RETROSPECT
AND PROSPECTS

LIBBY GOODMAN
LESTER MANN

This book examined the identification, management, and education of learning-disabled adolescents. Each of the contributing authors explored different facets of the education of older learning-disabled students. Together the contributors have built up a base of knowledge about the major concerns in this area and have formulated key questions for discussion and further study. The reader will find few easy or definitive answers, however. The book reflects the state of learning disabilities and the past neglect of learning-disabled adolescents.

The learning-disability efforts of the 1960s and early 1970s were focused on the needs of elementary-level handicapped children. The current concern for the learning-disabled in our schools is a relatively new one. The movement has little past to speak of, but an emerging present and a very challenging future.

Professionals who work with the older learning-disabled population have many unresolved issues and problems before them. Despite the many questions and complexities that face us, there is consensus on one critical point. We know that the problems will not be solved by simply transplanting the methodologies and technology of the elementary school to the secondary classroom. The graft will not take; the species are incongruent. Though they share the same identifying label, there are important differences between the younger and older student which prohibit exact duplication of treatment. The answer to the question "Are there fundamental differences between the older and younger learning-disabled individual?" is a resounding yes. There are differences in learning styles and learning problems, as well as in students' motivations, needs, and goals. To the accompanying question, "Is any of our knowledge about elementary learning-disabled children applicable to learning-disabled teenagers and young adults?" our replies are, as yet, unresolved. For the time, we may borrow from the first group to serve the second, but we should also be challenged to find innovative solutions to the problems of older learning-disabled students.

Where can we find solutions to the problems of older learning-disabled students? Suggestions for long-range inquiry have been included in this book, but for the immediate future we believe that activity and allocation of resources should focus on teacher preparation, materials and curriculum development research; studies of learning-disabled pupils; and provision of programs and services within the secondary school structure. Let us look at priorities in these areas more closely.

The number of teachers with the experience and skills to work effectively with older learning-disabled students is insufficient to meet existing needs; therefore, we should give high priority to the development of a corps of trained teachers. Education of older learning-disabled students makes unique demands on special and regular education teachers alike. But, even in regular education, researchers have yet to determine definitively the competencies required for successful teaching. Beyond that, we must ask if special skills and abilities are needed to educate learning-disabled adolescents (and other types of exceptional learners). Models of pre- and in-service education for insuring these competencies in teachers are still lacking. Controlled inquiry and research into this area are required.

While we train teachers for special education, we should also give some thought to the preparation of regular teaching personnel to work with learning-disabled adolescents. The joint efforts of both regular and special education will be required if we are to resolve the problems of older learning-disabled students.

We urgently need to develop and adopt curricula and materials to combat the learning deficiencies of older learning-disabled students. Most of the materials and technology of special education are designed to be used with the primary-aged child. Curricular options and products designed specifically for the older student are still scarce. Materials for instruction in basic skills, content subjects, and career and consumer education are needed. We must, however, proceed cautiously in the adoption (and adaptation) of existing materials and in the development of new curricular materials. We must avoid the meretricious and the mediocre. The teaching community should demand that materials be validated in the classroom with learning-disabled students prior to their broad application in training and remediation.

To date, curricular evaluation in learning disabilities has been generally neglected. Teachers have been left on their own in these matters, and traditionally they have been poorly prepared for curricular selection and evaluation. Yet choosing the materials and implementing them in the classroom have been and remain among the teacher's most important duties. Clearly, the curricular materials issue needs to be approached from several directions. First, we must undertake broad-based, systematic efforts at materials evaluation, but such endeavors go beyond the scope of an individual teacher. This is an area for massive federal support; the new NCEMMH/SO/ALRC Network was a step in this direction. Second, the various aspects of curricular selection, evaluation (within a given classroom), and modification need to be incorporated into teacher training and in-service programs. Finally, every effort should be made to familiarize teachers with existing resources.

Determining relevant psychoeducational characteristics of learning-disabled secondary students is most important. Although much has been written about the characteristics of the learning-disabled, little of this literature refers specifically to the secondary school student. Many of the characteristics attributed to learning-disabled adolescents will remain little more than generalities or stereotypic references if not supported by empirical data. There remains a critical need to delve into the social, emotional, cognitive, and educational character of learning-disabled teenagers. We need to know in which, if any, ways they differ from their nonhandicapped peers. We need to know if there are common qualities that recur among learning-disabled youths. We need to know which characteristics are significant to their educational needs and problems.

Such illumination of the cognitive-affective makeup of learning-disabled secondary students will require controlled investigation. Basic research should focus both on the learner and on the learning environment. The latter study is in vogue at the present time. Research on the learner, though somewhat in disrepute, should not be dismissed too quickly despite our previous disappointments. We need to study secondary-level learning-disabled pupils individually and interactively. For the individual, what psychoeducational profile and personological traits have significant bearings on his or her school performance, subsequent job performance, and social success? For the group, are there common traits or qualities that give a unique identity to the secondary learning-disabled as a whole?

The variables of the learning situation also require close scrutiny. We need to know how the instructional environment, methods, and materials can be selected, altered, or modified to increase the learning efficiency of learning-disabled adolescents. Close reading of each chapter of this book should suggest some plausible research avenues to take.

In our attempt to provide adequate programs and services for the older student, we need to approach solutions from both practical and research perspectives. Our methods for finding the answers to our questions should allow for basic research, experimental and correlative. Then, if we are to derive any practical implications from our investigations, we must apply careful field testing to this research. Basic research into learning disabilities has not received sufficient attention in recent years. Many of our current blind alleys and one-way streets in learning-disabilities practice might have been avoided had we investigated the problems thoroughly before developing the programs. Some of the lack of support for basic research programs, however, has stemmed from the disenchantment of the educational community with costly (both in terms of time and money) research activities that have often disrupted classroom programs and have shown few results or benefits for the students and teachers. To avoid a repetition of such disappointments, "basic" researchers should make every effort to make their findings applicable to real classroom situations. And while their research may start in the laboratory and/or clinic, it should culminate in applied fashion within the classroom. Unless we insist upon the application of basic research to the everyday problems of the learning-disabled, the schools will become even more resistant and negative to basic research.

Our most obvious need in the immediate future is the development of service programs. Activities here, however, bring on a confrontation with the issues of definition, identification, and incidence. These critical questions, which were never resolved for the younger learning-disabled population, now come into the limelight as we turn to learning-disabled secondary students. Resolution of these issues is vital for the future of the field of learning disabilities, for they will define the population, that is, the type and number of students to be served under the label *learning-disabled*. This label—the least pejorative (and most hopeful) of terms describing the handicapped—is now so popular in regular and special education that it may become meaningless through indiscriminate application.

The need for definitive criteria to identify the learning-disabled has been recognized by Congress. In November 1975 Congress passed the Education for All Handicapped Children Act. This legislation imposed a ceiling on the number of handicapped—and particularly on the numbers of learning-disabled—children who would be eligible for federal monetary funds; and it called for the development of specific identifying criteria and procedures for learning disabilities. The initial draft of the proposed standards for learning disabilities appeared in the Federal Register of November 1976, exactly one year after passage of the enabling legislation.

The original definition of the National Advisory Committee on Handicapped Children has been retained in toto, but very stringent criteria are set forth in the proposal for determining the degree of performance discrepancy between the student's actual and expected levels of achievement. Use of these criteria would limit eligibility for learning-disabilities programs to the most severe cases. The mildly and moderately disabled would, in effect, be excluded from services under special education and would remain the responsibility of regular education, even though they have failed in that environment. These criteria would restrict the number of students identified as learning-disabled to a very small proportion of our handicapped population— and would disqualify many of those learning-disabled children who have the best prognosis for improvement. True, the federal definition and standards will not prevent states and local school districts from employing different definitions or identifying criteria, but they will undoubtedly have a far-reaching effect upon state and local attitudes.

We are hopeful, however, that the proposed standards will be sufficiently modified before final adoption. We want to see the orderly development of learning-disabilities programs continue—not only those serving the most severely impaired but also those meeting the needs of the less severely disabled who have the best prognosis for remediation and return to the mainstream of academic activity.

We close our book with many unanswered questions and many unresolved issues. There are, however, certain clear and explicit points: Many pupils at the secondary level are suffering from learning disabilities. We need to know more about them and the best ways of educating them. Whatever the course of future legislation and standards, they constitute a reality that will not go away. They need help. We need to help them.

INDEX

BCDEFGHIJ—A—79